CASSEROLES

SALADS

SIDES

SWEETS

FOSTER'S MARKET FAVORITES

ANNIVERSARY 25TH COLLECTION

FOSTER'S MARKET FAVORITES

ANNIVERSARY
25TH
COLLECTION

SARA FOSTER

with EMILY WALLACE

PHOTOGRAPHY BY
PETER FRANK EDWARDS

STORY FARM

WINTER PARK · MIAMI · SANTA BARBARA

ALSO BY
Sara Foster

SARA FOSTER'S
SOUTHERN KITCHEN

SARA FOSTER'S
CASUAL COOKING

FRESH EVERY DAY

THE FOSTER'S MARKET
COOKBOOK

SARA AND FOOD STYLIST
MARIAN COOPER CAIRNS

Foster's Market Favorites: 25th Anniversary Collection

Published in the United States by Story Farm, LLC
www.story-farm.com

Library of Congress Cataloging-in-Publication Data
available upon request.
ISBN 978-0-9905205-7-3

EDITORIAL DIRECTOR Ashley Fraxedas
ART DIRECTOR Jason Farmand
FOOD STYLING Marian Cooper Cairns
PHOTO ASSISTANT/STYLIST Sandy Lang
COPY EDITORS Dorothea Hunter Sönne, Kathleen M. Kiely
EDITORIAL ASSISTANT Marcela Oliveira
INDEXING Amy Hall
PRODUCTION MANAGEMENT Tina Dahl
ILLUSTRATIONS Emily Wallace

10 9 8 7 6 5 4 3 2 1
First Edition

FOR PATRICK, who keeps me grounded
and keeps Foster's Market going,
hopefully for another 25 years

And for all of you who have supported us
over the years—our customers, farmers,
purveyors, friends and family

CONTENTS

INTRODUCTION

I SIT IN THE BACK of Foster's most mornings with the news and a Diet Coke. If you've been to the Market for breakfast, there's a good chance you've heard me. When I see someone I know—and after 25 years, that happens a lot—I tend to yell out across the dining room. I've never been one to hold back, which is why I'm the one writing this introduction. I'll tell you exactly how we got here.

Sara is modest when it comes to her story and success. She got her soft, cool demeanor from her mother and grandmother and infuses everything she does with those qualities. While I'm bellowing out hellos, she's generally grinning or lightly jabbing me to hush. And when the Market is buzzing with people, as it often is, she's a rock of calmness— quietly jumping in to take orders, refill the coffee machine or lend a hand at anything else that needs to be done. Regulars quickly learn they have to adopt Sara's own very laid-back attitude. Everything is created to order (except for the salads and baked goods, which are made in the early morning before the Market opens). Nothing gets rushed.

Here's how our story slowly unfolded and the stops along the way.

TENNESSEE

Sara grew up in rural Tennessee, where her paternal grandfather owned a country store—a community hub with well-stocked shelves that was certainly a genesis for what

would become Foster's. There were no big supermarket chains bursting with produce from Florida, California or Mexico. Produce came from the garden or the farm down the road. As a result, Sara grew up shopping and eating fresh, local and seasonal. Her family was known for frequent, large get-togethers that centered on meals cooked with homegrown vegetables. As Sara describes it, conversations overlapped and there was constant, cackling laughter. Basically, Foster's during Sunday brunch.

Granny Foster, as Sara's grandmother was called, cooked all the time, often with Sara by her side. Sara still references Granny's recipes, most of them scribbled on the back of used envelopes, bank deposit slips, grocery receipts and birthday cards. Those torn, stained and faded papers contain very few specifics: "a few pinches," "a couple of tablespoons," "if you have it," "a bunch of . . . " and—I love this one—"sometimes, I just . . . " This is exactly how Sara cooks, and it's always what she shares with students in her cooking classes. Experiment! Go your own way.

Sara did just that. She went to New York.

NEW YORK

We married in 1984, and I joined Sara in the city while she kick-started her career. I have always sensed that a defining moment took place in Sara's Honda Civic outside The New York Cooking School's administration offices in New York. She walked up to the car where I was waiting, slumped into the passenger seat and announced that tuition was a whopping $800. "Do you think I should do it?" she asked. "That's a lot of money." It was a lot for us at the time, but I believed in Sara's dream. Also, she could start school on Monday, which I saw as a real boon for our 5-by-8-foot kitchen, then home to teetering stacks of dishes and all of Sara's culinary experiments. With the wisdom of Solomon and a suitable beat for contemplation, I said, "Yes."

Following graduation, Sara pulled the disco shift with Ronnie Davis Productions to cater parties at Studio 54 and Limelight, ending in time to book it over to Soho Charcuterie at 4:30 a.m. for a morning stint there. I know from observation—and from Sara's own stories—that her time at the latter

served as a foundation for her cooking. Her task was to survey the produce in the walk-in and turn it into three or four salads for the day ahead, which forced her to think on her feet and be creative. For the record, she still cooks that way today. While I open our fridge and see nothing, she sees combinations that blow me away. And she hires cooks at the Market who are capable of the same.

Sara held two jobs not because she had to, but because she wanted the experience and her time in the kitchen. Eventually, she added a third to the rank, setting up a catering business with her classmate Renee Beauchamp in our tiny space, once home to the B-52's. Our stove had a two-burner top (usually enough room for just one pot) and the oven was barely suitable for reheating TV dinners. Ventilation for the gas burners was an open window that looked at the solid brick wall next door. But Sara and Renee prepped some impressive events under those conditions: a dinner for the three major network news anchors, *Rolling Stone's* Christmas party, plus events for New York Fashion Week, *Architectural Digest* and Seagram's.

They often used my past-sell-date Toyota Land Cruiser to transport the food across Manhattan and on more than one occasion had to lift the hood (while parked on Park Avenue, no less) and have a doorman pound the starter while Sara cranked the motor. But they always got rave reviews on their food. I believe Sara would agree that the first few events were by chance and luck. And as I recollect, they were probably confidence builders as much as resume highlights, one no more important than the other.

CONNECTICUT

Sara eventually tired of the city and the tiny kitchen. She longed for open space and something a little more small town. So one Saturday morning, she steered her Honda Civic toward Connecticut to check things out—or so she thought. Sara missed the on-ramp for FDR Drive and detoured through the Upper East Side, which turned out to be a very fortunate thing. Stalled at a stoplight, she spotted a friend in the window of a small shop and pulled over to talk. Her friend had a suggestion: a popular caterer in Westport, a young woman who had become very *in demand* locally, was looking for a chef. Her name was Martha Stewart.

Sara cooked dinner for Martha and her husband, Andy, and got the job, which took her far from the kitchens she knew in New York. Whereas small bunches of herbs and produce were delivered to dark basement spaces in the city, at Martha's place, Sara simply stepped out into the garden to pick white peaches or pull fresh greens. In a way, this brought Sara full circle, allowing her to put into practice the style of cooking she'd observed from her grandparents in Tennessee.

With Martha's national profile rising, Sara's attention shifted toward books, testing recipes, assisting at photo shoots and filling in as a regular girl Friday on tours. Martha's first book, *Entertaining*, became a huge success and many more projects followed. But demands on Martha's time became almost unmanageable, so she gave up catering and closed her kitchen. Sara used the occasion to open her own business and took a small space in Greenwich, Connecticut, fueled at first by clients and contracts that Martha generously sent over.

I have one vivid memory from those days: looking out of our upstairs window in Cos Cob on the Mianus River to find Sara managing a charcoal grill full of salmon and beef tenderloin. From spring through fall—wedding season—the grill was always going, which became the subject of a conversation in the winter of 1989. Sara was tired of cooking salmon and beef tenderloin and dreamt of doing something else. "I'm going back to the South. Are you coming?" she asked. I did, of course, so the story continues.

NORTH CAROLINA

Sara knew just where she wanted to go. Several summers earlier we'd rented a place between Chapel Hill and Pittsboro—an area brimming with small farms and big universities. So we took a trip down to Chapel Hill to scope things out once more, staying at The Carolina Inn and dining at Crook's Corner. (That alone helped seal the deal.)

Sara enlisted the help of a real-estate agent, who drove her around in search of the perfect space. But when she explained her idea—a casual restaurant on a large lot that would sell fresh produce, salads and sandwiches—he was dismayed. "No deep fryer?" he asked. "You won't last six months."

Sara swapped him for Jon Condoret, an architect who shared her vision. I have to admit, I thought they were a bit crazy when they chose, of all places, the former home of an old lawn mower repair business that was set among a bunch of pawnshops on Durham-Chapel Hill Boulevard. You should have seen it: a one-level cinder-block building with absolutely no charm (except the big windows along the street side). Jon assured her he could

fix it up and sketched out some drawings, which Sara loved. She'd found her spot.

The remodel started in late '89. On decor, we had Rick Landreth, whose tagline was "Make it look like 1864." He put barn wood down over oil-stained floors, built a long table with reclaimed wood that we still use to this day and secured two counters for a checkout area. We snagged a jewelry display case at the Raleigh Flea Market, deeming its long windows perfect for pastry gazing. And to cover holes in the ceiling from view, we hung tobacco baskets. Then a truck arrived with a bunch of goodies from Connecticut: aged kitchen tables that Sara and Martha collected on weekend trips during the mid-'80s. Foster's Market was simmering even back then.

A month before we opened, Sara's sister, Judy, and their best friend from high school, Boukie, moved in with us to help with the final touches—and believe me, there were many. Judy rented a brick cutter and laid the masonry that's still at the front of the shop after 25 years. Boukie painted a grapevine mural above what would become our produce section and created the logo for the wooden Foster's sign out front. Together we all made about 10 trips a day to the hardware store.

THE MARKET

We opened on May 2, 1990. The North Carolina growing season proved perfect for Sara's menu—from early spring lettuces to late fall turnips, sweet potatoes, parsnips and greens.

Sara quickly established relationships with many of the farmers and was rewarded with an endless source of fresh and interesting produce. Pigs, poultry, beef and lamb were also readily available from farms nearby.

At first, there was a handful of tables, but mostly folks grabbed muffins, scones, soups, salads and sandwiches to go. There were also shelves of fresh vegetables and flowers for sale (during a very ambitious period of time, Sara and I actually grew some of those ourselves). But the Market evolved thanks to our customers' subtle and not-so-subtle requests. With lines forming around the Market's few chairs, Sara removed some displays (reluctantly, at first) and decided to start serving full breakfast at the urging of

chef Wendell Wilson. We opened the outside for seating and added picnic tables and Adirondack chairs. Still, weekend brunches grew into raucous, lively affairs with long waits, no place to park and people eating while resting their plates on the grocery shelves.

In 1994, the Durham Chamber of Commerce named Sara the Small Business Person of the Year. Along with that recognition, Bridgette Lacy wrote an article for the Durham *Herald-Sun*, which exposed the Market to a much wider audience. The rest of the '90s flew by—busy, busy, busy.

In '99, I think, we were enjoying a reunion with Tennessee friends in Memphis, including artist Robert Malone. He wanted

Sara to write a cookbook and attempted to phone an agent friend in New York, Janis Donnaud, on the spot to tell her about Foster's Market. But Sara, the calm and calculated one among our group, decided to wait a few weeks until she could get the proposal just right with the help of co-author Sarah Belk King.

The Foster's Market Cookbook came to life over the ensuing months with recipe testing and retesting, photo shoots with James Baigre, writing and rewriting and the help of Sara's editor, Pamela Cannon. The result was a beautiful book for Random House. I'll never forget watching Sara promote it on Martha's television show while roasting squash and making a salad. When the program ended at 11 p.m. on the East Coast, I logged into Amazon and watched the book rocket up the cookbook charts, holding at number one for several hours. I'm struggling to find the right words for how proud I was of Sara that day. Her particular style and philosophy, her dedication to the business, her generosity with friends and staff and her humility and professionalism were all validated on the big stage. Sara's done four beautiful books since— *Sara Foster's Casual Cooking, Fresh Every Day, Sara Foster's Southern Kitchen* and, now, the *25th Anniversary Collection.*

Sara will fill in the gaps. Her recipes, presented in the pages that follow, are stories as much as they are also instructions. For instance, Say's Bread Pudding (page 298) tells of the Market's early days, when Sara's mother came to town wearing her trademark wide-brimmed hats. Known to everyone as "Say," she became a bit of a local celebrity among our customers and could be counted on to produce, in mass volumes, bread pudding, as well as chicken spaghetti and fresh

fruit cobblers. I was often a witness to the preparation and can attest that Say was no minimalist. Younger Market employees below the drinking age were barred from eating the rum-soaked bread pudding.

Bobbie's Cheese Dip (page 32) recalls Sara's days as a student at Ole Miss. Tarragon Chicken Salad (page 236) is right out of that early morning shift in the Soho Charcuterie kitchen. Foster's Scones Your Way (page 73) were developed on the catering team with Martha. Grilled Slab of Salmon (page 112)— well, you know the story there. Crustless Quiche (page 77) was created to quickly feed crowds of students at the Market's Sunday brunches. I could go on and on. But I know Sara's smiling, ready to give me a playful elbow to stop talking. And you should dig in.

CHAPTER 1

SNACKS

SCAN THE SHELVES OF FOSTER'S MARKET, and it's clear that I'm a pantry person. Our shop's larder never lacks for jams and chutneys, pickles and crackers, or honeys and oils. The same is true at home. My fridge may often verge on empty (just ask Peter), but the cupboard will always do—providing for formal parties, drop-in guests or just us two.

That said, I tend to avoid fussy hors d'oeuvres that take time away from cooking a meal or that give company too much to snack on in advance of dinner. Instead, I pull from the pantry, building platters or boards full of interesting small bites: olive oil with fresh herbs or spices, simple spreads that highlight in-season beans or greens and a mix of local and done-up (or done-down: see Bobbie's Cheese Dip, page 32) cheeses.

You could say I lost interest in intricate appetizers when I worked on Martha Stewart's catering team because we stuffed tens of thousands of little snow peas and dates with multistep fillings. But above all, I tend to avoid tedious snacks because I don't find them necessary. Before dinner, I prefer to fuss over the company I keep instead of the food—a point of view we also hold at the Market. That's not to say we dismiss what's on the plate, but rather that we value keeping it simple, and more so, that we value being a place for so many friends and families to gather. I love looking out on the Foster's lawn to see folks spread out at the picnic tables. That sense of community is what's kept us going for 25 years—though a bottle of wine and plate of pickles help, too.

Lentil Hummus

A VARIATION ON TRADITIONAL Chickpea Hummus (recipe follows), this earthy lentil and spinach dip pairs well with toasted wedges of pita or naan. **Makes about 3 cups**

¾ cup green lentils (about 2 cups cooked lentils)

¼ cup tahini paste

¼ cup almond butter

1 handful baby spinach, arugula or kale

Zest and juice of 2 lemons

2 garlic cloves, smashed

½ teaspoon crushed red pepper flakes

Sea salt and freshly ground black pepper

1 tablespoon extra-virgin olive oil

1. Place the lentils in a saucepan and add enough water to cover by about 3 inches. Place over medium-high heat and bring to a boil. Reduce heat to low and simmer, covered, until the lentils are tender, about 20 minutes. Drain the lentils (reserving the cooking liquid) and cool completely.

2. Place the lentils in the bowl of a food processor fitted with a metal blade. Add the tahini, almond butter, spinach, lemon zest and juice, garlic and red pepper flakes and puree until smooth, stopping to scrape down the sides of the bowl several times. Add just enough of the cooking liquid (about ¼ cup) and salt and black pepper to taste, and continue to blend to make a very smooth paste. Store refrigerated in an airtight container until ready to serve or for up to 5 days.

3. When ready to serve, drizzle with the olive oil and sprinkle with sea salt.

Chickpea Hummus

THIS CHICKPEA HUMMUS IS A STAPLE at the Market (and my house, too). For a simple lunch, we often spread it inside a toasted pita pocket filled with grated carrots, sliced cucumbers, sprouts and tomatoes. **Makes about 3 cups**

¾ cup dried chickpeas (about 2 cups cooked chickpeas) or 1 (15.5-ounce) can chickpeas

2 bay leaves

¾ cup tahini paste

3 garlic cloves, smashed

½ teaspoon crushed red pepper flakes

Sea salt and freshly ground black pepper

Juice of 2 lemons

2 tablespoons extra-virgin olive oil

Chopped fresh parsley

1. Rinse and pick over the chickpeas and place in a large saucepan with the bay leaves and water to cover by about 4 inches. Bring to a boil; reduce heat and simmer uncovered until the peas are tender, about 1½ hours. Drain (reserving cooking liquid), rinse and cool completely.

2. Place the chickpeas in the bowl of a food processor fitted with a metal blade and add the tahini, garlic, red pepper flakes, salt and black pepper to taste, and pulse several times, stopping to scrape down the sides of the bowl several times. Add the lemon juice and ⅓ to ½ cup of the reserved liquid and continue to puree to make a smooth paste that becomes pale in color. Store refrigerated in an airtight container until ready to serve or for up to 5 days.

3. When ready to serve, drizzle with the olive oil and sprinkle with parsley and additional sea salt.

CHICKPEA HUMMUS

LENTIL HUMMUS

BUTTERNUT SQUASH HUMMUS

Butternut Squash Hummus

LOSE THE LEGUMES—butternut squash creates a rich hummus perfect for fall, particularly when topped with Spicy Pumpkin Seeds (page 262). **Makes about 2½ cups**

½ **butternut squash, cut in half lengthwise and seeded (about 2 cups cooked squash)**

¾ **cup tahini paste**

1 tablespoon molasses

3 garlic cloves, smashed

½ **teaspoon crushed red pepper flakes**

Sea salt and freshly ground black pepper

Juice of 1 lemon

2 tablespoons extra-virgin olive oil

2 tablespoons chopped fresh cilantro

Spicy Pumpkin Seeds (page 262)

1. Preheat the oven to 400°F.

2. Place the squash cut side down on a rimmed baking sheet with ½ cup water. Place in the oven to roast until the squash is tender, about 40 minutes. Remove from the oven and turn right side up to cool completely. Scoop the flesh from the skin of the squash and place in the bowl of a food processor fitted with a metal blade.

3. Add the tahini, molasses, garlic, red pepper flakes, salt and black pepper to taste, and pulse several times, stopping to scrape down the sides of the bowl several times. Add the lemon juice and continue to puree to make a smooth paste that becomes pale in color. (If the mixture is too thick, add 1 to 2 tablespoons of water to make a smooth paste.) Store refrigerated in an airtight container until ready to serve or for up to 5 days.

4. When ready to serve, drizzle with the olive oil and sprinkle with cilantro, pumpkin seeds and sea salt.

Kale Artichoke Dip

THIS IS OUR TAKE ON A CLASSIC SPINACH DIP in what you might call the Era of Kale—though, as good Southerners, we often sub collards as the central green. **Makes about 2 cups**

1 (5-ounce) package baby kale

4 ounces reduced-fat cream cheese, softened

½ cup nonfat Greek yogurt

½ cup drained artichoke hearts, chopped

2 scallions, chopped

Zest and juice of 1 lemon

2 garlic cloves, smashed

2 tablespoons grated onion

1 tablespoon dried dill weed

1 tablespoon ground mustard

¼ teaspoon ground cayenne pepper

Sea salt and freshly ground black pepper

Combine the kale, cream cheese, yogurt and artichokes in the bowl of a food processor fitted with a metal blade and pulse until combined, stopping to scrape down the sides of the bowl several times. Add the scallions, lemon zest and juice, garlic, onion, dill, mustard, cayenne pepper and salt and black pepper to taste and pulse until smooth and thoroughly mixed, stopping to scrape down the sides of the bowl several times. Store refrigerated in an airtight container until ready to serve or for up to 5 days.

Spinach Dip

WE'VE MADE THIS SPINACH DIP SINCE DAY ONE, though we've lightened up and prefer the use of Greek yogurt in place of sour cream. **Makes about 2 cups**

½ cup nonfat Greek yogurt (substitute: sour cream)

8 ounces reduced-fat cream cheese, softened

3 handfuls baby spinach

¼ cup chopped fresh parsley

3 scallions, chopped

2 tablespoons grated onion

2 tablespoons grated carrot

2 garlic cloves, smashed

2 teaspoons dried dill weed

Zest and juice of 1 lemon

Sea salt and freshly ground black pepper

Combine the yogurt and cream cheese in the bowl of a food processor fitted with a metal blade and pulse until combined, stopping to scrape down the sides of the bowl several times. Add the spinach, parsley, scallions, onion, carrot, garlic, dill, lemon zest and juice, salt and black pepper to taste, and puree until smooth and thoroughly mixed. Store refrigerated in an airtight container until ready to serve or for up to 4 days.

Green Goddess Dip

WHEN IT COMES TO THIS GODDESS DIP, or the dressing on which it's based, we don't praise just one green or herb. We embrace handfuls of whatever is in season: spinach, kale, arugula, watercress, cilantro, dill, basil, chives or scallions. Beyond a dip for vegetables or crackers, try this spread on toast with avocado. **Makes about 2 cups**

1 cup nonfat Greek yogurt

¼ cup well-shaken buttermilk

1 small cucumber, peeled and chopped

1 handful baby spinach

1 handful baby kale or arugula

2 scallions, chopped

¼ cup fresh cilantro leaves

10 fresh basil leaves

2 teaspoons Dijon mustard

2 garlic cloves, smashed and chopped

Juice of 1 lime

Sea salt and freshly ground black pepper

Place the yogurt, buttermilk, cucumber, spinach, kale, scallions, cilantro, basil, mustard, garlic and lime juice in the bowl of a food processor fitted with a metal blade or the jar of a blender and pulse to mix, stopping to scrape down the sides of the bowl several times. Continue to puree until smooth. Season with salt and pepper to taste. Store refrigerated in an airtight container until ready to serve or for up to 1 week.

In the Kitchen

GREEK YOGURT These days, I tend to prefer Greek yogurt to sour cream—not only because it's lower in fat, but because it's also a tad tangier. Try using it as the base for sauces such as Herb Buttermilk Yogurt Sauce (page 142) or spicy chipotle crema to dress up Greek Lamb and Beef Kebabs (page 137) or Spinach and Cheese Enchiladas (page 189).

On the Lawn

FRESH HERBS I'm a huge proponent of fresh herbs, which partially explains why our rosemary bush has completely enveloped the Market's mailbox. Though our mail carrier may feel differently, we can't get enough—of any fresh herb, really. We grow varieties of basil, thyme, sage, oregano and mint in galvanized tubs around the Market's porch, plucking sprigs and leaves for most of our dishes. Fresh herbs are one of the simplest ways to add flavor. And they'll grow almost anywhere—on the lawn, in a bucket or on your windowsill—often returning year after year.

Spicy Field Pea Dip

DIXIE LEE, PRINCESS ANNE AND PINKEYE PURPLE HULL: there are as many names for field peas as there are ways to use them. Take this piquant dip, often called "Texas caviar," in which black-eyed peas are most common but any Southern field pea is welcome—the Mississippi Silver and Clemson Purple included. **Makes about 3 cups**

½ pound (about 2 cups) fresh or frozen field peas (such as black-eyed or Pinkeye Purple Hull)

½ cup Summer Tomato Salsa (page 34) or jarred salsa

¼ cup spicy pickle relish

1 red bell pepper, cored, seeded and diced

2 jalapeño peppers, cored, seeded and diced

4 scallions, minced

¼ cup chopped fresh cilantro

2 tablespoons olive oil

Zest and juice of 1 lime

Sea salt and freshly ground black pepper

Crostini (see Crostini, below)

1. Rinse the peas and place in a saucepan with enough water to cover by about 1 inch. Bring to a low boil and simmer until tender, 10 to 12 minutes. (Cooking time may vary if using frozen peas.) Drain, rinse and cool.

2. Place the peas and salsa in the bowl of a food processor fitted with a metal blade and pulse 5 or 6 times, stopping to scrape down the sides of the bowl several times, until thoroughly combined but still chunky. Place the pea mixture in a bowl and add the relish, red pepper, jalapeños, scallions, cilantro, olive oil, lime zest and juice; season with salt and black pepper to taste and stir to combine. Store refrigerated in an airtight container until ready to serve or for up to 5 days.

3. When ready to serve, pair with crostini, toasted pita or naan.

In the Kitchen

CROSTINI It's easy to make crostini, pita chips or toast with day-old bread. Slice into thin rounds or pieces before too hard. Brush with olive oil, sprinkle with salt and black pepper, and toast until golden brown. Freeze and keep on hand to serve with your favorite dip or spread.

Foster's Pimiento Cheese

I WON'T CALL THIS SPREAD THE MARKET'S DEFINITIVE pimiento cheese, as we've made dozens of varieties over the years and even hosted a pimiento cheese make-off. But this version with a tangy splash of cider vinegar and a sweet hint of honey is my personal favorite.

Makes about 3 cups

2 cups (8 ounces) grated extra-sharp Cheddar cheese

2 cups (6 ounces) grated Parmesan cheese

1 (4-ounce) jar pimiento peppers, drained and chopped

1 jalapeño pepper, cored, seeded and minced

⅔ cup your favorite mayonnaise or Homemade Mayonnaise (page 32)

1 tablespoon cider vinegar

1 teaspoon honey

½ teaspoon crushed red pepper flakes

Sea salt and freshly ground black pepper

Combine the Cheddar, Parmesan, pimientos, jalapeño, mayonnaise, vinegar, honey and red pepper flakes in a bowl. Season with salt and black pepper to taste and stir to blend. Store refrigerated in an airtight container until ready to serve or for up to 1 week. This is best if made a day before serving.

Pimiento Cheese Puffs

FOR THESE PUFFS—A STAPLE OF OLD, SPIRAL-BOUND JUNIOR LEAGUE COOKBOOKS— sourdough bread is cut into crustless rounds and dressed up with ruby red specks of pimientos. Served warm, they pair perfectly with a chilled glass of Prosecco or crisp Sauvignon Blanc.

Makes about 24 bite-size puffs

4 to 6 slices sourdough bread

1 cup Foster's Pimiento Cheese (recipe above)

2 tablespoons grated onion

2 tablespoons minced fresh parsley

¼ cup (¾ ounce) grated Parmesan cheese

1. Preheat the oven to 350°F.

2. Using a 1- to 1½-inch round cookie cutter, cut 4 to 6 rounds from each slice of bread (depending on its size), discarding the crusts. Place the rounds on a rimmed baking sheet and place in the oven to bake until golden brown around the edges, about 7 minutes. Remove from the oven and preheat the oven to broil.

3. While the bread is toasting, combine the pimiento cheese, onion and parsley in a bowl and stir to mix.

4. Scoop about 1 teaspoon of the mixture onto each round and sprinkle with Parmesan cheese. Place under the broiler until lightly brown and bubbling, 1 to 2 minutes, keeping a close eye on the puffs so as not to burn. Serve warm.

Bobbie's Cheese Dip

WHILE UNDERGRADS AT OLE MISS, my sister and I used to return from visits with her now mother-in-law, Bobbie, armed with a quart jar of cheese dip. We rarely took the stuff to tailgates or other gatherings, as it was too good to share. But we did eventually offer it to others at the Market when we first opened, admittedly skittish to reveal the signature "V" ingredient or Bobbie's penchant for Kraft mayonnaise (bless her heart). Do what you will. I suggest pepper Jack instead of Velveeta and Homemade Mayonnaise (recipe follows). **Makes about 2 cups**

8 ounces pepper Jack cheese, cut into small chunks, room temperature

1 cup your favorite mayonnaise or Homemade Mayonnaise (recipe follows)

½ white onion, grated

1 jalapeño pepper, cored, seeded and minced

2 garlic cloves, smashed and chopped

¼ teaspoon crushed red pepper flakes

Pinch of ground cayenne pepper

Kosher salt and freshly ground black pepper

Combine the cheese, mayonnaise, onion, jalapeño, garlic, red pepper flakes, cayenne pepper, and salt and black pepper to taste in the bowl of a food processor fitted with a metal blade or the jar of a blender and puree until smooth, stopping to scrape down the sides of the bowl several times. Store refrigerated in an airtight container until ready to serve or for up to 1 week. This is best if made a day before serving.

In the Kitchen

HOMEMADE MAYONNAISE Place **2 large egg yolks** in a bowl and slowly whisk in **1 tablespoon of canola oil**. Slowly add **1 cup canola oil** to the eggs, 1 tablespoon at a time, whisking constantly. Continue to whisk, alternating additions of the **juice of 1 lemon** and **2 teaspoons white vinegar** with the remaining oil, until all the oil has been added. Add the **zest of 1 lemon, 1 teaspoon Colman's dry mustard, a pinch of ground cayenne pepper, a pinch of paprika, and kosher salt and black pepper to taste,** continuing to whisk until the mayonnaise is thick. This can also be done in a food processor or blender. Whisk in **1 teaspoon hot water**. Store refrigerated in an airtight container until ready to serve or for up to 1 week.

Sun-Dried Tomato Spread

WHEN SUMMER ENDS AND TOMATOES LOSE THEIR LUSTER, this spread more than fills in, especially on a sandwich with prosciutto or Serrano ham. **Makes about 2 cups**

8 ounces reduced-fat cream cheese, softened

1 cup (4 ounces) crumbled feta

½ cup sun-dried tomatoes (packed in oil or reconstituted), drained and chopped

½ cup slivered almonds

¼ cup fruit chutney

4 garlic cloves, smashed

2 scallions, chopped

Sea salt and freshly ground black pepper

Place the cream cheese, feta, tomatoes, almonds, chutney, garlic, scallions, and salt and black pepper to taste in the bowl of a food processor fitted with a metal blade and pulse until smooth and thoroughly combined, stopping to scrape down the sides of the bowl several times. Store refrigerated in an airtight container until ready to serve. This will keep refrigerated for up to 1 week.

Fresh Butter Bean Dip

THERE'S NO NEED FOR JUST ONE SUMMER LOVE. Butter beans rank up there with vine-ripe tomatoes and crisp silver corn (the list goes on), and this butter bean dip is one of my favorite ways to get in an extra helping before dinner is even served. Fresh green peas or fava beans work well, too. **Makes about 2 cups**

2 tablespoons olive oil

½ pound fresh butter beans

½ onion, chopped

2 garlic cloves, smashed

½ cup (1½ ounces) grated Parmesan cheese

Juice of 1 lemon

¼ cup chopped fresh parsley

10 fresh mint leaves

½ teaspoon sea salt

½ teaspoon freshly ground black pepper

½ teaspoon crushed red pepper flakes

1. Heat the olive oil in a large skillet over medium-high heat and add the butter beans and onion with ¼ cup water. Reduce the heat to medium and cook, stirring, until the beans are just tender and most of the water has reduced, about 10 minutes. Add the garlic and continue to cook and stir 1 minute more. Remove from the heat and set aside to cool completely.

2. Place the bean mixture, scraping any oil from the bottom of the pan, in the bowl of a food processor fitted with a metal blade or the jar of a blender. Add the cheese, lemon juice, parsley, mint, salt, black pepper and red pepper flakes and puree until smooth, stopping to scrape down the sides of the bowl several times. Store refrigerated in an airtight container until ready to serve. This will keep refrigerated for up to 4 days.

3. When ready to serve, drizzle with olive oil and sprinkle with chopped parsley and mint.

Summer Tomato Salsa

A CROWDED LAWN IN FRONT, A BLOOMING FIELD OUT BACK and this salsa: blessed are summers at Foster's Market. Particularly blessed are summers when a box of Cherokee Purple tomatoes arrives. The heirloom variety—known for its dark hue and sweet bite—ranks at the top for me, though I won't (can't) stop testing other tomatoes (German Johnsons, Green Zebras and Nebraska Weddings, among them) to confirm my belief. **Makes about 3 cups**

2 pounds mixed vine-ripe tomatoes, cored and diced

1 small onion, diced

1 jalapeño pepper, cored, seeded and minced

2 garlic cloves, smashed and minced

2 teaspoons crushed red pepper flakes

Zest and juice of 1 lime

2 tablespoons extra-virgin olive oil

1 tablespoon cider vinegar

1 bunch chopped fresh cilantro

1 teaspoon sugar

Sea salt and freshly ground black pepper

1. Place the tomatoes, onion, jalapeño, garlic, red pepper flakes, and lime zest and juice in a large bowl.

2. Drizzle the olive oil and vinegar over the tomato mixture. Sprinkle with cilantro, sugar, and salt and black pepper to taste. Stir to combine; do not overmix or the tomatoes will start to break down. Taste for seasoning and add additional salt and black pepper, if desired. Store refrigerated in an airtight container until ready to serve or for up to 4 days.

In the Kitchen

SALSA VARIATIONS Don't limit summer's bounty: add fresh corn or watermelon to a mix of heirloom tomatoes. Or make a sturdier salsa by including avocado or black beans. Tomatoes are just the beginning.

Corn: add 1 cup cooked or fresh corn kernels to the recipe above.

Watermelon: add 1 cup chopped watermelon to the recipe above.

Avocado: add 1 cup chopped avocado to the recipe above right before serving.

Black Bean: add 1 cup cooked black beans and ½ cup diced red peppers to the recipe above.

On the Lawn

SOL PATCH FARMS In the beginning, Peter and I had a brilliant idea: grow flowers to sell at our brand-new business. As you can imagine, that didn't last long; we had to let the field go fallow so the Market didn't, too. Thankfully, Sol Patch Farms has recently taken up the helm. What began as a mobile classroom in 2011 has since taken root in our backyard, thanks to the vision of one of our former employees, Ellen Duda. She and her partners transformed the lawn into a colorful farm, where wooden pallets and pastel tires frame a field of tomatoes, kale and peppers. Much of their produce shows up on the Market's menu, with offerings also available at a small stand on the property.

Herb and Onion Flatbread

I HAVE MY SISTER TO THANK for this crispy flatbread. She used to make it at the Market when we first opened and nobody could get enough. Stock up: once baked, the bread freezes well and can be popped in the oven to warm for unexpected guests. To finish, top with fresh herbs and sweet red onions—or whatever else you have on hand. **Makes four (10- to 12-inch) flatbreads**

1 cup warm water

1 (¼-ounce) package active dry yeast

¼ teaspoon sugar

¼ cup olive oil

2½ cups all-purpose flour

½ cup cornmeal

¼ teaspoon kosher salt

1 red onion, thinly sliced

8 sprigs fresh thyme or rosemary

Sea salt and freshly ground black pepper

1. Mix the warm water, yeast and sugar in a bowl and set aside in a warm place to proof until doubled in size and light and airy, about 10 minutes. Add 1 tablespoon of the olive oil and stir to mix.

2. In a large bowl, combine the flour, cornmeal and kosher salt and stir to mix. Make a well in the center, add the water-yeast mixture and stir to combine thoroughly until it forms soft dough. Turn to coat in an oiled bowl, cover with a damp cloth and let rise in a warm place until it has doubled in size and forms a soft dough, about 1 hour.

3. When ready to bake, preheat the oven to 400°F.

4. Punch the dough down, divide into 4 pieces, form into flat, round disks and let rest, about 10 minutes. Dust a piece of parchment or wax paper with flour and cornmeal and roll each piece of flatbread into an oval about 10 inches long. Top with thin slices of red onion and herb leaves, brush with remaining olive oil and sprinkle with sea salt and black pepper to taste. Place in the oven to bake until golden brown and crisp, about 20 minutes. Remove from oven and serve warm.

On the Menu

OTHER TOPPINGS Keep it simple or go all out. Here are a few extras I'm prone to throw on this dough, depending on what's in season: thinly sliced zucchini or yellow squash; green or red peppers; eggplant; plum tomatoes; scallions; sweet or red potatoes; spinach or kale leaves.

Savory Cheese Crisps

WHEN MARTHA STEWART LAUNCHED A FURNITURE LINE out of High Point, North Carolina, we catered parties using recipes from her books. These zesty cheese wafers were one of our go-tos, though we often swap the sesame seeds for the likes of benne, millet and poppy.

Makes about 24 wafers

---

8 tablespoons (1 stick) unsalted butter, softened

1 cup (4 ounces) grated sharp Cheddar cheese

1 cup (4 ounces) grated Gruyère cheese

1½ cups all-purpose flour

2 teaspoons sea salt

1 tablespoon sesame seeds

1 teaspoon crushed red pepper flakes

1. Cream the butter and cheese together in the bowl of an electric mixer fitted with the paddle attachment or with a wooden spoon until smooth and combined.

2. In a separate bowl, combine the flour, salt, sesame seeds and red pepper flakes and stir to mix.

3. Add the flour mixture to the cheese mixture. Stir to combine thoroughly and form a soft dough.

4. Shape the dough into a 2-inch-wide rectangular bar or roll into a log and chill at least 2 hours or overnight. Freeze the dough at this point if you are making ahead of time. It freezes well for up to 1 month.

5. When ready to bake, preheat the oven to 375°F. Lightly grease a baking sheet or line with parchment paper and set aside.

6. Cut the formed dough into slices, about ¼ inch thick, and place on the prepared baking sheet. Sprinkle with additional sesame seeds if desired.

7. Place in the oven to bake until lightly brown around the edges, about 15 minutes. Remove from the oven and serve warm, or place on baking racks to completely cool before storing.

On the Menu

SERVE WITH For a cocktail hour, dress these crisps up with one of the following:
- Chopped avocado and Summer Tomato Salsa (page 34)
- Tuna or beef tartare with red onion and capers
- Fresh mozzarella, Basil Pesto (page 143) and fresh basil leaves
- Salami and apricot jam
- Country ham and pepper jelly
- Fresh figs and ricotta

Potato Pancakes

THESE PAN-FRIED POTATO CAKES pair well with almost anything—applesauce, sour cream, crème fraîche, caviar and goat cheese among my favorites. **Makes 14 to 16 small cakes**

1 russet potato

1 Yukon Gold potato

1 tablespoon cornstarch

¼ cup all-purpose flour

2 large eggs, lightly beaten

2 tablespoons grated onion

2 tablespoons chopped fresh parsley

1 tablespoon chopped fresh rosemary

½ teaspoon sea salt

½ teaspoon freshly ground black pepper

Pinch of ground cayenne pepper

Vegetable oil, for frying

1. Preheat the oven to 300°F.

2. Scrub the potatoes and coarsely grate into a large bowl. Add the cornstarch and toss to coat.

3. Add the flour, eggs, onion, parsley, rosemary, salt, black pepper and cayenne and stir to combine.

4. Heat enough oil to just cover the bottom of a large nonstick skillet until sizzling hot over medium-high heat. Spoon a heaping tablespoon of the mixture into the skillet and flatten into a cake, about 3 inches wide. Repeat with enough to fill the bottom of the skillet, but do not overcrowd. Cook until golden and crispy, turning only once, about 2 minutes per side. Transfer to a wire rack over a rimmed baking sheet, sprinkle with additional salt and place in the oven to keep warm. Repeat the process with the remaining potato mixture, stirring as you scoop the mixture to keep the egg distributed throughout the potatoes. Serve warm topped with applesauce and sour cream or your favorite topping.

In the Kitchen

VARIATIONS I prepare these potato cakes all year long, but also enjoy the following seasonal variations, replacing the potatoes with the same grated quantity:

- **Summer:** Yellow squash with basil and scallions
- **Fall:** Sweet potatoes with leeks and thyme
- **Spring:** Carrots and parsnips with chives

Gravlax

Vodka improves brunches beyond just Bloody Marys. With the aid of fennel, dill and two days' time, it cures salmon for Saturday morning bagels with herb cream cheese or Herb Buttermilk Yogurt Sauce (page 142), as well as Saturday evening hors d'oeuvres, presented with a crisp, cool vodka-soda. **Serves 15 to 20**

1 (2- to 2½-pound) salmon fillet, skin on

¼ cup good-quality vodka

3 tablespoons sea salt

3 tablespoons sugar

1 tablespoon freshly ground black pepper

1 bunch fresh dill leaves, plus more for garnish

½ fennel bulb, cored and thinly sliced

Herb Buttermilk Yogurt Sauce (page 142)

1. Rinse the salmon and pat dry with a paper towel. Place in a baking dish flesh side up and pour the vodka over the salmon. Mix the salt, sugar and pepper together, sprinkle over the salmon and rub into the flesh. Press the dill and fennel into the top of the salmon. Spoon any vodka that runs off to the side over the salmon again.

2. Flip the salmon over, flesh side down, and cover tightly with plastic wrap. Place a cutting board on top to weight it down and set aside in the refrigerator 2 days.

3. Remove the dill and fennel, sprinkle with freshly chopped dill and thinly slice, starting from the tail end, on a diagonal. Serve with Herb Buttermilk Yogurt Sauce (page 142).

On the Menu

SERVE WITH Beyond a traditional bagel and a smear of cream cheese, try gravlax one of the following ways:
- On pumpernickel bread with thinly sliced cucumbers and onion or Red Onion Horseradish Gremolata (page 142)
- Mixed in an omelet with creamy goat cheese and wilted spinach
- On crostini with Summer Tomato Salsa (page 34) and sliced avocado

PARTY ON A PLATTER

PARTY TRAYS DON'T REQUIRE RECIPES—just well-stocked shelves and a little assembly. Here are a few components I commonly pair using what I have on hand (plus a few extra items you can make or acquire ahead of time if you want to do a little more). With advance notice, I often choose a theme. Here are a few examples.

SOUTHERN PLATTER

Bite-size pieces of fried chicken with Green Goddess Dip (page 28); mini Sweet Potato Sorghum Biscuits (page 63); pickled okra, carrots or green beans; bread-and-butter pickles; deviled eggs; cheese straws or Savory Cheese Crisps (page 39).

ITALIAN PLATTER

Breadsticks, crostini or crackers; olives; fresh mozzarella marinated in olive oil and herbs; wedge of Pecorino cheese; thinly sliced salami or prosciutto; roasted peppers; dried figs and dates; Marcona almonds.

FARMERS' MARKET PLATTER

(Use these ideas from my farmers' market in Durham as inspiration for what you might find in your area.)

Wedges of Chapel Hill Creamery's New Moon or Calvander cheeses; rolls of Elodie Farms' goat cheese; Farmer's Daughter Brand Pear Preserves with Black Pepper; rainbow radishes and carrots from Bluebird Meadows; wildflower honey with the comb; Arkansas Black apples; a baguette from Scratch Baking.

GREEK PLATTER

Greek olive mixture, green and black; Chickpea Hummus (page 24) drizzled with olive oil and sprinkled with sea salt; Herb Buttermilk Yogurt Sauce (page 142) and toasted wedges of pita bread; cubed feta cheese tossed with olive oil and fresh herbs; cherry tomatoes and cucumber slices.

A FEW MORE SIMPLE IDEAS

- Seasonal crudités with seasoned olive oil and Harissa or Curry Buttermilk Yogurt Sauce (page 142)
- Make Your Own Bruschetta Board: crostini, Kale Pesto (page 143) and flavored oils
- Mixed Grilled Sausage Board: sausage, mustard, pickles and chutney
- Chips with a selection of dips: Summer Tomato Salsa (page 34), Green Goddess Dip (page 28) or Lentil Hummus (page 24)
- Syrian bread and naan with Bobbie's Cheese Dip (page 32) and Lentil Hummus (page 24), Chickpea Hummus (page 24) or Butternut Squash Hummus (page 25)

On the Menu

MORE PANTRY PAIRINGS Try the following together on crostini or crackers:

- Sour cherry preserves and pecorino cheese
- Strawberry preserves, fresh ricotta cheese and spicy pecans
- Pear preserves with blue cheese and watercress
- Apple slices and sharp Cheddar
- Fresh mozzarella and Kale Pesto (page 143)
- Gravlax (page 43) or smoked salmon, fresh dill and honey mustard
- Serrano ham, Foster's Pimiento Cheese (page 31) and pepper jelly
- Salami, whole-grain mustard, Sun-Dried Tomato Spread (page 33) and peach preserves
- Figs, arugula, goat cheese and prosciutto

BREAKFAST

WE ALMOST SKIPPED THE MOST IMPORTANT MEAL of the day—or so it seems in retrospect compared to what we serve today (at least 400 omelets each weekend). In the beginning, there were just quick breads, muffins and one tiny coffee pot that practically percolated itself to death. A turning point, you could say, was the morning I came in to find a note that read, "I can't work here anymore until we get a sufficient coffeemaker." Our disgruntled employee was right; lines were looming, as there was hardly another place on the Boulevard to get a cup of coffee back then. There was absolutely nowhere to get espresso, which we added to the menu in 1994 with the help of Cindy Chang. Whereas Peter and I were nervous—there was no coffee culture in the Triangle yet and espresso machines were expensive and seemingly otherworldly—Cindy was all in (it was no surprise to us that she was later named executive director of the World Barista Championship). Foster's is deeply indebted to the vision of its customers and employees, and Cindy is high among them.

Tim Youngblood is another who prodded us along. It was he who suggested we try our hand at omelets about two years after the Market first opened. I'll never forget the whiteboard we kept in the kitchen to track how many we sold: the first Sunday, four, the next, eight, and so on. Eventually, we stopped counting omelets and started adding more dishes—from our Grits Bowl Your Way (page 74) to Foster's take on Eggs Sardou (page 79).

Of course, we never gave up the things that got us started (except for that pitiful first coffee machine). We've still got the Scones (page 72) and Herb Cheddar Biscuits (page 60) that helped us build a foundation—for the Market and each day.

Banana Foster's Bread

CLOAKED WITH CARAMELIZED BANANAS AND SPIKED WITH BOURBON, we call this bread Banana Foster's. It's a perfect combination of two classics: New Orleans' famed Bananas Foster and my grandmother's banana bread. All you need to finish it off (perhaps past breakfast) is a scoop of vanilla ice cream. **Makes one (9 x 5 x 3-inch) loaf**

½ cup **light brown sugar**

5 ripe **bananas**

2 tablespoons **bourbon**

2¼ cups **all-purpose flour**

2 teaspoons **baking powder**

1 teaspoon **ground cinnamon**

½ teaspoon **freshly grated nutmeg**

½ teaspoon **ground cardamom**

¼ teaspoon **kosher salt**

8 tablespoons (1 stick) **unsalted butter, softened**

1 cup **granulated sugar**

2 large **eggs**

½ cup **chopped pecans**

1 teaspoon **pure vanilla extract**

1. Preheat the oven to 350°F. Grease and lightly flour a 9 x 5 x 3-inch loaf pan.

2. Spread the brown sugar evenly on the bottom of a cast-iron skillet over medium heat. Peel and slice 1 of the bananas in half lengthwise and place cut side down on the sugar. Sprinkle the bourbon over the top and cook, without flipping, just shaking the pan occasionally until the sugar melts and the banana begins to caramelize, about 5 minutes. Remove from the heat and set aside until ready to use.

3. Combine the flour, baking powder, cinnamon, nutmeg, cardamom and salt in a large bowl and stir to mix.

4. In a separate bowl, with an electric mixer beat together the butter and sugar until soft and creamy, stopping to scrape down the sides of the bowl several times. Slowly add the eggs, one at a time, mixing well after each addition. Add the remaining bananas, pecans and vanilla and mix to break up the bananas and combine.

5. By hand, stir the flour mixture into the banana mixture just until the dry ingredients are incorporated, being careful not to overmix. Pour the batter into the prepared pan and place on a rimmed baking sheet (this makes it easier to handle in and out of the oven).

6. Place the caramelized banana on top of the loaf and drizzle with any remaining caramel. Bake 1 hour to 1 hour and 10 minutes, until the bread rises and a wooden skewer comes out clean when inserted in the center.

7. Remove from the oven and let sit to cool, about 15 minutes. Run a knife around the inside edge of the pan, turn the loaf out onto a cooling rack and continue to cool more before slicing and serving, about 10 minutes.

Pecan Sweet Potato Sticky Buns

I'M A SUCKER FOR SWEET POTATOES and welcome them at all times of the day (perhaps this is what landed me a seat as an advising chef to the North Carolina Sweet Potato Commission). For these breakfast buns, the potato is folded into the dough and dressed with bourbon, brown sugar and chopped pecans. **Makes about 1 dozen (3-inch) buns**

DOUGH

6 tablespoons (¾ stick) unsalted butter

½ cup milk

¼ cup plus 1 teaspoon sugar, divided

½ cup warm water

1 teaspoon kosher salt

1 (¼-ounce) package active dry yeast

1 large egg

1 cup mashed sweet potato (about 1 medium sweet potato)

3½ to 4 cups all-purpose flour

continues »

DOUGH

1. Melt the butter in a large saucepan with the milk and scald. (For the rolls to rise properly, you really must scald the milk, heating it just below the boiling point until it slightly bubbles around the edges.) Add ¼ cup of the sugar and the salt and stir until the sugar dissolves. Remove from the heat and set aside to cool slightly.

2. Dissolve the yeast and remaining sugar in warm water and set aside in a warm place, until frothy, about 5 minutes. Lightly grease a large bowl with vegetable oil and set aside.

3. Whisk the egg and sweet potato together in a large bowl until smooth and well combined.

4. When the milk mixture has cooled, add the yeast mixture and stir to combine. Add this to the egg mixture and stir to mix.

5. Slowly add 3 cups of the flour and mix until incorporated. If needed, add more flour, about ¼ cup at a time, to make a soft, sticky dough. (The dough will be very sticky at this point but after refrigerated it will become firm enough to work.)

6. With lightly floured hands remove the dough from the bowl, place in the oiled bowl, cover and set aside in a warm area to rise until doubled in size, or refrigerate overnight.

continues »

In the Kitchen

MAKE AHEAD For ease—especially if making this recipe for guests—you can prepare this dough ahead of time and refrigerate for up to several days. Before using, remove the dough from the refrigerator and punch down and let rest in a warm place before rolling out, about 20 minutes.

STICKY BUNS

1 cup golden raisins

2 tablespoons bourbon (substitute: apple juice)

2 tablespoons unsalted butter, softened

1½ cups light brown sugar

8 tablespoons (1 stick) unsalted butter, melted

1 teaspoon ground cinnamon

½ cup honey

1 cup coarsely chopped pecans

STICKY BUNS

1. Combine the raisins and bourbon in a bowl and set aside to soak until plumped, about 20 minutes.

2. Grease a deep, 9-inch round baking dish with the softened butter and set aside.

3. Stir together ¾ cup of the brown sugar, melted butter and cinnamon in a separate bowl and set aside.

4. In another bowl, mix together the remaining brown sugar, honey and pecans. Spread evenly in the bottom of the prepared baking dish and set aside.

5. On a lightly floured surface, roll the dough about ⅛ inch thick to form a 12 x 6-inch rectangle. Spread the brown sugar-butter mixture evenly over the dough, leaving about 1 inch of exposed dough all the way around the edges. Sprinkle the raisins and bourbon evenly over the top of the dough. Roll up the dough lengthwise into a 12-inch-long log.

6. Place the log, seam side down, on the work surface and use a sharp knife to cut the log crosswise into about 12 slices. Place the slices in the baking dish, cut side down, on top of the pecan mixture. (The slices should touch one another and should fit snugly in the dish.) Set aside in a warm place to rise until puffy, 15 to 20 minutes.

7. When ready to bake, preheat the oven to 350°F.

8. Place the baking dish on a rimmed baking sheet and bake 50 minutes to 1 hour, until the buns are golden brown and a wooden skewer inserted in the center comes out clean.

9. Remove from the oven and cool, 5 to 10 minutes. While still warm, run a knife around the inside edge of the dish to loosen the buns. Place a platter or plate on top of the baking dish, and turn the dish over to unmold the sticky buns onto the platter, scraping out all the excess pecans and sugar from the bottom. Serve warm.

Ginger Pumpkin Bread

LIKE CANNED TOMATOES, CANNED PUMPKINS OFFER CONSISTENCY. But the beauty of pumpkins is that they're anything but consistent, at least in shape and size. If time is not a factor, try roasting small "sugar pie" varieties—round Baby Pams, ghost-white Luminas or flat-topped Cinderellas—to use in this quick bread. Then bake a batch of Spicy Pumpkin Seeds (page 262).

Makes one (9 x 5 x 3-inch) loaf

2 cups all-purpose flour

2 teaspoons baking powder

2 teaspoons ground ginger

2 teaspoons ground cinnamon

½ teaspoon ground allspice

¼ teaspoon kosher salt

⅓ cup vegetable oil

1 cup sugar

2 large eggs

1 cup canned or cooked mashed pumpkin

¼ cup molasses

1 (1-inch) piece ginger, peeled and finely grated

1 teaspoon pure vanilla extract

1. Preheat the oven to 350°F. Grease and lightly flour a 9 x 5 x 3-inch loaf pan.

2. Combine the flour, baking powder, ground ginger, cinnamon, allspice and salt in a large bowl and stir to mix.

3. In a separate bowl, whisk together the oil, sugar and eggs. Add the pumpkin, molasses, grated ginger and vanilla and stir to blend.

4. Add the flour mixture to the egg mixture and stir just until the dry ingredients are incorporated, being careful not to overmix.

5. Scrape the batter into the prepared pan and place on a rimmed baking sheet (this makes it easier to handle in and out of the oven). Place in the center of the oven and bake until the bread rises and a wooden skewer comes out clean when inserted in the center, 1 hour to 1 hour and 10 minutes.

6. Remove from the oven and let sit about 15 minutes before removing from the pan. Continue to cool more before slicing and serving, about 10 minutes.

In the Kitchen

GINGER Keep a cache of ginger. Powdered, it warms up baked goods. Fresh, it livens up soups, stews, vegetables and vinaigrettes. And crystalized, it sweetly stings in cookies or cakes.

New York Crumb Cake

WE COULDN'T LEAVE NEW ENGLAND WITHOUT TAKING THE CRUMB CAKE with us. It's been a staple at the Market since we opened, particularly embraced by New York transplants in the Triangle. But though it hails from elsewhere in spirit, we actually got our recipe in North Carolina from one of our first bakers, Gretchen Sedaris. Her version calls for a heap of crumbly topping, which partially bakes into the batter. **Makes one (9 x 13 x 2-inch) pan**

TOPPING

3 cups all-purpose flour

1½ cups light brown sugar

1 tablespoon ground cinnamon

1 teaspoon freshly grated nutmeg

½ teaspoon ground allspice

½ teaspoon kosher salt

½ pound plus 4 tablespoons (2½ sticks) unsalted butter, melted

CAKE

3 cups all-purpose flour

1 cup sugar

1 tablespoon baking powder

½ teaspoon kosher salt

2 large eggs

1¼ cups milk

¼ cup vegetable oil

1 tablespoon pure vanilla extract

¼ cup confectioners' sugar

TOPPING

Combine the flour, sugar, cinnamon, nutmeg, allspice and salt together in a large bowl and stir to mix. Stir in the butter until all dry ingredients are moist and incorporated.

CAKE

1. Preheat the oven to 350°F. Generously grease and flour a 9 x 13 x 2-inch baking dish.

2. Stir together the flour, sugar, baking powder and salt in a large bowl.

3. In a separate bowl, combine the eggs, milk, oil and vanilla and stir to blend well.

4. Add the flour mixture to the egg mixture and stir just until the dry ingredients are incorporated, being careful not to overmix. Spread the batter evenly into the prepared dish. Sprinkle the crumb topping evenly over the top and press gently into the batter.

5. Place in the center of the oven and bake until the cake rises and the topping bakes into the cake and a wooden skewer inserted in the center comes out clean, 40 to 45 minutes.

6. Remove from the oven and cool in the dish. Cut into desired serving sizes and sprinkle with confectioners' sugar.

In the Kitchen

VARIATION For a Southern twist, add sweet potatoes to the recipe (pumpkin makes a nice addition, too): decrease the milk to ¾ cup and add **1 cup mashed sweet potato or pumpkin purée** to the cake batter in step 4 with the eggs, milk, oil and vanilla.

Spiced Sour Cream Coffee Cake with Chocolate and Chiles

CONSIDER THIS COFFEE CAKE LIKE A DOUBLE SHOT OF ESPRESSO, amped up a notch by the addition of dried chiles in place of more common chopped nuts. It may be crumbly if served warm, but it is delicious. **Makes one (10-inch) Bundt or tube cake / Serves 10 to 12**

FILLING

⅓ **cup shaved chocolate**

⅓ **cup light brown sugar**

2 teaspoons ground cinnamon

½ **teaspoon crushed dried chiles**

CAKE

3½ cups all-purpose flour

1 tablespoon baking powder

1 teaspoon freshly grated nutmeg

¼ **teaspoon kosher salt**

½ **pound (2 sticks) unsalted butter, softened**

1 cup sugar

3 large eggs

1 cup light sour cream

1 cup nonfat Greek yogurt

2 teaspoons pure vanilla extract

FILLING

Place the chocolate, sugar, cinnamon and chiles in a bowl and stir to mix.

CAKE

1. Preheat the oven to 350°F. Generously grease and flour a 10-inch Bundt or tube pan.

2. Stir together the flour, baking powder, nutmeg and salt in a large bowl.

3. Beat the butter and sugar in a large bowl with an electric or stand mixer until pale and fluffy, stopping to scrape down the sides of the bowl several times. Add the eggs, one at a time, stopping to scrape down the sides of the bowl several times and mixing thoroughly after each addition. Add the sour cream, yogurt and vanilla and mix to combine. Reduce the speed to low and slowly add the flour mixture, combining just until all the dry ingredients are moist, being careful not to overmix and stopping to scrape the sides of the bowl several times.

4. Spoon half of the batter into the bottom of the prepared pan and spread evenly. Sprinkle with about two-thirds of the chocolate mixture. Top with the remaining batter and spread evenly into the pan, and tap the pan several times on the counter to settle. Sprinkle with the remaining chocolate mixture.

5. Place on the middle rack of the oven to bake until the cake rises and starts to pull away from the sides and a wooden skewer inserted into the center comes out clean, 40 to 50 minutes.

6. Remove from the oven and cool in the pan, about 30 minutes. Run a knife around the outer and inner edges of the pan before turning the cake out onto a rack to cool. Serve warm or room temperature.

Herb Cheddar Biscuits

THESE HERB-PACKED BISCUITS ARE A MARKET STAPLE—in the morning, tucked with egg and cheese; at lunch or dinner, dipped into a cup of Chicken and Black-Eyed Pea Soup (page 92).

Makes about 1 dozen (2½- to 3-inch) biscuits

3½ cups all-purpose flour

2 teaspoons baking powder

1 teaspoon baking soda

1 teaspoon kosher salt

½ pound (2 sticks) cold unsalted butter, cut into ¼-inch cubes

1 cup (4 ounces) grated sharp Cheddar cheese

2 scallions, trimmed and minced

2 tablespoons chopped fresh parsley

1¼ cups well-shaken buttermilk, plus more if needed

Egg wash: 1 large egg beaten with 2 tablespoons milk

1. Preheat the oven to 425°F. Lightly grease a baking sheet or line with parchment paper and set aside.

2. Sift together the flour, baking powder, baking soda and salt in a large bowl.

3. Add the butter to the flour mixture. Using a pastry cutter or two knives, cut the butter into the flour mixture until it resembles coarse meal (or pulse 10 to 12 times in the bowl of a food processor fitted with a metal blade). Transfer the mixture to a large bowl to continue making the dough by hand. Add the cheese, scallions and parsley and stir to combine.

4. Add the buttermilk and mix lightly just until the dough begins to stick together, being careful not to overmix. Add up to 4 tablespoons more buttermilk, 1 tablespoon at a time, if the dough is still crumbly and not sticking together.

5. Turn the dough onto a large piece of lightly floured waxed or parchment paper (this makes for easy cleanup) and knead several times just until the dough comes together, adding only as much flour as you need to keep the dough from sticking to the work surface or to your hands. Form the dough into a flat round. Pat or roll the dough to ½ to ¾ inch thick.

6. Using a floured biscuit or cookie cutter, cut the dough into rounds about 2½ inches, dipping the cutter into the flour as needed to keep the dough from sticking and pressing directly down while careful not to turn the cutter.

7. Place the biscuits on the prepared baking sheet and brush the tops with the egg wash.

8. Bake until golden brown, 12 to 15 minutes. Remove the biscuits from the oven and serve warm.

SIX ORIGINAL EGG SCRAMBLES

SERVES 4

TO MAKE A CREAMY, FOOLPROOF SCRAMBLE: Melt **1 tablespoon unsalted butter** with **1 tablespoon olive oil** in a large nonstick skillet over medium heat. While the butter melts, whisk together **8 large eggs**, until the whites and yolks are completely combined. Season with sea salt and freshly ground black pepper to taste.

When the butter begins to foam, pour in the egg mixture. Do not stir until the eggs begin to set. Stir gently with a heatproof rubber spatula or wooden spoon until the eggs are creamy and still moist, 2 to 3 minutes; they will continue to cook and firm up after they are removed from the heat. Serve immediately. If you are adding cheese or herbs, stir in during the last minute, just before serving.

Cream Cheese and Wilted Spinach: stir in **2 tablespoons cream cheese** and about **1 handful spinach** until spinach wilts.

Summer Tomato Salsa and Crumbled Goat Cheese: stir in **2 tablespoons crumbled goat cheese** and top with **Summer Tomato Salsa** (page 34).

Sautéed Mushrooms and Crispy Bacon: stir in or top with about **½ cup sautéed mushrooms** and **2 slices crumbled crispy bacon**.

Smoked Salmon or Gravlax (page 43) and Scallions: stir in **¼ cup thinly sliced smoked salmon or Gravlax (page 43)** and **1 tablespoon minced scallions**.

Chorizo and Cheddar with Salsa Verde: stir in **½ cup chopped cooked chorizo sausage** and **½ cup grated Cheddar cheese** and top with **Italian Salsa Verde** (page 140).

Herbs and Cheese: using your favorite herbs and cheeses, stir in **1 tablespoon chopped fresh herb leaves** and **½ cup grated or crumbled cheese**.

On the Menu

SIX EGG VEHICLES These scrambles go great with (or better yet, on):
- Herb Cheddar Biscuits (page 61)
- Grilled or Toasted Cornbread Slices (page 145)
- Rustic Toast with Olive Oil and Sea Salt (page 145)
- Flame-Toasted Tortillas (page 145)
- Peter's Breakfast Potatoes (page 251)
- Potato Pancakes (page 40)
- Grits Bowl Your Way (page 74)
- Creamy Polenta (page 269)

Sweet Potato Sorghum Biscuits

NORTH CAROLINA'S GO-TO POTATO (our state potato, in fact, thanks to a letter-writing crusade led by elementary-school students) lends its sunny hue and a hint of sweetness to these savory biscuits. Deck them out with other staples from the Tar Heel state, including Foster's Pimiento Cheese (page 31) or vinegary pulled pork. **Makes about 1 dozen (2½- to 3-inch) biscuits**

3½ cups all-purpose flour

2 teaspoons baking powder

1 teaspoon baking soda

¼ teaspoon kosher salt

8 tablespoons (1 stick) cold unsalted butter, cubed

4 tablespoons vegetable shortening

1¼ cups well-shaken buttermilk, plus more if needed

1 cup mashed sweet potato (about 1 medium sweet potato)

2 tablespoons sorghum molasses

In the Kitchen

SORGHUM MUSTARD Give your mustard more depth. Try this simple recipe, which relies on sorghum syrup in place of more common honey, and spread on ham biscuits.

Mix together ½ **cup Dijon mustard** with **2 tablespoons sorghum syrup** and ½ **teaspoon freshly ground black pepper** and stir to combine. Store refrigerated in an airtight container until ready to serve.

1. Preheat the oven to 425°F. Lightly grease a baking sheet or line with parchment paper and set aside.

2. Sift together the flour, baking powder, baking soda and salt in a large bowl.

3. Add the butter and shortening to the flour mixture. Using a pastry cutter or two knives, cut the butter and shortening into the flour mixture until it resembles coarse meal (or pulse 10 to 12 times in the bowl of a food processor fitted with a metal blade).

4. Combine the buttermilk, sweet potato and sorghum in a separate small bowl and stir until thoroughly mixed. Add this mixture to the flour-butter mixture and stir until the dough just begins to stick together, being careful not to overmix. Add up to 4 tablespoons more buttermilk, 1 tablespoon at a time, if the dough is still crumbly and not sticking together.

5. Turn the dough onto a large piece of lightly floured waxed or parchment paper (this makes for easy cleanup) and knead several times just until the dough comes together, adding only as much flour as you need to keep the dough from sticking to the work surface or to your hands. Form the dough into a flat round. Pat or roll the dough to ½ to ¾ inch thick.

6. Using a floured biscuit or cookie cutter, cut the dough into 2½- to 3-inch rounds, dipping the cutter into the flour as needed to keep the dough from sticking and pressing directly down while careful not to turn the cutter.

7. Place onto the prepared pan, leaving at least ½ inch between biscuits.

8. Bake 15 to 17 minutes, until golden brown around the edges. Remove the biscuits from the oven and serve warm.

Apple Cider Doughnut Muffins

WITH WARM SPICES AND A SPLASH OF APPLE CIDER, these muffins may recall fall. But they remind me of Sunday mornings—every Sunday morning, as a kid—when my grandfather delighted in making doughnuts. Tip: I usually use a pan release for muffins because the pans are so hard to grease. **Makes about 1 dozen muffins**

MUFFINS

3 cups all-purpose flour

2 teaspoons baking powder

1½ teaspoons ground cinnamon

1 teaspoon freshly grated nutmeg

½ teaspoon ground cloves

¼ teaspoon kosher salt

12 tablespoons (1½ sticks) unsalted butter, melted

1 cup sugar

2 large eggs

½ cup apple cider

½ cup well-shaken buttermilk

1 teaspoon pure vanilla extract

DIPPING SUGAR

4 tablespoons unsalted butter

¼ cup apple cider

¾ cup sugar

2 teaspoons ground cinnamon

MUFFINS

1. Preheat the oven to 375°F. Generously coat a 12-cup muffin tin with pan release (do not use paper liners for this recipe) and set aside.

2. Combine the flour, baking powder, cinnamon, nutmeg, cloves and salt in a large bowl and stir to mix.

3. In a separate bowl, stir together the butter, sugar and eggs and whisk to thoroughly combine. Mix the apple cider, buttermilk and vanilla in the measuring cup as you measure and stir to combine. Add this to the sugar mixture.

4. Add the buttermilk mixture to the flour mixture and stir just until the dry ingredients are incorporated, being careful not to overmix.

5. Scoop the batter into the prepared muffin tins using a ⅓-cup measure or an ice-cream scoop to fill each cup about three-quarters full.

6. Bake 25 to 30 minutes, until springy to the touch and a wooden skewer inserted in the center comes out clean. Remove the muffins from the oven and let cool enough to handle, but don't cool completely before rolling into dipping sugar.

DIPPING SUGAR

While the muffins are baking, melt the butter in a small bowl and stir in the apple cider. In a separate bowl, combine the sugar and cinnamon. Remove the warm muffins from the tin, one at a time, and dip the tops into the cider mixture. Roll all over in the cinnamon-sugar to completely coat. Serve warm.

Very Berry Muffins

BLUE IS JUST THE BEGINNING: toss in handfuls of ruby-red raspberries and dark-hued blackberries for muffins as good-looking as they are good-tasting. **Makes about 1 dozen muffins**

2½ cups all-purpose flour

2 teaspoons baking powder

1 teaspoon ground cinnamon

1 teaspoon ground cardamom

½ teaspoon freshly grated nutmeg

¼ teaspoon kosher salt

2 cups mixed berries (blueberries, blackberries and raspberries), divided

8 tablespoons (1 stick) unsalted butter, melted

1 cup sugar

2 large eggs

¾ cup well-shaken buttermilk

2 teaspoons pure vanilla extract

Zest and juice of 1 lemon

1. Preheat the oven to 375°F. Place paper baking cups in a muffin tin or coat lightly with pan release.

2. Combine the flour, baking powder, cinnamon, cardamom, nutmeg and salt in a large bowl and stir to mix.

3. In a separate bowl, whisk together 1 cup of the berries, butter, sugar, eggs, buttermilk, vanilla, and lemon zest and juice.

4. Add the egg mixture to the flour mixture and stir just until the dry ingredients are incorporated, being careful not to overmix. Gently fold in the remaining berries to distribute throughout the batter.

5. Scoop the batter into the prepared muffin tins using a ⅓-cup measure or an ice-cream scoop to fill each cup about three-quarters full.

6. Bake 25 to 30 minutes, until springy to the touch and a wooden skewer inserted in the center comes out clean. Remove from the oven and let sit for about 5 minutes before turning out of the pan. Serve warm with sweet butter.

In the Kitchen

BLUEBERRY MUFFINS We've offered classic blueberry muffins since day one. To make, just replace the other berries from the recipe above with all blues, pureeing half.

Oatmeal Orange Raisin Muffins

WITH THE ZEST OF ORANGES AND THE TANG OF BUTTERMILK, these muffins are guaranteed to brighten up your morning. **Makes about 1 dozen muffins**

MUFFINS

12 tablespoons (1½ sticks) unsalted butter, softened

1⅓ cups sugar

2 large eggs

2 cups all-purpose flour

1 cup old-fashioned rolled oats

2 teaspoons baking powder

1 teaspoon ground cinnamon

1 teaspoon ground cardamom

¼ teaspoon kosher salt

1 cup well-shaken buttermilk

Zest and juice of 1 orange

1 cup golden raisins

GLAZE

Juice of 1 orange

½ cup sugar

MUFFINS

1. Preheat the oven to 350°F. Place paper baking cups in a muffin tin or coat lightly with pan release.

2. Cream the butter and sugar in a large bowl with a mixer until light and fluffy, stopping to scrape down the sides of the bowl several times. Slowly beat in the eggs, one at a time, stopping to scrape down the sides of the bowl several times and mixing thoroughly after each addition.

3. In a separate bowl, stir together the flour, oats, baking powder, cinnamon, cardamom and salt. Combine the buttermilk and orange zest and juice in another separate bowl and stir to mix.

4. Add the flour mixture and buttermilk mixture to the sugar mixture and stir just until the dry ingredients are incorporated. Gently fold in the raisins to distribute throughout the batter.

5. Scoop the batter into the prepared muffin tin using a ⅓-cup measure or an ice-cream scoop to fill each cup about three-quarters full.

6. Bake 25 to 30 minutes, until springy to the touch and a wooden skewer inserted in the center comes out clean. Remove from the oven and allow to cool slightly before glazing.

GLAZE

While the muffins are baking, combine the orange juice and ¼ cup of the sugar in a small saucepan and bring to a boil. Cook and stir until the sugar dissolves, about 1 minute. Remove from the heat and set aside until ready to use. Remove the muffins from the tin and brush with the orange juice glaze while still warm. Sprinkle the tops with the remaining ¼ cup of the sugar to coat. Serve warm.

Sorghum Sweet Potato Muffins with Crumb Topping

ONE OF THE MANY REASONS I LOVE SWEET POTATOES is for their subtlety, the same reason I love sorghum syrup. Compared to molasses, it's a little less cloying and a little more complex. Here, the two are combined—then admittedly topped with brown sugar, which is also in the batter).

Makes about 1 dozen muffins

CRUMB TOPPING

4 tablespoons (½ stick) cold unsalted butter

½ cup chopped pecans

¼ cup all-purpose flour

¼ cup brown sugar

1 teaspoon ground cinnamon

¼ teaspoon sea salt

MUFFINS

2 cups all-purpose flour

2 teaspoons baking powder

2 teaspoons ground cinnamon

1 teaspoon freshly grated nutmeg

½ teaspoon ground allspice

¼ teaspoon kosher salt

1 cup brown sugar

¾ cup vegetable oil

2 large eggs

1½ cups mashed sweet potato (about 1 large sweet potato)

¼ cup sorghum molasses

½ cup chopped pecans

CRUMB TOPPING

Place the butter, pecans, flour, sugar, cinnamon and salt in the bowl of a food processor fitted with a metal blade and pulse until crumbly and the butter is combined with the dry ingredients. (Alternatively, mix together in a large bowl with a pastry blender or your fingertips.) Set aside until ready to use.

MUFFINS

1. Preheat the oven to 375°F. Place paper baking cups in a muffin tin or coat lightly with pan release.

2. Sift together the flour, baking powder, cinnamon, nutmeg, allspice and salt in a large bowl and stir to mix.

3. In a separate bowl, stir together the sugar, oil and eggs. Add the sweet potato and sorghum to this mixture and stir until well combined.

4. Add the egg mixture to the flour mixture and stir just until the dry ingredients are incorporated, being careful not to overmix. Gently fold in the pecans to distribute throughout the batter.

5. Scoop the batter into the prepared muffin tin using a ⅓-cup measure or an ice-cream scoop to fill each cup about three-quarters full. Top each with a heaping tablespoon of the crumb topping.

6. Bake 25 to 30 minutes, until springy to the touch and a wooden skewer inserted in the center comes out clean. Remove from the oven and let sit for about 5 minutes before turning out of the pan. Serve warm.

Black Bottom Muffins

FULL DISCLOSURE: THIS IS BASICALLY A CAKE BATTER (meaning these are basically cupcakes). But our customers tend to turn a blind eye or perhaps just embrace them whole-heartedly, as these are one of our best-selling muffins each morning. We certainly understand. They go great with a cup of coffee for breakfast or dessert. **Makes about 1 dozen muffins**

TOP

6 ounces reduced-fat cream cheese, softened

⅓ cup sugar

1 large egg yolk, lightly beaten

½ cup semisweet chocolate chips

BOTTOM

2 cups all-purpose flour

1 cup sugar

¼ cup unsweetened cocoa powder, sifted

2 teaspoons baking powder

½ teaspoon kosher salt

¾ cup warm water

⅓ cup canola oil

2 teaspoons pure vanilla extract

TOP

With an electric mixer, cream together the cream cheese and sugar until smooth and fluffy. Add the egg yolk and beat until well combined. Gently fold in the chocolate chips until distributed throughout. Set aside until ready to use.

BOTTOM

1. Preheat the oven to 375°F. Place paper baking cups in a muffin tin or coat lightly with pan release.

2. In a large bowl, combine the flour, sugar, cocoa, baking powder and salt and stir to mix.

3. In a separate bowl, whisk together the warm water, oil and vanilla.

4. Add the oil mixture to the flour mixture and stir just until all the dry ingredients are incorporated, being careful not to overmix.

5. Scoop the batter into the prepared muffin tins using a ¼-cup measure or an ice-cream scoop to fill each cup about halfway full. Top each with a heaping tablespoon of the cream cheese mixture.

5. Bake 25 to 30 minutes, until springy to the touch and a wooden skewer inserted in the center comes out clean. Remove from the oven and cool in the tin, about 5 minutes. Turn the muffins out of the pan and serve warm, or continue to cool completely before storing.

Foster's Scones Your Way

TO OUR DISMAY, THERE WERE NO SCONES IN THE TRIANGLE when Peter and I first arrived. Thankfully we moved south armed with Dorian Leigh Parker's recipe. Beyond modeling for Revlon and others during the 1950s, Parker catered for Martha Stewart and taught us the art of baking soft, lightly sweetened scones with a crisp outer shell. Good thing! Since we opened the Market 25 years ago, we've offered three different kinds each morning—meaning, some 9,000 days and some tens of thousands of scones. **Makes about 1 dozen scones**

4½ cups all-purpose flour

½ cup sugar

2 teaspoons baking powder

½ teaspoon baking soda

½ teaspoon kosher salt

¾ pound (3 sticks) cold unsalted butter, cut into small pieces

1¼ cups well-shaken buttermilk, plus more if needed

Egg wash: 1 large egg beaten with 2 tablespoons milk or cream

1. Preheat the oven to 400°F. Lightly grease 2 baking sheets or line with parchment paper and set aside.

2. Sift together the flour, sugar, baking powder, baking soda and salt in a large bowl and stir to mix.

3. Add the butter to the flour mixture. Using a pastry cutter or two knives, cut the butter into the flour mixture until it resembles coarse meal (or pulse 10 to 12 times in the bowl of a food processor fitted with a metal blade). Transfer the mixture to a large bowl to continue making the dough, being careful not to overmix.

4. Add the buttermilk and mix lightly until just combined and the dough begins to stick together. Add up to 2 tablespoons more buttermilk, 1 tablespoon at a time, if the dough is still crumbly and not sticking together.

5. Turn the dough onto a large piece of lightly floured waxed or parchment paper (this makes for easy cleanup) and roll or pat into two 6-inch rounds, about 1½ inches thick. Cut each round in half and cut each half into 3 triangles (pie-shaped wedges).

6. Place on the prepared baking sheets, and brush the tops with the egg wash.

7. Bake 30 to 35 minutes, until golden brown and firm to the touch. Remove from the oven and serve warm.

In the Kitchen

FLAVOR VARIATIONS These flavors are on frequent rotation at the Market, except for the plain scone—our most popular—which is a mainstay and never takes a break. To make variations, add the following dry ingredients at the end of step 3, before adding the buttermilk. If the added ingredient is soft or runny (like sweet potato or coffee), add with the buttermilk in step 4.

- **Butterscotch:** add 1 cup butterscotch chips.
- **Cherry Chocolate:** add ½ cup chocolate chips and ½ cup dried tart cherries.
- **Pumpkin White Chocolate:** cut the buttermilk by ¼ cup and add ½ cup pumpkin puree and ½ cup white chocolate chips.
- **Strawberry:** cut the buttermilk by ¼ cup and add 1 cup hulled chopped strawberries.

Grits Bowl Your Way

THE GLORY OF GRITS IS THAT THEY ARE GOOD SIMPLY DONE, with just a pat of butter and a sprinkle of salt and pepper, or done up. At the Market, we adorn our grits bowl with Spicy Black Beans (recipe below), Summer Tomato Salsa (page 34), an extra grate of cheese and a runny fried egg—and sometimes a crumble of bacon or chorizo, too. At home, some of my favorite toppings include sautéed garlic shrimp and wild mushrooms, Everyday Bolognese (page 160) and grated Parmesan or Pickle-Brined Fried Chicken (page 120) and Sriracha Honey (page 120). **Serves 4 to 6**

3 cups water

2 teaspoons sea salt

1 cup yellow stone-ground grits

1 cup milk, plus up to ½ cup more if needed

4 tablespoons (½ stick) unsalted butter

1 cup (4 ounces) grated sharp Cheddar cheese

1 teaspoon freshly ground black pepper

Spicy Black Beans (recipe follows), for serving

Fried or scrambled eggs

Summer Tomato Salsa (page 34) or your favorite salsa

1. Bring the water to a boil in a large saucepan over high heat and add the salt. Slowly add the grits in a steady stream, whisking constantly. Reduce the heat to low and cook, stirring frequently, until thick and creamy, 20 to 30 minutes (depending on the grits).

2. Stir in the milk to combine, and continue to cook until the grains are tender to the bite and most of the milk is absorbed, 5 to 10 minutes more.

3. Remove from the heat and stir in the butter, cheese and pepper until the butter and cheese have melted. Taste and season with additional salt and black pepper, if desired. The grits should be loose and creamy. If they are too stiff, stir in up to ½ cup of milk to obtain the desired consistency. Serve immediately or cover to keep warm until ready to serve.

4. Scoop the grits into bowls and top with Spicy Black Beans (recipe follows); fried or scrambled eggs; Summer Tomato Salsa (page 34); and sausage, ham or bacon, if you like.

SPICY BLACK BEANS

MAKES ABOUT 3 CUPS

Heat **1 tablespoon olive oil** in a saucepan over medium-high heat until sizzling hot. Add **4 diced scallions, 1 jalapeño pepper (cored, seeded and diced)** and **2 minced garlic cloves** and cook, stirring, about 1 minute, until fragrant. Add **1 (15½-ounce) can black beans (drained and rinsed)** and **1 cup Summer Tomato Salsa (page 34) or your favorite salsa,** reduce the heat to medium and cook, stirring, until the beans are heated through, about 5 minutes. Serve warm over the grits or refrigerate until ready to serve and reheat just before serving.

Crustless Quiche

FOR OUR BUSIEST DAYS, when the wait for a hot breakfast verges on an hour—graduation, Mother's Day and the Fourth of July—we make a large pan of this crustless, gluten-free quiche to have on hand. Serve it to your next crowd, bulking it up according to their tastes: sausage, bacon, roasted red peppers, kale or asparagus. **Serves 6 to 8**

1 tablespoon olive oil

1 tablespoon unsalted butter

½ onion, minced

2 handfuls baby spinach or supergreens mix (see Mix It Up, below)

1 cup (4 ounces) shredded Gruyère or Swiss cheese

1 cup (4 ounces) shredded sharp Cheddar cheese

6 large eggs

1 cup heavy cream

1 teaspoon ground mustard

½ teaspoon sea salt

⅛ teaspoon freshly ground black pepper

Pinch of ground cayenne pepper

Pinch of freshly grated nutmeg (2 to 3 grates)

1. Preheat the oven to 350°F. Generously grease a 9- or 10-inch quiche or pie dish and set aside.

2. Heat the oil and butter in a large skillet over medium heat until sizzling hot. Add the onion and cook, stirring, until translucent, about 5 minutes. Add the spinach and cook, stirring, just until wilted, about 1 minute. Remove from the heat and set aside to cool.

3. Sprinkle the cheese over the bottom of the prepared dish. Top with the onions and spinach.

4. In a large bowl, whisk together the eggs, cream, mustard, salt, black pepper, cayenne and nutmeg and pour over the cheese and spinach mixture.

5. Place in the oven to bake until the filling is puffed and golden and the eggs are set around the edges and slightly loose in the center, about 35 minutes. Let cool slightly before slicing into wedges, about 5 minutes. Serve warm.

On the Menu

SERVE WITH To round out a full meal, pair with a fresh Kale Salad with Tangerines, Avocado and Crispy Country Ham (page 229) or BLT Salad with Arugula, Avocado and Corn (page 230).

In the Kitchen

MIX IT UP When I call for greens in a recipe, such as spinach or arugula, feel free to use what is available or in season. Here are a few of my favorites: spinach, arugula, tatsoi and Swiss chard. Or buy the supergreens mix and get all in one.

Eggs Sardou Your Way

TO HONOR THE ARRIVAL OF FRENCH DRAMATIST EDWARD SARDOU to New Orleans in 1908, Antoine's created poached eggs garnished with fine black truffles and crisp ham, and set atop a bed of creamed spinach and artichoke hearts. Our version is a bit simpler, calling for fewer ingredients than the original, but it's also spicier, with the addition of Sriracha. **Serves 4**

EGGS

1 teaspoon kosher salt

2 teaspoons white vinegar

8 large eggs

SPINACH

1 tablespoon unsalted butter

1 tablespoon olive oil

1 (14-ounce) can artichoke hearts, drained and flattened

4 handfuls baby spinach or supergreens mix (see Mix It Up, page 77)

1 scallion, minced

1 garlic clove, smashed and minced

Pinch of ground cayenne pepper

Sea salt and freshly ground black pepper

Blender Sriracha Hollandaise (recipe follows)

2 tablespoons chopped fresh chives

EGGS

1. Pour enough water in a large skillet to fill to about 3 inches and bring to a boil. Add the salt and vinegar and reduce the heat to a low simmer so there are only a few bubbles on the surface.

2. Break 1 egg into a small bowl or measuring cup, taking care not to break the yolk. Turn the egg out of the bowl into the water in a quick motion so the egg keeps its shape when it hits the water. Repeat with the remaining eggs.

3. Cook the eggs for 2 to 3 minutes, until the whites set and a thin translucent film forms over the yolk. For a firmer yolk, cook the eggs another 1 to 2 minutes.

SPINACH

1. While the eggs are cooking, heat the butter and olive oil in a large skillet over medium-high heat until sizzling hot. Add the artichoke hearts and cook until golden brown around the edges, about 1 minute per side. Remove and place on a large platter or 4 individual plates and keep warm.

2. Add the spinach, scallion, garlic, cayenne, and salt and black pepper to taste to the same skillet and cook, stirring, just until the spinach wilts, about 1 minute.

3. Top the artichokes with the spinach mixture, dividing it evenly. Use a slotted spoon to gently lift the eggs out of the water and blot on a paper towel. Place 2 eggs on each plate, and spoon the Blender Sriracha Hollandaise sauce over the top. Sprinkle with chives and season with additional salt and pepper if desired. Serve immediately.

BLENDER SRIRACHA HOLLANDAISE

MAKES ABOUT 1 CUP

Place the **yolks of 2 large eggs (room temperature)** in the jar of a blender. Add the **juice of 1 lemon**, sprinkle with **1 teaspoon sea salt** and blend until frothy. While the blender is running, slowly add **8 tablespoons (1 stick) melted butter** that has been cooled to room temperature through the feed tube until all is incorporated. Add **1 tablespoon Sriracha** and pulse several times until well blended. Season with **freshly ground black pepper** to taste. Serve immediately or store at room temperature, covered, for up to 3 hours. This sauce cannot be refrigerated or reheated.

Foster's House-Made Granola

HERE, IT'S ALL ABOUT CONTRASTS: sweetened coconut and tart cherries; crunchy almonds and chewy cranberries; healthy rolled oats and a mess of maple syrup.

Makes about 8 cups / Serves 6 to 8

2 cups old-fashioned rolled oats

1 cup shredded sweetened coconut

1 cup sliced almonds

1 cup pecan halves

1 teaspoon kosher or sea salt

¾ cup maple syrup

¼ cup canola or safflower oil

1 tablespoon pure vanilla extract

½ cup dried tart cherries

½ cup dried cranberries

1. Preheat the oven to 275°F.

2. Combine the oats, coconut, almonds and pecans on a large rimmed baking sheet and spread evenly in a single layer. (It is important to have this in a thin layer, not piled up. Depending on the size of your baking sheet, you may need two.)

3. Place in the oven and bake, stirring occasionally, until the ingredients are lightly toasted but not quite golden in color, 12 to 15 minutes.

4. Remove from the oven and transfer the mixture to a large bowl. Add the salt and stir to mix.

5. Increase the oven temperature to 350°F. Lightly grease the same baking sheet.

6. Stir the syrup, oil and vanilla in a small bowl, pour over the oat mixture and toss to coat evenly. Spread the mixture in a single layer onto the oiled baking sheet and place in the oven to toast, stirring occasionally, until golden brown, 25 to 30 minutes. (It will not get crispy until it cools.)

7. Remove from the oven and allow to cool completely on the baking sheet, stirring often to prevent sticking.

8. When the mixture has completely cooled, add the cherries and cranberries and toss to mix. Store at room temperature in an airtight container for up to 2 weeks. Serve topped with Greek yogurt and your favorite fruit.

Chorizo Sweet Potato Hash

SPICY CRUMBLED CHORIZO provides the perfect foil for this sweet chopped hash. **Serves 4 to 6**

2 sweet potatoes, chopped

1 russet potato

2 tablespoons olive oil, divided

½ pound fresh bulk chorizo sausage

1 tablespoon unsalted butter

1 red bell pepper, cored, seeded and chopped

½ onion, chopped

2 tablespoons chopped fresh parsley

Sea salt and freshly ground black pepper

6 to 12 large eggs

1. Place the potatoes in a pot with enough water to cover by about 2 inches. Bring to a boil, reduce the heat to simmer and cook, about 5 minutes. The potatoes should be barely tender, still firm enough to hold their shape. Remove from the heat and drain well.

2. Heat 1 tablespoon of the oil in a large skillet over medium-high heat until sizzling hot and add the sausage, breaking it up as it cooks. Cook, stirring, until the sausage is brown and cooked through, 4 to 5 minutes. Remove from the skillet and place on a paper towel to drain.

3. Add the butter and remaining olive oil to the same skillet and heat until sizzling hot. Add the potatoes and cook, stirring occasionally, until slightly brown around the edges, about 5 minutes.

4. Add the pepper and onion and cook, stirring, until the potatoes are soft, about 5 minutes more. Add the sausage back to the skillet and cook just to warm the sausage, about 1 minute more. Add the parsley, season to taste with salt and pepper and stir to mix. Remove from the heat and cover to keep warm.

5. Fry or poach the eggs to your desired doneness and divide the hash among individual plates, top with 1 or 2 eggs and serve hot.

On the Menu

A LITTLE MORE Top this hash with Summer Tomato Salsa (page 34) or Avocado Crema (page 143) and pair it with Herb Cheddar Biscuits (page 61).

In the Kitchen

VARIATIONS Think of the above recipe as a basic blueprint, then go your own way—mixing up the potatoes, herbs or fixings. Removing the chorizo, here are some of my preferred combinations:
- Summer Squash, Tomatoes, Corn and Spicy Shrimp
- Sweet and Hot Peppers, Eggplant, Onions and Andouille Sausage
- Butternut Squash, Kale and Chicken Apple Sausage
- Hominy, Country Ham and Banana Peppers

SOUPS & STEWS

SOUPS AND STEWS

I LIKE TO THINK SOUP SUMS US UP. Not because we've kept two different varieties on the menu every day since we opened, but because it's stuff to share—stuff that's warm and comforting and intended to bring folks together, which is what we aim to do at the Market. (Soup can be daunting on one's own without a giant freezer to stow away second, third and fourth helpings.)

My mother was revered for the Brunswick Stew she made in a black cast-iron kettle for the Fourth of July, Labor Day and other family gatherings. We all watched eagerly as it stewed slowly over a wood fire in our backyard. From this, I came up understanding soup and its ability to unite—but not how to make it. That came later at Soho Charcuterie in New York, my first real kitchen job, where I was tasked with reviewing produce in the walk-in cooler that was on its way out, then turning it into soups and salads. That experience forced me to be creative and unencumbered by recipes (for the record, we didn't have any anyway), which you'll see I encourage throughout this book. If a recipe calls for kale and you have a different green, try that instead, as I suggest in the notes for Toasted Farro Stew with Kale and Roasted Butternut Squash (page 102). Or, if you have golden beets but no sweet potatoes, why not give those a go, as I recommend for Lentil, Spinach and Sweet Potato Soup (page 99). Don't be afraid to experiment with what you have on hand or what is in season. Those are the best inspirations.

Of course, more goes into making good soup than a list of ingredients. I got my best tip from Wendell Wilson, one of the Market's first chefs, whose soups were always more flavorful than mine, even when we used the exact same recipes. Finally, I asked him what it was that gave his an extra edge. His answer: don't rush the onions. Cook them for at least 10 minutes, allowing them to caramelize (a man of true patience, he preferred to cook them for 30 to 40 minutes). It's advice that transfers beyond onions. Slow down, gather good company and enjoy a warm bowl of soup.

Short Rib Chili

TENDER, BEER-BRAISED SHORT RIBS make this far from your average chili. If timing allows, make it a day in advance, allowing the flavors to fully meld. Then all you have to do is warm the soup, add garnishes and crack open one of the beers left over from the short rib prep.

Makes about 3½ quarts / Serves 8 to 10

2 pounds boneless short ribs (3½ to 4 pounds bone-in)

Kosher salt and freshly ground black pepper

3 tablespoons olive oil

1 (12-ounce) dark beer

4 sprigs fresh rosemary

2 onions, chopped

1 red bell pepper, cored, seeded and diced

2 jalapeño peppers, cored, seeded and diced

4 garlic cloves, smashed and minced

¼ cup chili powder

1 tablespoon ground cumin

2 teaspoons dried basil

8 cups low-sodium chicken or beef broth (use reserved broth from short ribs first)

1 (28-ounce) can diced tomatoes

¼ cup Worcestershire sauce

2 tablespoons tomato paste

2 bay leaves

1 teaspoon crushed red pepper flakes

1 (15-ounce) can black beans, drained and rinsed

1 (15-ounce) can chickpeas, drained and rinsed

1. Season the short ribs all over with salt and black pepper. Heat 1 tablespoon of the olive oil in a large saucepan or Dutch oven over medium-high heat and add the short ribs. Sear on both sides until dark brown, about 4 minutes per side. Add the beer, 2 cups of water (or enough to cover the ribs about two-thirds of the way up with liquid) and rosemary and cover tightly. Reduce the heat to low and simmer until fork-tender, about 2 hours. (Alternatively, you can place in a preheated 325°F oven for the same amount of time.) When the beef is fork-tender and cool enough to handle, remove from the liquid (reserving the liquid) and shred into small pieces. Discard any excess fat from the ribs. You should have 4 to 5 cups of shredded beef.

2. Heat the remaining olive oil in a separate large saucepan or Dutch oven over medium heat until sizzling hot and add the onions. Reduce the heat to low and cook, stirring, until soft and golden brown, about 10 minutes. Add the red bell pepper and jalapeños and cook, stirring often, until peppers are soft, about 5 minutes more. Add the garlic and cook, stirring, about 1 minute more.

3. Add the shredded beef, chili powder, cumin and basil and continue to cook, stirring, about 4 minutes more.

4. Stir in the broth, tomatoes, Worcestershire sauce, tomato paste, bay leaves and red pepper flakes, and season with salt and black pepper to taste. Bring to a low boil and reduce the heat, simmering, until the liquid has reduced slightly and the flavors have time to meld, about 1 hour.

5. Remove the bay leaves from the chili and discard. Add the beans and continue to cook until the beans have heated through, about 15 minutes more. Serve warm with a dollop of sour cream or yogurt, grated cheese and chopped fresh cilantro or scallions.

Black Bean and Sweet Potato Chili

CUSTOMERS OFTEN THINK WE'VE MADE A MISTAKE—that we've left "beef" off our sign for this chili. But it's bulgur here at play. The nutty grain makes a substantial soup that can be bulked up even more with a combination of toppings: grated sharp Cheddar or pepper Jack cheeses, minced fresh chiles, diced onions, crisp tortilla chips or a dollop of sour cream.

Makes about 3 quarts / Serves 8 to 10

2 tablespoons olive oil

1 onion, chopped

2 medium sweet potatoes, diced

1 red bell pepper, cored, seeded and chopped

1 green bell pepper, cored, seeded and chopped

2 jalapeño peppers, cored, seeded and diced

3 garlic cloves, smashed and minced

3 tablespoons chili powder

2 teaspoons ground cumin

2 teaspoons dried basil

1 teaspoon dried marjoram

1 teaspoon crushed red pepper flakes

3 bay leaves

1 teaspoon kosher salt

½ teaspoon freshly ground black pepper

6 cups low-sodium vegetable or chicken broth

1 (28-ounce) can chopped tomatoes

1 (12-ounce) beer

½ cup bulgur (substitute: barley)

2 (15-ounce) cans black beans, rinsed and drained

½ cup chopped fresh cilantro

3 scallions, minced

2 limes, cut into wedges

1. Heat the olive oil in a large saucepan or Dutch oven over medium heat until sizzling hot and add the onion. Reduce the heat to low and cook, stirring often, about 10 minutes. Add the sweet potatoes, red and green bell peppers and jalapeños and cook, stirring occasionally, 5 minutes more. Stir in the garlic and cook, stirring, about 1 minute longer.

2. Add the chili powder, cumin, basil, marjoram, red pepper flakes, bay leaves, salt and black pepper and cook, stirring, about 2 minutes. Add the broth, tomatoes, beer and bulgur and stir to combine, bringing to a low boil. Reduce the heat to a simmer and cook uncovered, stirring occasionally, about 40 minutes.

3. Remove the bay leaves from the chili and discard. Add the beans, stir to mix and continue to cook, stirring occasionally, until the beans are heated through, about 15 minutes more. Garnish with the cilantro and scallions and serve warm with wedges of lime to squeeze into the chili.

On the Menu

SIDE DISHES Keep it easy. Serve Easy Quesadillas (page 123), Grilled Cornbread or Toasted Slices (page 145) or Grilled Romaine Caesar with Rustic Crunchy Croutons (page 213). Then conclude with an Ice Cream Mix-Ins Buffet (page 289).

In the Kitchen

TOPPINGS When I have a chili party I like to offer at least two versions: a meat and a vegetarian option. But the real variety is served in small dishes filled with grated sharp Cheddar cheese, Avocado Crema (page 143), Summer Tomato Salsa (page 34), chopped chile peppers, minced onions, fresh cilantro leaves, lime wedges and Fritos so people can dress their chili according to their preference. In addition, I often serve Grilled or Toasted Cornbread Slices (page 145) or Flame Toasted Tortillas (page 145).

Chicken and Black-Eyed Pea Soup

WHAT COULD MAKE THIS BOWL OF BLACK-EYED PEAS AND SWEET POTATOES more Southern? A few handfuls of collard greens. Just throw them in during the last 10 minutes of cooking. To go all out, substitute shredded pork for chicken. **Makes about 3½ quarts / Serves 8 to 10**

1 tablespoon olive oil

1 tablespoon unsalted butter

1 onion, diced

4 celery stalks, diced

1 red bell pepper, cored, seeded and diced

2 jalapeño peppers, cored, seeded and minced

3 garlic cloves, smashed and minced

4 cups cooked shredded chicken (meat from roasted or boiled chicken)

2 teaspoons dried basil

1 teaspoon ground cumin

½ teaspoon crushed red pepper flakes

1 teaspoon sea salt

½ teaspoon freshly ground black pepper

8 cups low-sodium chicken broth

2 sweet potatoes, chopped

2 bay leaves

2 cups fresh or frozen black-eyed peas, rinsed and drained

¼ cup chopped fresh cilantro

1. Heat the olive oil and butter in a large saucepan over medium heat until sizzling hot and butter melts. Add the onion, reduce heat to low and cook, stirring occasionally, until golden brown, about 10 minutes. Add the celery and bell pepper and cook, stirring often, until the vegetables are soft, about 5 minutes. Add the jalapeños and garlic and cook, stirring, 1 minute more, taking care not to let the garlic brown.

2. Add the chicken, basil, cumin, red pepper flakes, salt and black pepper and cook, stirring, about 2 minutes. Add the broth, potatoes and bay leaves and stir to mix, bringing to a low boil. Reduce the heat and simmer until potatoes are soft, about 30 minutes. Skim any foam from the top of the soup while cooking and discard. Remove the bay leaves from the soup and discard. Add the peas and continue to cook until the peas are tender, about 15 minutes more.

3. Remove the soup from the heat and stir in the cilantro. Serve warm with Grilled or Toasted Cornbread Slices (page 145) on the side, if desired.

On the Menu

SERVE WITH I love to top this soup with crumbled Grilled or Toasted Cornbread Slices (page 145). For starters, try a Spring Chopped Vegetable Salad (page 211) or one of its seasonal variations. Also goes well with Kale Salad with Tangerines, Avocado and Crispy Country Ham (page 229) and Brown Sugar Apple Crisp with Crumb Topping (page 301) for a perfect fall dinner.

Mulligatawny

OUR VERSION OF MULLIGATAWNY—a British-Indian hybrid whose name means "pepper water"—is softened by the addition of coconut milk. For it, we thank Wendell Wilson, one of the Market's first chefs and a great soup maker. **Makes about 3 quarts / Serves 8 to 10**

2 tablespoons olive oil

1 teaspoon cumin seeds

1 teaspoon coriander seeds

1 teaspoon yellow mustard seeds

2 dried Thai chile peppers

2 tablespoons unsalted butter

1 onion, diced

2 carrots, diced

1 jalapeño pepper, cored, seeded and diced

1 (2-inch) piece ginger, peeled and minced

4 garlic cloves, smashed and minced

3 tablespoons all-purpose flour

2 tablespoons curry powder (see Homemade Curry Powder, page 101)

2 teaspoons ground cumin

1 teaspoon ground coriander

10 cups low-sodium chicken broth

4 cups cooked shredded chicken (meat from 1 roasted or boiled chicken)

1 cup green lentils

1 teaspoon kosher salt

½ teaspoon freshly ground black pepper

1 bunch kale, stems removed and roughly chopped

1 (15½-ounce) can chickpeas, drained and rinsed

1 cup fresh or frozen green peas

1 cup light coconut milk

Juice of 1 lemon

1 bunch fresh cilantro, chopped

Curry Buttermilk Yogurt Sauce (page 142)

1. Heat 1 tablespoon of the olive oil in a large saucepan or Dutch oven over medium heat until sizzling hot. Add the cumin seeds, coriander seeds, mustard seeds and chili peppers and cook, stirring, until fragrant and seeds begin to pop, about 1 minute. Remove from the pan and set aside.

2. Add the remaining olive oil and butter to the same pan and heat until sizzling hot. Add the onion, reduce the heat to low and cook, stirring, until the onion is soft and golden brown, about 5 minutes. Add the carrots and jalapeño and cook, stirring, about 5 minutes more. Add the ginger and garlic and cook, stirring, until fragrant, about 2 minutes. Add the flour, curry, cumin and coriander and cook, stirring constantly, until smooth and light brown, about 3 minutes.

3. Slowly add the broth, scraping up any brown bits from the bottom of the pan, and stir until smooth. Add the chicken, reserved spice seeds and chile peppers, lentils, salt and black pepper and stir to combine, bringing to a low boil. Reduce the heat to low and simmer uncovered until the lentils are tender, about 40 minutes.

4. Stir in the kale, chickpeas, green peas, coconut milk and lemon juice and simmer to thoroughly heat and wilt kale, about 10 minutes. Remove from the heat and stir in the cilantro. Serve warm topped with Curry Buttermilk Yogurt Sauce (page 142).

Beef and Barley Stew

HEARTY BEEF AND BARLEY MAKE THE TITLE, but I often create this simple stew with Roasted Vegetables (page 254) in mind. Sweet and sturdy—not having succumbed to hours in a simmering pot—the vegetables are a great foil for this winter dish. Make a heaping bowl, then spoon the stew on top, almost like a gravy. For an extra kick, add a splash of bourbon to each bowl.

Makes about 3 quarts / Serves 8 to 10

2 tablespoons olive oil

1 onion, diced

3 celery stalks, diced

2 carrots, diced

3 garlic cloves, smashed and minced

9 cups low-sodium beef or chicken broth

4 cups (about 2 pounds) cooked shredded chuck roast (see How to Cook a Pot Roast, below)

¾ cup barley

2 tablespoons Worcestershire sauce

2 teaspoons ground cumin

2 teaspoons dried marjoram

2 teaspoons ground mustard

1 teaspoon ground paprika

½ teaspoon crushed red pepper flakes

1 teaspoon kosher salt

½ teaspoon freshly ground black pepper

2 handfuls baby spinach

1 tablespoon chopped fresh oregano

1 teaspoon chopped fresh marjoram

1. Heat the olive oil in a large saucepan or Dutch oven over medium-high heat until sizzling hot. Add the onion, reduce the heat to medium and cook, stirring, until golden brown, about 5 minutes. Add the celery and carrots and cook, stirring, about 5 minutes longer. Add the garlic and continue to cook, stirring often, about 1 minute more.

2. Add the broth, beef, barley, Worcestershire sauce, cumin, dried marjoram, mustard, paprika and red pepper flakes and stir to combine. Stir in salt and black pepper, reduce the heat to low and simmer until the barley is tender and the flavors have time to meld, about 45 minutes.

3. Add the spinach, oregano and fresh marjoram and cook, stirring, just to wilt the spinach, about 2 minutes. Remove from the heat and serve warm.

In the Kitchen

HOW TO COOK A POT ROAST Season a 2½ to 3-pound **chuck roast** with salt and black pepper all over. Heat just enough **vegetable oil** to cover the bottom of a deep ovenproof skillet over medium-high heat until sizzling hot and sear the roast on both sides. Add a few quartered **carrots** and **sprigs of rosemary or thyme** for extra flavor. Add enough **water** to cover about halfway up the roast, cover tightly and place in a 325°F preheated oven, undisturbed, until fork tender, about 2½ to 3 hours.

MUSHROOM BARLEY SOUP For a robust vegetarian version of this stew, replace the beef with **4 cups of assorted sautéed mushrooms**. Try a combination of wild and cultivated varieties, such as chanterelles, hen-of-the-woods, oyster, portobello, cremini or hedgehog.

Tuscan Bean, Cabbage and Sausage Soup

HEARTY BEANS AND GREENS ARE OFFSET BY A DELICATE BROTH. Soak up every drop with Rustic Toast with Olive Oil and Sea Salt (page 145). **Makes about 3 quarts / Serves 8 to 10**

2 tablespoons olive oil

2 onions, diced

½ pound fresh bulk pork, chicken or turkey sausage

3 celery stalks, diced

2 carrots, diced

6 garlic cloves, smashed and thinly sliced

8 cups low-sodium chicken broth

1 cup dried Navy beans, rinsed and picked through (substitute: cannellini)

2 bay leaves

1 teaspoon dried rosemary

1 teaspoon fennel seeds

1 teaspoon kosher salt

½ teaspoon freshly ground black pepper

½ head cabbage, cored and thinly sliced

1 bunch kale, stems removed and roughly chopped

1 tablespoon chopped fresh rosemary

Rustic Toast with Olive Oil and Sea Salt (page 145)

1. Heat the olive oil in a large saucepan or Dutch oven over medium heat until sizzling hot. Add the onions, reduce heat to low and cook, stirring, until soft and light brown, about 10 minutes.

2. Add the sausage and cook, breaking up sausage into small pieces, about 5 minutes. Add the celery and carrots and cook, stirring, until the celery is soft, about 5 minutes longer. Add the garlic and cook, stirring constantly, about 1 minute more.

3. Add the broth, beans, bay leaves, dried rosemary, fennel seeds, salt and black pepper and stir to mix, bringing the soup to a low boil. Reduce the heat to simmer and cook partially covered until the beans are tender, about 1 hour and 30 minutes.

4. Remove the bay leaves from the soup and discard. Stir in the cabbage and cook until tender, about 15 minutes. Add the kale and fresh rosemary and simmer just until the kale begins to wilt, about 5 minutes. Serve warm with big slices of Rustic Toast with Olive Oil and Sea Salt (page 145).

In the Kitchen

QUICK-COOKED BEANS These aren't canned, nor are they soaked for hours on end. These are in-between beans—dry beans that are prepped to cook in less than an hour, which retain their flavor and texture. To make, place the dried beans in a large pot and cover with 3 inches of water. Bring to a boil over high heat. Reduce to medium and cook uncovered about 45 minutes. Drain and rinse the beans. You can always substitute canned beans for a quicker-cooking soup.

East Coast Clam Chowder

TECHNICALLY, THIS IS A TRADITIONAL CREAM-BASED NEW ENGLAND CLAM CHOWDER, but I like to think of it more as an Eastern Seaboard stew—reflective not of the broth, but of the clams and their origins. For me, that often means pungent mahoganies from Maine's coast (Peter and I always seek them out while on summer trips to Lake Placid, New York) or cherrystones from North Carolina's Core Sound. **Makes about 3½ quarts / Serves 8 to 10**

2 tablespoons olive oil, divided

2 ounces prosciutto or country ham, diced

1 onion, diced

2 tablespoons unsalted butter

4 celery stalks, diced

2 carrots, diced

2 garlic cloves, smashed and minced

3 tablespoons all-purpose flour

1 teaspoon kosher salt

½ teaspoon freshly ground black pepper

6 cups low-sodium fish or chicken broth

½ cup bottled clam juice

2 tablespoons Worcestershire sauce

1 tablespoon hot sauce

4 Yukon Gold potatoes (about 1 pound), scrubbed and chopped

2 cups fresh or frozen corn kernels

1 pound chopped fresh or frozen clam meat

½ cup heavy cream

¼ cup chopped fresh parsley

2 tablespoons chopped fresh chives

1. Heat 1 tablespoon of the olive oil in a large saucepan or Dutch oven over medium heat until sizzling hot. Add the prosciutto and cook, stirring often, until crispy, 2 to 3 minutes. Remove from the pan with a slotted spoon, leaving any remaining oil, and place on a paper towel to drain. Add the remaining olive oil to the same pan and heat until sizzling hot.

2. Add the onion, reduce the heat to medium-low and cook, stirring, until the onion is thoroughly cooked and light brown, about 5 minutes.

3. Add the butter, celery and carrots and continue to cook, stirring, until the vegetables are soft, about 5 minutes more. Add the garlic and cook, stirring, about 1 minute. Add the flour, salt and black pepper and cook, stirring constantly, until golden brown, about 3 minutes.

4. Slowly add the broth, scraping up any brown bits from the bottom of the pan. Add the clam juice, Worcestershire sauce, hot sauce, potatoes and corn and bring to a low boil. Reduce the heat and simmer uncovered until the potatoes are tender, 30 to 35 minutes. Mash the soup with a potato masher; this will thicken the soup and give it body.

5. Add the clams and cook until tender, about 10 minutes. Remove from the heat and stir in the cream, parsley and chives. Taste for seasoning and add additional salt and pepper, if desired. Serve warm with pieces of crispy prosciutto sprinkled on top.

Lentil, Spinach and Sweet Potato Soup

IN THIS DISH, GREEN LENTILS—drab but as comforting as an old sweater—are perked up by sunny sweet potatoes and rich-hued spinach. Make a heartier meal by topping it with grilled chicken, lamb or pork sausage. **Makes about 3 quarts / Serves 8 to 10**

1 tablespoon olive oil

1 tablespoon unsalted butter

1 onion, diced

3 celery stalks, diced

2 carrots, diced

2 garlic cloves, smashed and minced

2 bay leaves

2 teaspoons dried tarragon

1 teaspoon dried marjoram

8 cups low-sodium vegetable or chicken broth

1 (15-ounce) can chopped tomatoes

1 cup dry red wine

1½ cups green lentils

2 sweet potatoes, chopped

1 teaspoon kosher salt

½ teaspoon freshly ground black pepper

1 (5-ounce) package baby spinach

1 cup chopped fresh parsley

1. Heat the olive oil and butter in a large saucepan or Dutch oven over medium heat until sizzling hot. Add the onion, reduce the heat to low and cook, stirring, until soft and golden brown, about 5 minutes. Add the celery and carrots and cook, stirring constantly, until soft, about 5 minutes more. Add the garlic and cook, stirring, about 1 minute longer.

2. Add the bay leaves, tarragon and marjoram and continue to cook, stirring, 1 minute more. Add the broth, tomatoes, wine, lentils and sweet potatoes and stir to combine. Season with salt and pepper and bring to a low boil. Reduce the heat to low and simmer until the liquid has reduced slightly and the lentils and potatoes are soft, about 45 minutes.

3. Remove the bay leaves from the soup and discard. Add the spinach and stir to mix, cooking just until the spinach wilts, about 2 minutes. Remove from the heat, add the parsley and serve warm.

In the Kitchen

SUBSTITUTIONS In place of the sweet potatoes, try substituting 3 to 4 golden beets, peeled and chopped. You can mix up the greens as well. In addition to (or instead of) the spinach, try kale, mustard greens or collards. In the summer, I add chopped tomatoes from the garden instead of canned.

Curried Carrot Ginger Soup

SPIKED WITH CURRY POWDER AND GINGER, this blazing orange soup tastes as warm as it appears. To add more zest, top it off with a dollop of Harissa Buttermilk Yogurt Sauce (page 142).

Makes about 3½ quarts / Serves 8 to 10

2 tablespoons olive oil

1 onion, chopped

2 tablespoons unsalted butter

10 to 12 carrots (about 1½ pounds), scrubbed and chopped

3 celery stalks, chopped

2 parsnips, chopped

2 red bell peppers, cored, seeded and chopped

2 garlic cloves, smashed and diced

1 (2-inch) piece ginger, peeled and minced

2 tablespoons Homemade Curry Powder (recipe below)

1 teaspoon ground cumin

½ teaspoon ground cardamom

8 cups low-sodium vegetable or chicken broth

1 teaspoon kosher salt

½ teaspoon freshly ground black pepper

Zest and juice of 2 oranges

1 (13½-ounce) can light coconut milk

½ cup chopped fresh cilantro

1 tablespoon honey

1 tablespoon Sriracha

Harissa Buttermilk Yogurt Sauce (page 142)

Lime wedges

1. Heat the olive oil in a large saucepan over medium heat until sizzling hot. Add the onion, reduce the heat to low and cook, stirring, until golden brown, about 5 minutes. Add the butter and melt. Add the carrots, celery, parsnips and peppers and cook, stirring often, until the carrots are just cooked, about 10 minutes. Add the garlic, ginger, curry, cumin and cardamom and continue to cook, stirring, until fragrant, about 2 minutes more.

2. Stir in the broth, salt and pepper and reduce the heat to low, simmering, until the carrots are tender, about 30 minutes. Remove from the heat and stir in the orange zest and juice, coconut milk, cilantro, honey and Sriracha.

3. Allow the soup to cool slightly and place an immersion blender into the pot, or pour the cooled soup into the bowl of a food processor fitted with a metal blade, and puree until smooth. Serve warm with additional cilantro sprinkled on top and a swirl of Harissa Buttermilk Yogurt Sauce. This soup can also be served chilled with wedges of lime to squeeze in.

In the Kitchen

HOMEMADE CURRY POWDER Make your own fresh and aromatic curry powder. In a small bowl or airtight container fitted with a lid, combine **1 tablespoon ground Hungarian paprika, 1 tablespoon ground cumin, 1 tablespoon ground coriander, 1 tablespoon ground turmeric, 2 teaspoons ground cardamom, 2 teaspoons ground yellow mustard, 2 teaspoons ground fennel seed, 1 teaspoon ground cayenne pepper, 1 teaspoon ground ginger, ½ teaspoon ground cinnamon** and **½ teaspoon ground cloves**. Stir or shake to blend. Store in an airtight container until ready to use, up to several months. Makes about ½ cup.

BEYOND SOUP I often repurpose pureed soups like this one to flavor a simple broth for other dishes. If making a risotto, add ½ cup to the broth. Or if steaming mussels or scallops, thin 1 cup of the soup with a little white wine or fish stock.

Toasted Farro Stew with Kale and Roasted Butternut Squash

THE KEY TO THIS DISH (AND MANY MORE) IS PARMESAN—not just the grated cheese, but also the rind. Adding it to the pot as the soup simmers infuses it with Parmesan's distinctive nutty undertones, which pair well with farro. For a bright finish, I swirl a spoonful of pesto in after the soup has finished cooking. **Makes about 3 quarts / Serves 6 to 8**

2 tablespoons olive oil

1 tablespoon unsalted butter

1 onion, chopped

¾ cup farro (substitute: barley)

1 teaspoon kosher salt

½ teaspoon freshly ground black pepper

1 butternut squash, peeled, seeded and cubed

2 carrots, chopped

2 celery stalks, chopped

4 garlic cloves, smashed and minced

2 tablespoons chopped fresh rosemary

1 teaspoon crushed red pepper flakes

10 cups low-sodium vegetable or chicken broth

Rind of Parmesan cheese

1 bunch kale, stems removed and roughly chopped

1 ounce shaved Parmesan cheese

Basil Pesto (page 143) or extra-virgin olive oil

Rustic Toast with Olive Oil and Sea Salt (page 145)

1. Heat the olive oil and butter in a large saucepan or Dutch oven over medium heat until sizzling hot. Add the onion and farro and season with salt and black pepper. Cook and stir until the onion is soft and translucent and the farro is lightly toasted, about 5 minutes.

2. Add the butternut squash, carrots and celery and cook, stirring, about 5 minutes longer. Add the garlic, rosemary and red pepper flakes and cook, stirring, 1 minute more.

3. Add the broth and rind, reduce the heat to low and simmer, stirring occasionally, until the farro and squash are tender but slightly chewy, about 40 minutes.

4. Add the kale and cook, stirring, just until the kale is wilted, about 2 minutes. Serve warm with a few shards of shaved Parmesan and a swirl of Basil Pesto (page 143) or a drizzle of olive oil on each serving, and with Rustic Toast with Olive Oil and Sea Salt (page 145) on the side.

In the Kitchen

SUBSTITUTIONS In the summer, I make this with fresh tomatoes instead of butternut squash or with navy and cannellini beans. It is also good with the addition of fennel, cabbage or bok choy, or with collard greens, Swiss chard, spinach or freshly shelled fava beans in place of kale. Feel free to improvise, making use of what's available or in season.

Potato Leek Soup

PICK YOUR POTATO—OR POTATOES, IN MY CASE. I like to make this soup with a combination, including buttery Yellow Finns, sweet California whites, creamy Carolas or Rose Golds and requisite russets. Pulled chicken makes a nice addition, too. **Makes about 3 quarts / Serves 8 to 10**

1 tablespoon olive oil

1 tablespoon unsalted butter

4 leeks (about 2 pounds), cleaned, trimmed, split lengthwise and thinly sliced (see Cleaning Leeks, below)

3 celery stalks, chopped

2 parsnips, chopped

4 garlic cloves, smashed and minced

6 Yukon Gold potatoes, chopped

8 cups low-sodium chicken or vegetable broth

1 teaspoon kosher salt

½ teaspoon freshly ground black pepper

¼ cup chopped fresh parsley

1 tablespoon chopped fresh thyme

Herb Buttermilk Yogurt Sauce (page 142)

1. Heat the olive oil and butter in a large saucepan over medium heat until the butter melts and is sizzling hot. Add the leeks and cook, stirring often, until the leeks are very tender, about 10 minutes. If the leeks begin to brown, reduce the heat to low and continue cooking. Add the celery and parsnips and cook, stirring occasionally, until soft, about 5 minutes more. Add the garlic and cook, stirring, 1 minute longer.

2. Add the potatoes and broth. Season with salt and black pepper and bring the soup to a low boil over medium heat. Reduce the heat to low and simmer uncovered, stirring occasionally, until the potatoes are tender, 25 to 30 minutes.

3. Ladle half of the soup into the bowl of a food processor fitted with a metal blade or the jar of a blender and puree until smooth. (You can puree half the soup with an immersion blender directly in the pot; just make sure to remove half to leave some of the vegetables chunky for texture.) Return the pureed soup back to the pot and stir to mix.

4. Remove the soup from the heat and stir in the parsley and thyme. Serve warm, topped with a dollop of yogurt or swirl of heavy cream.

In the Kitchen

CLEANING LEEKS Leeks are notorious for packing dirt between their delicate layers. To remove: trim the leeks, split them lengthwise and place them in a bowl of water to soak, 10 to 15 minutes. The dirt will sink to the bottom while the leeks remain at the top, so make sure the water is deep enough. Carefully remove the leeks and rinse under cool water to remove any remaining dirt.

MAKE-YOUR-OWN-SANDWICH BOARD

OPEN-FACED OR LOOSELY shut with two slices of bread; veggie-packed or meat-stacked; dry or smeared; simple or all out: there's a sandwich for everyone. At my home, that's the mantra. So for guests, I often set out things for them to mix and match of their own accord and pace. The number of choices and amounts depend on how many I am serving, but I suggest providing three to four options from each category.

MEATS
sliced ham, turkey, chicken, salami, mortadella or prosciutto; tuna packed in oil

CHEESE
thinly sliced Cheddar, provolone, Swiss, Havarti, or smoked Gouda; creamy fresh mozzarella; goat cheese or Brie

CONDIMENTS
mayonnaise, mustard, pickles, roasted peppers, pepperoncini peppers, pickled peppers, olives, chutney, jam or capers

VEGETABLES
lettuce, sprouts, spinach, kale, thinly sliced tomatoes, onions, cucumbers, carrots or peppers

SPICES
sea salt and freshly ground black pepper—must-haves!

CHAPTER 4

FAMILY DINNERS

WE HAVE THE LONG, WELL-LOVED TABLES that are perfect for a big family dinner. But in the beginning, we didn't have the menu, as Foster's focused more on biscuits and scones, sandwiches and salads, produce and pantry wares. Thankfully, one of our catering managers, Kara Pate, had an idea for the customers who dropped in after work or a Little League game: a weekly menu of made-from-scratch dishes that a busy family could pick up, take home and simply reheat.

The recipes in this chapter represent some of our most beloved Foster's Family Dinners—those that comfort us, like Market Meatloaf (page 110); those that are worthy of a celebration and a seat at a big table, such as Moroccan-Rubbed Grilled Boneless Leg of Lamb (page 136) or Pork Tenderloin with Olives and Tangerines (page 128); those that inspire a raucous time around the grill, including Beer Can Chicken (page 118) and Sweet and Sticky Baby Back Ribs (page 132); and those that remind us that, while family (or a family of friends), we're all a little different—Chile-Braised Pork Shoulder with Taco Fixings (page 130) and a Ginger Rice Bowl with Vietnamese Chili Sauce (page 114) allow everyone to do their own thing, throwing in toppings and sauces to their liking.

All of the dishes here will make perfect family dinners for you at home. They'll also make ample leftovers. And as is the case with Market Meatloaf and Chile-Braised Pork Shoulder with Taco Fixings, I can't decide what I like better: the initial meal or its day-old resurrection (see Meatloaf Sandwich, page 110, and be your own judge). What I do know for sure is that these are meals I don't want to miss. You'll see that in order to savor every bite I've included notes on Four Bready Things for Sopping Up Sauce (page 145), though for me the real treat is the company.

Market Meatloaf

MEATLOAF IS A MARKET STANDARD, though we've never standardized it. We're always changing up the recipe (you'll find two very different versions in our earlier cookbooks). Here, we use a mix of beef and pork, plus a whole host of herbs. **Serves 6 to 8**

2 large eggs, lightly beaten

1 onion, grated

1 carrot, grated

1 bunch fresh parsley, stems removed, chopped

2 tablespoons Dijon mustard

2 tablespoons Worcestershire sauce

3 garlic cloves, smashed and minced

2 teaspoons dried marjoram

2 teaspoons dried oregano

2 teaspoons sea salt

1 teaspoon freshly ground black pepper

2½ pounds ground chuck

½ pound ground pork

2 cups shredded mozzarella

2 cups fresh breadcrumbs

1 cup Everyday Marinara sauce (page 163) (substitute: ketchup or your favorite tomato sauce)

1. Preheat the oven to 375°F.

2. Combine the eggs, onion, carrot, parsley, mustard, Worcestershire, garlic, marjoram, oregano, salt and pepper in a large bowl and mix well.

3. Add the beef, pork, mozzarella, breadcrumbs and half of the marinara to the egg mixture and gently mix to combine and evenly distribute the seasoning, being careful not to overmix.

4. Place the meat mixture on a rimmed baking sheet and mold into a loaf, about 10 x 4-inches in shape. Brush the remaining marinara on top and bake until cooked through and the juices run clear when pierced with a small knife, or an instant thermometer inserted in the center reads between 145°F and 150°F, about 1 hour to 1 hour and 15 minutes. Remove from the oven and let sit, loosely covered with foil, about 10 minutes before slicing and serving. Serve warm with extra Everyday Marinara (page 163) or ketchup on the side.

On the Menu

MEATLOAF SANDWICH As far as I'm concerned, meatloaf is one of those dishes that is almost better in its leftover form—especially when it's sliced and piled high on sourdough with spicy mustard and crisp dill pickles.

On the Shelves

MUSTARD In my refrigerator—and on the Market's shelves—I believe the more mustard, the merrier. Peter's favorite is Stonewall Kitchen's Ballpark Mustard, a classic, which we spread on Foster's meatloaf sandwiches. We also keep Stonewall's Horseradish and Traditional Pub Style varieties on hand. For a sweet spread, I like to make my own Sorghum Mustard (page 63).

Korean Barbecue Swordfish Kebabs

SWORDFISH WORKS PERFECTLY FOR KEBABS because it has a firm, meaty texture that won't flake apart when cooked. We douse it with our Korean Barbecue Sauce—essentially a cross between teriyaki and the thick, sweet marinade found in Memphis—and serve the kebabs with Sriracha Aioli (page 140) or Vietnamese Chili Sauce (page 142) for dipping. **Serves 6 to 8**

2½ **pounds skinless swordfish fillets, cut into 1½-inch chunks (substitute: salmon)**

1 cup Sauce (page 133)

¼ **cup chopped fresh cilantro leaves**

Sea salt and freshly ground black pepper

1 lemon, cut into thin rounds

1 lime, cut into thin rounds

4 scallions, trimmed and cut into 2-inch-long pieces

2 jalapeño peppers, cut into thin rounds

Grilled Lemon Halves (recipe follows)

1. About 30 minutes before ready to grill, build a fire in a gas or charcoal grill. If using a charcoal grill, let the coals burn to a gray ash with a slight red glow. If using a gas grill, preheat to medium-high.

2. Place the fish in a shallow container or a large resealable plastic bag and pour the sauce over, turning to coat the fish evenly. Close the bag and refrigerate to marinate about 15 minutes, but no longer (see Marinating Fish, below).

3. Remove the fish from the marinade and season with the cilantro, salt and pepper to taste. Thread onto skewers, alternating with slices of lemon, lime, scallions and jalapeños.

4. Place the skewers on the grill over direct heat and grill, turning every 2 to 3 minutes, until the fish is slightly charred on all sides and slightly pink in the center, 6 to 7 minutes total. Remove the fish from the grill and serve the skewers on a platter surrounded by the Grilled Lemon Halves.

In the Kitchen

MARINATING FISH Contrary to other proteins, don't marinate fish overnight. It can change the texture, especially if there is citrus in the mix. The rule of thumb is about 10 to 15 minutes. All you want to do is impart the flavor, adding more of the marinade as the fish cooks.

GRILLED LEMON HALVES Grilling lemons brings out the fruit's natural sweetness. Cut **3 lemons** in half and place cut side down on a hot grill until slightly charred, about 2 minutes. Sprinkle the cooked side with **sea salt** and squeeze over the fish.

On the Menu

SERVE WITH For a light meal, pair the kebabs with Fried Rice Pilaf with Quinoa and Crispy Lentils (page 256) and Carrot, Beet, Apple and Raisin Slaw (page 220) or Tangy Cabbage and Kale Slaw (page 223).

Grilled Slab of Salmon

PETER SWEARS THAT THIS RECIPE FOR A WHOLE SIDE OF SALMON is the reason I got out of solely catering. I'd sometimes grill as many as 20 sides of salmon on early summer mornings before running off to serve a wedding party—a whole side salmon is a crowd-pleaser. I did learn the perfect method for grilling it. And for the home cook, it's a fail-safe way to prepare salmon for a group. **Serves 6 to 8**

1 (2- to 2½-pound) salmon fillet, skin on, scales removed

2 tablespoons olive oil

Sea salt and freshly ground black pepper

5 to 6 sprigs fresh dill, cilantro, basil or a combination

Rouille (page 143) or Herb Buttermilk Yogurt Sauce (page 142)

In the Kitchen

PLAN AHEAD I cook the fish with the skin on, which prevents its flesh from drying out and helps it stay together when flipped. You can grill the salmon up to 1 day in advance of serving and warm it in the oven before guests arrive. To do this, grill the fish on the flesh side only, cool it to room temperature, wrap it in foil and set it aside in the refrigerator. When ready to serve, place it in a preheated 400°F oven until it's warmed through, about 20 minutes.

1. Lay the salmon skin side down on a baking sheet and drizzle the flesh side with the olive oil. Rub the flesh side of the fish with olive oil to coat evenly and season liberally with salt and pepper. Sprinkle the herbs over the salmon, pressing slightly to help them adhere. Cover with plastic wrap and refrigerate until ready to grill, for up to 1 day.

2. About 30 minutes before ready to grill, build a fire in a gas or charcoal grill. If using a charcoal grill, let the coals burn to a gray ash with a slight red glow. If using a gas grill, preheat to medium.

3. Lightly oil the grill grates. Lay the salmon flesh side down on the grill grates and cook, undisturbed, until the salmon is slightly golden and releases easily from the grill, about 5 minutes. Have a spray bottle of water handy to spray the flames out if needed.

4. Lay a piece of foil on the grill beside the salmon and, using 2 metal spatulas, flip the fish onto it. Move the foil with the salmon on it so that it is over direct heat and cover the grill. Cook the salmon until flaky but slightly pink and fleshy in the center, 5 to 6 minutes more. To check for doneness, insert the tip of a small knife in the thickest part of the fish and gently pry the fish open to see the color and texture inside. The fish will continue to cook slightly more after removed from the grill. Lift the foil with salmon off the grill, carefully transfer to a baking sheet and set aside to cool slightly.

5. Flip the fillet over to remove the skin. Flip the fish onto a platter so the skinned side is down. Serve warm or at room temperature with Rouille (page 143), Herb Buttermilk Yogurt Sauce (page 142) or your choice of sauce spooned over and around.

Ginger Rice Bowl with Vietnamese Chili Sauce and Variations

BUILD A BAR. For this Ginger Rice Bowl with Vietnamese Chili Sauce, I like to set out a mess of fresh toppings for guests to choose what they like to mix in. I think a bar makes a fun presentation. It also takes the pressure off the host at serving time. Have everything ready so that all you have to do at the last moment is cook the chicken, salmon or other protein you're serving.   **Serves 6 to 8**

GINGER RICE

2 tablespoons olive oil

1 tablespoon unsalted butter

1 onion, diced

1½ cups white jasmine rice

2 teaspoons sea salt, plus more to taste

1 cup light coconut milk

1 (1-inch) piece ginger, peeled and grated

¼ cup chopped fresh parsley leaves

4 scallions, thinly sliced

Zest and juice of 1 lime

Freshly ground black pepper

continues »

GINGER RICE

1. Heat the oil and butter in a saucepan over medium heat until sizzling hot. Add the onion and cook, stirring occasionally, until soft and translucent, about 5 minutes.

2. Rinse the rice in a colander until the water runs clear. Drain and add the rice to the pan with the onion. Season with salt and cook over medium heat, stirring occasionally, until it easily slides around the pan, 2 to 3 minutes.

3. Add the coconut milk, ginger and 1½ cups of water. Stir to combine the ingredients, making sure to release any rice stuck to the bottom of the pan. Bring the liquid to a low boil. Reduce the heat to very low and simmer, covered, until all the liquid is absorbed, about 15 minutes. Turn off the heat and let the rice sit, covered, about 5 minutes; it will become fluffy and soft in texture.

4. Add the parsley, scallions, lime zest and juice, and pepper to taste. Stir gently to combine the ingredients. Taste for seasoning and add more salt and pepper, if desired.

continues »

THAI CHICKEN THIGHS

8 boneless, skinless chicken thighs (about 2½ pounds)

Juice and zest of 1 orange

2 tablespoons hoisin sauce

2 tablespoons tamari or low-sodium soy sauce

1 tablespoon smooth peanut butter

1 tablespoon honey

1 (1-inch) piece ginger, peeled and grated

1 small Thai chile pepper, thinly sliced

2 garlic cloves, smashed and minced

1 scallion, minced

¼ cup chopped fresh cilantro leaves

Sea salt and freshly ground black pepper

1. Rinse the chicken thighs and pat dry. Place the chicken in a shallow container or large resealable plastic bag.

2. Combine the orange zest and juice, hoisin sauce, tamari, peanut butter, honey, ginger, chile pepper, garlic, scallion and half of the cilantro in a blender and puree until smooth, stopping to scrape down the sides of the blender several times. Add the pureed mixture to the bag with the chicken and turn to coat the chicken all over. Place in the refrigerator to marinate at least 2 hours or overnight.

3. About 30 minutes before ready to grill, build a fire in a gas or charcoal grill. If using a charcoal grill, let the coals burn to a gray ash with a slight red glow. If using a gas grill, preheat to high. (Alternatively, heat a grill pan over high heat to just before the smoking point and preheat the oven to 400°F.) Bank the coals on one side of the grill for direct and indirect heat.

4. Remove the chicken from the marinade and season all over with salt and pepper to taste. Reserve the marinade for basting.

5. Place the chicken over the coals and baste with the marinade. Grill 5 to 6 minutes per side, turning only once and basting again when you flip, until golden brown and slightly charred with grill marks. Move the chicken to the side of the grill with indirect heat, close the lid and cook until the chicken is cooked through, 4 to 5 minutes more. (If you are cooking the chicken in a grill pan, at this point transfer to the preheated oven to cook the last 4 to 5 minutes.)

6. Transfer the chicken to a platter, cover loosely with foil and let sit about 5 minutes before serving. Serve warm with the remaining cilantro leaves sprinkled over the top and rice and vegetables on the side.

In the Kitchen

MAKE AHEAD The chicken and salmon can be cooked several hours in advance of serving them. To do so, cook the salmon on the flesh side only, until it is golden brown around the edges. Place it on a rimmed baking sheet, spoon the reserved marinade over the top and chill until you're ready to serve it. Likewise, grill the chicken and skip the last 5 minutes over the indirect heat. When you're ready to serve your meal, preheat the oven to 400°F. Place the baking sheet with the salmon and/or chicken in the oven to cook through, about 5 minutes.

THAI-STYLE SALMON

Zest and juice of 1 orange

1 tablespoon tamari or low-sodium soy sauce

1 tablespoon rice wine vinegar

1 (1-inch) piece ginger, peeled and grated

½ teaspoon crushed red pepper flakes

8 (4- to 6-ounce) skinless salmon fillets

3 tablespoons olive oil

Sea salt and freshly ground black pepper

1. Combine the orange zest and juice, tamari, vinegar, ginger and red pepper flakes in a shallow container or large resealable bag and stir to mix. Place the salmon in the dish with the marinade and drizzle the fish with 2 tablespoons of the olive oil. Turn to coat the fish evenly with the marinade. Place the fish in the refrigerator, covered, to marinate about 15 minutes (no longer or the marinade will cook the fish). Remove the salmon from the marinade, reserving the marinade for basting, and season with salt and pepper to taste.

2. Pour the remaining olive oil into a nonstick skillet and heat until the oil is sizzling hot. (Alternatively, heat a grill pan to just before its smoking point.) Add the salmon to the skillet and cook, turning only once, spooning the reserved marinade over the fish while cooking, until the salmon is golden brown on both sides and flaky but still slightly pink on the inside, 3 to 4 minutes per side. (Note that the fish will continue to cook after it is removed from the heat.)

3. Place the salmon on a platter and cover loosely with foil until ready to serve. Serve warm with rice and vegetables on the side.

BUILD-YOUR-OWN-BOWL BAR

2 carrots, julienned

2 red, yellow or orange bell peppers (or a combination), cored, seeded and julienned

1 bunch fresh cilantro sprigs

1 cup sprouts (bean, pea, sunflower or a combination)

4 Thai chile peppers, thinly sliced

Sriracha Aioli (page 140)

Vietnamese Chili Sauce (page 142)

Ginger Rice (page 115)

Thai Chicken Thighs (page 116)

Thai-Style Salmon (recipe above)

Put the carrots, bell peppers, cilantro, chile peppers, Sriracha Aioli and Vietnamese Chili Sauce each in its own bowl. Place the rice in individual bowls or a large dish and the chicken and salmon on platters. Put out enough bowls—and forks or chopsticks—for your guests to create their own combinations and serve themselves.

Beer Can Chicken

THIS BEER IS FOR THE BIRDS. A whole chicken roosts atop a half-full tallboy to absorb extra moisture and flavor. Perched above a hot bed of coals, it also takes on a golden, smoke-tinged hue. There's not much to do except stand back and turn the bird a few times while sipping on the extra beers. In fact, the method is so easy that I tend to cook two at a time, ensuring leftovers for chicken salad and tacos. **Serves 4 to 6**

1 (3½- to 4-pound) chicken

1 tablespoon sea salt

2 teaspoons freshly ground black pepper

2 teaspoons crushed red pepper flakes

1 (16-ounce) can dark beer

2 tablespoons olive oil

Juice of 1 lemon

1 lime or lemon, cut into wedges

On the Menu

SERVE WITH When grilling, I often make cool sides like Watermelon Arugula Tabbouleh with Feta and Mint (page 214) and Tangy Cabbage and Kale Slaw (page 223). And for dessert, Mixed Berry Pie with Crumb Topping (page 295) with a scoop of vanilla ice cream.

1. About 30 minutes before ready to grill, build a fire in a gas or charcoal grill. If using a charcoal grill, let the coals burn to a gray ash with a slight red glow. Bank the coals on one side of the grill for direct and indirect heat. If using a gas grill, preheat one side only to medium.

2. Rinse the chicken, pat dry and remove any excess skin or fat. Season inside and out with half of the salt, black pepper and red pepper flakes. Open the can of beer, drain half and place in the cavity of the chicken, legs down over the can so that the chicken sits upright. Place the chicken on the side of the grill without the coals or heat with the back facing the heat, making sure it is secure enough on the grate not to tip over.

3. Mix the olive oil, lemon juice and remaining salt, black pepper and red pepper flakes in a small bowl and stir to combine. Brush the outside of the chicken all over with about one-third of this mixture.

4. Place the cover on the grill and cook, about 20 minutes. Uncover, carefully rotate the chicken a quarter turn, keeping the breast side away from the direct heat, and baste again with the olive oil mixture. Cover and cook the chicken about 20 minutes more. Repeat the process two more times until the chicken is cooked through and an instant thermometer inserted in the thickest part of the thigh reads 165°F, a total of 1 hour and 15 to 20 minutes. If using a charcoal grill, you may need to add more coals while cooking. If using a gas grill, the chicken may cook faster because the heat is more even.

5. Carefully remove the chicken from the grill (the liquid in the can will be extremely hot) and place on a rimmed baking sheet to rest, about 15 minutes. When the chicken is cool enough to handle, carefully remove the beer can from the cavity and discard. Chop the chicken into pieces and serve warm with ice-cold beer and wedges of lemon or lime.

Pickle-Brined Fried Chicken with Sriracha Honey

THE END OF A PICKLE JAR (which I greet quite often) makes an easy excuse for this dish, and this dish makes an easy excuse to open a new jar of pickles. It's a cycle I'm not keen to break. **Serves 4 to 6**

BRINE

1 tablespoon yellow mustard seeds

1 tablespoon coriander seeds

1 teaspoon whole black peppercorns

1 teaspoon whole cloves

2 tablespoons white wine vinegar

¼ cup kosher salt

¼ cup sugar

1 tablespoon dill seeds

1 bunch fresh dill leaves, chopped, or 1 tablespoon dried dill

CHICKEN

6 bone-in, skinless chicken thighs

2 boneless, skinless chicken breast halves, cut into halves or thirds, depending on the size

2 cups well-shaken buttermilk

2 cups all-purpose flour

1 teaspoon sea salt

½ teaspoon freshly ground black pepper

Pinch of ground cayenne pepper

Vegetable oil, for frying (enough to fill the skillet about a third of the way up)

¼ cup Sriracha

2 tablespoons honey

BRINE

Toast the mustard seeds, coriander seeds, peppercorns and cloves in a dry skillet over medium heat, stirring constantly, until the seeds become aromatic, about 2 minutes. Add the vinegar, salt, sugar and dill seeds and bring to a boil, stirring, until the salt and sugar dissolve. Remove from the heat and stir in fresh dill and 2 cups of cold water.

CHICKEN

1. Transfer the brine to a large bowl, and add the chicken and enough water to completely submerge. Cover and refrigerate at least 3 hours or overnight.

2. When ready to cook the chicken, remove from the brine and scrape off any seeds or dill leaves. Place the buttermilk in a large bowl and add the chicken.

3. Place the flour, sea salt, black pepper and cayenne pepper in a separate large, shallow bowl or plastic bag and stir or shake to mix. (I like to use a bag because the chicken gets coated all over and it makes for an easy cleanup.)

4. Place the oil about ¼ inch deep in a large cast-iron skillet over medium-high heat until the temperature reaches between 360°F and 375°F. The oil should be deep enough to submerge the chicken about halfway; the level of the oil will rise slightly when you add the chicken.

5. Working in batches, remove the chicken from the buttermilk and dredge or shake in the flour mixture, one piece at a time, to coat evenly on all sides, beginning with the large pieces. Shake off any excess flour.

6. Place the chicken, 6 to 8 pieces at a time, in the hot oil and fry until golden brown and cooked through, turning once, 6 to 7 minutes per side. Do not overcrowd the skillet for even frying. Check the pieces to make sure they are not browning too quickly, if so, reduce the heat or turn the pieces on their sides. Bring the oil back up to temperature before starting the next batch.

7. Transfer to a wire rack on top of a baking sheet to drain, and season with additional salt and pepper to taste, if desired. Keep in a warm oven while the next batch is frying.

8. While the chicken is cooking, combine the Sriracha and honey in a small bowl and stir to mix. Serve the chicken hot or at room temperature with the Sriracha Honey drizzled on top or served alongside for dipping.

Mixed Grilled Chicken Thighs and Sausages

IN SUMMER, OUR DOOR IS OFTEN OPEN. So when last-minute guests appear at our home in Lake Placid, New York, I dash down to Kreature butcher shop for chicken thighs and a mix of sausages—sweet Italian with fennel, chicken and apple, lamb with feta and veggie brats. They don't require a lot of prep or cook time and there's something for everyone. **Serves 4 to 6**

6 boneless, skinless chicken thighs

6 fresh sausages, such as sweet Italian with fennel, chicken-apple or lamb-feta

3 tablespoons olive oil

3 tablespoons balsamic vinegar

¼ cup chopped fresh rosemary

Sea salt and freshly ground black pepper

6 basil leaves, thinly sliced

1. About 30 minutes before ready to grill, build a fire in a gas or charcoal grill. If using a charcoal grill, let the coals burn to a gray ash with a slight red glow. If using a gas grill, preheat to medium-high.

2. Rinse the chicken and pat dry. Place the chicken and sausage on a rimmed baking sheet and drizzle with the olive oil and vinegar, sprinkle with the rosemary, salt and pepper to taste and turn to coat.

3. Place the chicken over the coals. Grill 5 to 6 minutes per side until golden brown and slightly charred with grill marks. Move to the outside of the grill to continue to cook, 4 to 5 minutes more.

4. At the same time, grill the sausages over the direct heat, turning occasionally until golden brown on all sides, 8 to 10 minutes. Place the lid on the grill and continue to cook, 2 to 3 minutes more.

5. Remove the chicken and sausages from the grill and place on a platter. Cover loosely with foil to keep warm until ready to serve. Sprinkle with the basil and serve warm.

On the Menu

SERVE WITH Pull out whatever mustards you have in the refrigerator (I like to keep a variety on hand). And if time permits, mix up Italian Salsa Verde (page 140) and South of the Border Buttermilk Yogurt Sauce (page 142). On the side, try Sweet and Sour Cabbage (page 246) and to end, Chocolate Chess Pie (page 294).

Spicy Backyard Barbecue Chicken

HOT VINEGAR OR STICKY, SWEET TOMATO. Douse this grilled chicken with your favorite sauce and top with a mix of fresh herbs. It also makes for great leftovers in tacos or Easy Quesadillas (recipe follows). **Serves 4 to 6**

1 (3- to 3½-pound) chicken, cut into 8 pieces

2 tablespoons olive oil

Juice of 1 lemon

Sea salt and freshly ground black pepper

2 cups your favorite barbecue sauce

¼ cup mixed chopped fresh herbs, such as rosemary, thyme, parsley, oregano or marjoram

1. Preheat the oven to 350°F.

2. Rinse the chicken, pat dry and trim any excess fat and skin. Place on a rimmed baking sheet and drizzle with the oil and lemon juice. Season all over with salt and pepper and bake, 30 minutes.

3. About 30 minutes before ready to grill, build a fire in a gas or charcoal grill. If using a charcoal grill, let the coals burn to a gray ash with a slight red glow. If using a gas grill, preheat to medium.

4. Remove the chicken from the oven and brush both sides with the barbecue sauce. Place the chicken, skin side down, on the grill. Grill 6 to 8 minutes until golden brown and slightly charred with grill marks, turning as needed depending on the heat of your fire. Have a spray bottle of water handy to spray the flames out if needed. Flip the chicken over and brush with barbecue sauce again until slightly charred with grill marks, cooking 6 to 8 minutes more and basting halfway through. Move from the direct heat, baste again and cover and continue to cook about 5 minutes more until the chicken is cooked through.

5. Remove the chicken from the grill and let rest about 5 minutes, loosely covered with foil, before serving. Serve warm with additional barbecue sauce on the side, if desired.

EASY QUESADILLAS

SEARED TORTILLAS BECOME HOME TO MANY OF MY LEFTOVERS—from Chile-Braised Pork Shoulder (page 130) to Spicy Backyard Barbecue Chicken (recipe above) and Summer Tomato Salsa (page 34) with Cheddar and goat cheeses. **Makes 1 Quesadilla**

Heat **1 tablespoon vegetable oil** in a cast-iron skillet over medium-high heat until sizzling hot. Place **1 tortilla** (flour or corn) in the skillet. Scatter evenly with **cheese, vegetables, herbs or other fillings**. Top with a little **more cheese** and drizzle with **Summer Tomato Salsa (page 34) or your favorite salsa**. Place **another tortilla** on top and press down gently. Cook until crispy on the bottom, about 2 minutes. Flip over and cook the other side until crispy, about 2 minutes more. Place on a cutting board and let sit for a few minutes, slice into wedges and serve warm topped with **additional Summer Tomato Salsa and mixed baby greens** or **shredded cabbage**.

Chicken Piccata

POUNDED THIN AND LIGHTLY BREADED, this chicken is a cinch to cook—seared for a mere three minutes on each side, then simmered just three more in a bright sauce of lemon, wine and butter. **Serves 4 to 6**

4 boneless, skinless chicken breast halves (about 2 pounds)

Sea salt and freshly ground black pepper

1 cup all-purpose flour

3 to 4 tablespoons canola or safflower oil, plus more if needed

4 tablespoons unsalted butter

2 garlic cloves, smashed and minced

3 tablespoons capers, drained

1 lemon, thinly sliced into rounds

1 cup dry white wine

2 cups low-sodium chicken broth

Juice of 1 lemon

¼ cup chopped fresh parsley

In the Kitchen

CREATING CUTLETS Place a boneless, skinless chicken breast on a cutting board. Depending on the size of the breast, slice into 2 or 3 pieces, starting at the thickest end and cutting horizontally. Ideally, you will end up with cuts that are approximately ¼ inch thick, which makes the pounding much easier. For extra ease, most butchers and specialty grocers sell cutlets.

1. Rinse the chicken and pat dry. Slice and pound the chicken into cutlets (see Creating Cutlets, below). Season generously with salt and pepper to taste.

2. Place the flour in a shallow bowl, season with salt and pepper and stir to mix.

3. Heat 2 tablespoons of the oil and 1 tablespoon of the butter in a large skillet over medium-high heat until sizzling hot. Dredge both sides of each piece of chicken in the flour, pressing gently to help the flour adhere and shaking off any excess before placing in the skillet.

4. Sauté until golden brown around the edges, working in batches and careful not to overcrowd the skillet, about 3 minutes per side. Remove, place on a platter and cover loosely with foil to keep warm. Repeat with the remaining chicken, adding more oil, 1 tablespoon at a time, if needed. If the flour in the bottom of the skillet starts to get too dark, clean the skillet halfway through by removing it from the heat and carefully wiping the skillet dry with paper towels, but keep a little flour in the bottom of the skillet, as it will help your sauce thicken.

5. Add 1 tablespoon of oil to the same skillet and heat until sizzling hot. Add the garlic, capers and lemon slices and cook, stirring occasionally, about 1 minute. Add the wine, scraping up any brown bits from the bottom of the pan. Bring to a boil and cook until the wine reduces by half, about 3 minutes. Add the broth and lemon juice and continue to cook, stirring occasionally, until the sauce thickens. Reduce the heat to low and stir in the remaining butter to melt.

6. Add the chicken and any juices that have collected in the bottom of the platter back to the skillet with the sauce and heat through, about 3 minutes. Place the chicken back on the platter with the sauce poured over. Sprinkle with parsley and serve warm.

Pork Chops Milanese

THINLY CUT PORK CHOPS ARE OFTEN LABELED "breakfast chops." But lightly breaded with panko crumbs that form a crisp, golden crust, they make an excellent lunch or dinner served with a glass of chilled white wine. **Serves 4 to 6**

6 thin-cut pork loin chops

Sea salt and freshly ground black pepper

1 tablespoon fresh thyme leaves

2 cups panko breadcrumbs

1 cup all-purpose flour

½ cup finely grated Parmesan cheese

2 large eggs, lightly beaten

¼ cup well-shaken buttermilk

¼ cup canola oil, plus more if needed

2 handfuls mixed greens

2 tomatoes, cored and chopped

½ cup shaved Parmesan cheese

2 tablespoons olive oil

2 tablespoons red wine vinegar

Herb Buttermilk Yogurt Sauce (page 142)

1. Place the pork chops between 2 pieces of plastic wrap and flatten with a mallet or the bottom of a heavy skillet until about ¼ inch thick. Season both sides with the salt, pepper and thyme.

2. Place the breadcrumbs, flour and grated Parmesan in a large, shallow bowl, season with salt and pepper and stir to combine. Mix the eggs and buttermilk in a separate shallow bowl and stir to combine.

3. Working with one pork chop at a time, dip into the egg mixture and press into the breadcrumb mixture to coat evenly on both sides. Set on a rimmed baking sheet and repeat with the remaining chops. Place covered in the refrigerator until ready to cook.

4. Heat the canola oil in a large skillet until sizzling hot over medium-high heat. The oil should just cover the bottom of the skillet; you may need more depending on the size of your skillet. Working in batches, add 2 to 3 pork chops to the skillet, reduce the heat to medium and sauté until golden brown and crispy, 3 to 4 minutes per side.

5. Place on a separate rimmed baking sheet, season with salt and pepper to taste and place in the oven to keep warm while the others are cooking. Repeat the process with the remaining chops, adding a little more oil to the skillet if needed.

6. Serve warm piled high with a heap of mixed greens, chopped tomatoes and shaved Parmesan cheese and drizzled with the olive oil and vinegar or Herb Buttermilk Yogurt Sauce (page 142) over the top.

In the Kitchen

HOMEMADE CRUMBS Panko breadcrumbs add a crisp layer to Pork Chops Milanese, but for most recipes I recommend having ready-made crumbs on hand in your freezer. At the Market, we make them out of most any day-old bread, including rolls, biscuits, baguettes and cornbread (the only thing I avoid is whole grain). To make, tear bread apart into smaller bits, or crumble cornbread. Place in a food processor fitted with a metal blade or the jar of a blender and pulse to desired crumb. Store in a resealable freezer bag for up to 2 months.

Pork Tenderloin with Olives and Tangerines

I AM ALWAYS LOOKING FOR SOMETHING DIFFERENT to do with pork tenderloin—a tender cut of meat, as its name suggests, that I consider near-perfect. For this dish, I was inspired by the waning contents of my fridge: plump Italian Castelvetrano olives and a handful of tangerines. I so loved the salty and sweet combination that I've since turned to it time and time again. **Serves 6 to 8**

2 (1½ pounds each) pork tenderloins

½ cup dry white wine

Zest and juice of 1 tangerine

2 tablespoons sherry vinegar

1 tablespoon chopped fresh rosemary

1 teaspoon crushed red pepper flakes

2 garlic cloves, smashed and minced

Sea salt and freshly ground black pepper

1 tablespoon olive oil

1 tablespoon unsalted butter

½ cup green olives, pitted and halved

3 tangerines, peeled and sliced

On the Menu

SERVE WITH On cool nights, try this dish alongside Roasted Butternut Squash and White Bean Salad with Crispy Prosciutto (page 218) or Scalloped Potatoes (page 179) and Grilled Romaine Caesar with Rustic Crunchy Croutons (page 213).

1. Rinse the pork and pat dry. Remove the silver skin from the top of the loins. Place the tenderloins in a shallow container or a large resealable plastic bag.

2. Whisk together the wine, tangerine zest and juice, vinegar, rosemary, red pepper flakes, garlic, salt and black pepper to taste in a small bowl to combine. Pour the marinade over the pork, turning the meat to coat evenly. (Or, if using a resealable bag, pour the marinade into the bag, seal and shake to coat the pork.) Cover the dish with plastic wrap and place it in the refrigerator. Marinate for at least 4 hours or overnight, turning the pork several times to distribute the marinade evenly over the pork.

3. When ready to cook, preheat the oven to 375°F.

4. Heat the olive oil and butter in a large ovenproof skillet over medium-high heat until sizzling hot. Remove the pork from the marinade, shaking off any excess and reserving the marinade. Place in the skillet to cook until golden brown, 3 to 4 minutes per side, about 8 minutes total time.

5. Pour the reserved marinade over the pork, add the olives and tangerines and place the skillet in the oven to roast until an instant thermometer inserted into the tenderloins reads 145°F for medium or 160°F for medium-well, basting several times during cooking, about 20 minutes. The pork will continue to cook a few degrees more when removed from the oven, but it is best if light pink inside.

6. Remove the pork from the oven and place on a cutting board, loosely covered with foil, and allow to rest 5 to 10 minutes before slicing. Slice the tenderloin into ¼-inch-thick portions, season with additional salt and pepper, if desired, and serve warm with sauce, olives and tangerines spooned over and around.

Chile-Braised Pork Shoulder with Taco Fixings

KEEP IT COOL. Offset this spicy pork with a heap of fresh fixings—from Avocado Crema (page 143) and cilantro to Summer Tomato Salsa (page 34) with a spritz of lime. **Serves 6 to 8**

PORK

2 tablespoons brown sugar

1 tablespoon chili powder

1 tablespoon ground paprika

2 teaspoons sea salt

1 teaspoon freshly ground black pepper

1 teaspoon crushed red pepper flakes

1 (4- to 4½-pound) bone-in pork shoulder or butt

1 cup apple cider or unfiltered apple juice

¼ cup apple cider vinegar

Juice of ½ grapefruit

Juice of ½ orange

½ bunch fresh cilantro sprigs

FIXINGS

20 corn tortillas

4 cups shredded mixed romaine and cabbage

Summer Tomato Salsa (page 34) or your favorite salsa

1 cup (4 ounces) grated Cheddar cheese

1 cup (4 ounces) crumbled queso fresco

½ white onion, minced

1 cup fresh cilantro leaves

1 bunch radishes, trimmed and thinly sliced

Avocado Crema (page 143)

4 limes, cut into wedges

PORK

1. Preheat the oven to 325°F.

2. Combine the sugar, chili powder, paprika, salt, black pepper and red pepper flakes in a small bowl and stir to mix.

3. Place the pork, fatty side up, in a large roasting pan or Dutch oven with a tight-fitting lid. Pour the apple cider and vinegar over the pork. Squeeze the juice from the grapefruit and orange over and add the cilantro sprigs. Rub the spice mixture into the pork to coat completely.

4. Cover the pan tightly with the lid or foil and place in the oven to roast, undisturbed, 2½ hours. Uncover, raise the oven temperature to 375°F and cook until the skin is crispy and the pork breaks apart easily when tested with a fork, about 30 minutes longer. Remove from the oven and let rest about 15 minutes before pulling it into chunks.

FIXINGS

1. While the pork is resting, heat the tortillas over an open flame or in a grill pan, about 30 seconds per side. Stack the heated tortillas and wrap in a clean dish towel or foil to keep warm. Put each of the topping ingredients in its own bowl and set the bowls out for guests to serve themselves.

2. Pull the pork into chunks and pile on a platter. Scatter the limes around the pork roast and let guests dig in, adding a little of the pulled pork to a warm tortilla with their choice of toppings.

In the Kitchen

PORK TOSTADAS Trade tacos for tostadas. When you remove the pork from the oven, increase the temperature to 400°F. Lay the tortillas on a baking sheet and brush both sides lightly with oil. Place in the oven to crisp, about 10 minutes. Remove and add your favorite toppings.

Sweet and Sticky Baby Back Ribs

DRAWING ON MY CHILDHOOD NEAR MEMPHIS, where ribs were ever-present, I have included a recipe for them in every cookbook I've ever published. The method is always the same—why mess with tender, fall-off-the-bone ribs? For me, the fun is in switching up the sauce. Here, the mix is sweet, sticky, salty and spicy. The best thing about this sauce is that no cooking is required. Just mix and baste. **Serves 4 to 6**

RIBS

1 onion, sliced

2 racks baby back ribs (about 2½ pounds each)

1 (12-ounce) beer

2 teaspoons crushed red pepper flakes

Sea salt and freshly ground black pepper

SAUCE

1 cup ketchup

½ cup light brown sugar

½ cup chili paste

½ cup sweet chili sauce

¼ cup apple cider vinegar

¼ cup molasses

¼ cup strong coffee, cold

Juice of 1 orange

2 tablespoons Sriracha

RIBS

1. Preheat the oven to 325°F.

2. Spread the onion on a rimmed baking sheet in a single layer and place the ribs on top. Pour the beer over and around. Sprinkle with red pepper flakes and salt and black pepper to taste. Cover tightly with foil and place in the oven to bake, undisturbed, 2 hours, until the ribs are tender.

SAUCE

1. While the ribs are cooking, make the sauce by combining the ketchup, sugar, chili paste, chili sauce, vinegar, molasses, coffee, orange juice and Sriracha in a medium bowl and stir to combine.

2. About 30 minutes before ready to grill, build a fire in a gas or charcoal grill. If using a charcoal grill, let the coals burn to a gray ash with a slight red glow. If using a gas grill, preheat to medium.

3. Uncover the ribs and let cool slightly before removing from the pan. Place on the grill and baste with enough of the sauce to cover generously. Cover and cook, turning and basting as needed, until lightly charred with grill marks, about 30 minutes. Any extra sauce can be used for serving on the side.

4. Remove the ribs from the grill and place on a cutting board, loosely covered with foil, until cool enough to handle. Slice the racks into 3- to 4-rib segments, pile on a platter and serve warm with extra sauce on the side to spoon over, if desired.

On the Menu

SERVE WITH Twice-Baked Yukon Gold and Sweet Potatoes with Toppings (page 248), Carrot, Beet, Apple and Raisin Slaw (page 220) and Foster's Brownies (page 289).

Grilled Racks of Lamb

WHEN GRILLED, A WHOLE RACK OF LAMB FORMS A CRISP, CHARRED EXTERIOR and keeps a pink, succulent interior. After cooking, simply cut into individual chops for serving alongside Grilled Romaine Caesar with Rustic Crunchy Croutons (page 213) and Heirloom and Shell Bean Salad with Sherry Vinaigrette (page 224). **Serves 4 to 6**

2 (1 to 1½ pounds each) Frenched lamb racks (see Frenched Lamb and Other Tips, below)

Sea salt and freshly ground black pepper

¼ cup olive oil

¼ cup chopped fresh mint

¼ cup chopped fresh parsley

4 garlic cloves, smashed and minced

Zest and juice of 1 lemon

1 teaspoon crushed red pepper flakes

Pounded Mint Chimichurri (page 140), Mint Pesto (page 143), Italian Salsa Verde (page 140) or Harissa Buttermilk Yogurt Sauce (page 142)

1. Season the lamb racks all over with salt and pepper to taste and place in a shallow container or a large resealable bag. In a small bowl, combine the olive oil, mint, parsley, garlic, lemon zest and juice, and red pepper flakes and stir to mix thoroughly. Pour the marinade over the racks, turning the meat to coat evenly with the marinade. (Or, if using a resealable bag, pour the marinade into the bag, seal and shake to coat the racks.) Refrigerate the lamb until you're ready to grill, at least 2 hours or overnight.

2. About 30 minutes before ready to grill, remove the lamb from the container and bring to room temperature. Build a fire in a gas or charcoal grill. If using a charcoal grill, let the coals burn to a gray ash with a slight red glow and bank them on one side. If using a gas grill, preheat only one side to medium.

3. Place the lamb racks on the grill over the direct heat and cook, turning occasionally, until the lamb is slightly charred with grill marks all over, 10 to 12 minutes. Do not leave unattended. The fat will cause the flames to flare up. Have a spray bottle of water handy to spray the flames out if needed. If the flames persist, move the lamb racks away from the direct heat just until the flames die down, then return. After the lamb is evenly browned, move to the side of the grill with indirect heat, bone side down. Cover the grill and cook, turning occasionally, about 15 minutes for medium-rare or until an instant thermometer inserted into the center of each rack reads 125°F.

4. Remove the lamb from the grill and let rest, loosely covered with foil, about 10 minutes. Cut the lamb into individual or double chops and serve with Pounded Mint Chimichurri (page 140), Italian Salsa Verde (page 140) or Harissa Buttermilk Yogurt Sauce (page 142).

In the Kitchen

FRENCHED LAMB AND OTHER TIPS   Frenching refers to removing tough meat so you're left with nothing but clean bones and tender chops. It makes them easy to eat, too. Oftentimes, lamb racks and chops are sold Frenched. If not, ask your butcher to do it for you. This recipe assumes that you are using small racks because that's what is most commonly available. Larger racks will require longer time on the grill.

Moroccan-Rubbed Grilled Boneless Leg of Lamb

LEG OF LAMB IS THE ULTIMATE FAMILY (OR FRIEND) DINNER—a luxurious cut that's fit for a crew and the center of a table. Here, harissa—a garlic-heavy chili paste popular in North Africa—heats things up in the marinade and in an otherwise cool Harissa Buttermilk Yogurt Sauce (page 142). **Serves 6 to 8**

1 (4½- to 5-pound) boneless butterflied leg of lamb, trimmed of excess fat and silver skin

6 to 8 garlic cloves, smashed and thinly sliced

2 tablespoons fresh rosemary leaves

½ cup dry red wine

¼ cup chopped fresh mint

3 tablespoons olive oil

3 tablespoons chopped fresh marjoram

2 tablespoons harissa

Grated zest and juice of 1 orange

1 teaspoon sea salt

1 tablespoon freshly ground black pepper

Harissa Buttermilk Yogurt Sauce (page 142) or Pounded Mint Chimichurri (page 140)

1. Make about 10 small incisions on the fatty side of the lamb and stuff each slit with a few slivers of the garlic and several rosemary leaves. Place the lamb in a shallow dish or large resealable bag.

2. Put the wine, mint, olive oil, marjoram, harissa, orange zest and juice and the remaining garlic together in a small bowl and stir to mix. Rub the marinade into both sides of the lamb, or if using a resealable bag, pour the marinade into the bag, seal and shake to coat. Refrigerate at least 2 hours or overnight. Remove from the refrigerator about 1 hour before cooking to bring to room temperature.

3. About 30 minutes before ready to grill, build a fire. If using a charcoal grill, let the coals burn to a gray ash with a slight red glow. If using a gas grill, preheat to medium.

4. Remove the lamb from the marinade and let any excess drip off, reserving the marinade for basting. Season both sides with salt and pepper.

5. Place the lamb on the grill over direct heat and cook, turning occasionally and basting frequently with the marinade, until slightly charred with grill marks all over, 10 to 15 minutes per side. Do not leave unattended. After the lamb is evenly browned, move to the side of the grill with indirect heat. Cover the grill and cook, turning once, 10 to 15 minutes more until an instant thermometer inserted in the center reads from 130°F to 135°F for medium-rare or from 140°F to 145°F for medium. Remove the lamb from the grill and let rest, loosely covered with foil, about 15 minutes before slicing. Carve the lamb into thin slices and serve with the sauces on the side.

On the Menu

SERVE WITH At summer's height, pair with Watermelon Arugula Tabbouleh with Feta and Mint (page 314) and Maque Choux (page 242). The next day (if any is lamb is left), stuff it into a warm pita or piece of naan with sliced cucumbers and Harissa Buttermilk Yogurt Sauce (page 142).

Greek Lamb Kebabs with Variations

DOWN IN OXFORD, MISSISSIPPI, where I went to undergrad, the Chevron station sells ice-cold beers till midnight and legendary chicken-on-a-stick for hours afterward to those who have had a few too many. I seek out the kebabs (at a reasonable hour) when I'm back in Mississippi. But at home in North Carolina, I make an array, including lamb, beef, Korean Barbecue Swordfish Kebabs (page 111) and, yes, chicken. **Serves 6 to 8**

2½ pounds boneless leg of lamb, trimmed of excess fat and silver skin, cut into 1½-inch pieces

Sea salt and freshly ground black pepper

½ onion, minced

2 garlic cloves, smashed and minced

½ cup dry red wine

¼ cup chopped fresh rosemary

3 tablespoons olive oil

2 tablespoons balsamic vinegar

2 red bell peppers, cored, seeded and cut into 1½-inch chunks

1 red onion, cut into 6 to 8 wedges

½ cup chopped fresh cilantro

4 lemons, cut into wedges

Buttermilk Yogurt Sauce (page 142), Pounded Mint Chimichurri (page 140) or Red Onion and Horseradish Gremolata (page 142)

1. Season the lamb all over with salt and pepper to taste and place in a shallow dish or large resealable plastic bag.

2. In a small bowl, combine the minced onion, garlic, wine, rosemary and 1 tablespoon of the oil and stir to mix. Pour the marinade over the lamb, turning the meat to coat evenly with the marinade. (Or, if using a resealable bag, pour the marinade into the bag, seal and shake to coat the lamb.) Refrigerate at least 2 hours or overnight.

3. Put the vinegar and remaining olive oil in a bowl and stir to combine. Add the peppers and onion, toss to coat and season with salt and pepper.

4. About 30 minutes before ready to grill, remove the lamb from the refrigerator to bring to room temperature and build a fire in a gas or charcoal grill. If using a charcoal grill, let the coals burn to a gray ash with a slight red glow and bank on one side. If using a gas grill, preheat only one side to medium.

5. Remove the lamb from the marinade and thread onto skewers, alternating with the onions and peppers. Reserve the marinade for basting.

6. Put the skewers on the hot side of the grill, turning every 2 to 3 minutes, until slightly charred with grill marks on all sides, 6 to 8 minutes total, depending on the heat of the fire. Baste the lamb as it cooks with the reserved marinade. Move the skewers to the side of the grill with indirect heat. Cover and cook 6 to 8 minutes more for medium-rare (or to your desired doneness). Remove the skewers from the grill, place on a platter, sprinkle with the cilantro and scatter the lemon wedges around the platter to squeeze over the lamb. Serve warm with the sauce of your choice on the side.

In the Kitchen

VARIATIONS This recipe is equally as good with ribeye, skirt or hanger steaks, or boneless, skinless chicken thighs cut in half and threaded onto the skewer. Depending on the thickness of the meat you choose, cooking times will vary. When making beef or lamb skewers, marinate the meat overnight to tenderize. And for extra flavor, save the marinade to baste the meat while it's grilling.

TEN SAUCES THAT WILL CHANGE YOUR MEAL

THE QUESTION I RECEIVE MOST FROM FAMILY and friends or students in a cooking class is how to make something simple like grilled chicken, a piece of fish or a bowl of pasta more exciting. It's easy: a simple, fresh sauce. A spoonful of just the right dressing eliminates plain and boring. Below are ten sauces that I use in constant rotation to add flavor and a pop of color. All of them are easy to make and can be created in advance. When guests arrive—or when you want to simply dress up boneless, skinless chicken breast—stir together one of these sauces and spoon it on.

SRIRACHA AIOLI / Makes about 2 cups

Here, trusty mayonnaise takes the heat from Sriracha and is better for it.

Place **1 cup good-quality mayonnaise or Homemade Mayonnaise** (page 32), **2 tablespoons Sriracha, 4 garlic cloves** and the **juice of 1 lemon** in the bowl of a food processor or the jar of a blender fitted with a metal blade and pulse to mix. With the motor running, slowly add ¼ **cup olive oil** until the mixture is smooth and combined, stopping to scrape down the sides of the bowl several times. Season with **sea salt** and **freshly ground black pepper** to taste. Refrigerate in an airtight container until ready to serve or for up to 4 days.

ITALIAN SALSA VERDE / Makes about 1 cup

Italy's "green sauce," similar to pesto in texture, calls for chopped parsley dressed in olive oil, lemon zest, garlic and capers. Beyond parsley, I make use of any herb in my crisper drawer and always call upon salty capers. For me, they are what make salsa verde so distinctive and well-suited for grilled lamb or steak.

In a bowl combine ½ **cup extra-virgin olive oil** with **1 cup finely chopped mixed fresh herbs (such as basil, parsley, mint, cilantro, chives, oregano, marjoram, rosemary, thyme or celery leaves), 1 minced shallot, 1 tablespoon capers, a pinch of sugar**, and **sea salt** and **freshly ground black pepper** to taste and stir to mix. Refrigerate in an airtight container until ready to serve or for up to 4 days. Bring the salsa to room temperature before serving.

POUNDED MINT CHIMICHURRI
Makes about 1 cup

A mortar and pestle provide more than a workout; they give control, allowing you to slowly mix (or pound) ingredients to achieve a texture that's just right. Don't worry: for coarse chimichurri, the process only takes a few minutes and a little bit of elbow grease.

Combine **2 cups fresh mint leaves, 1 cup fresh cilantro leaves, grated zest and juice of 1 lime, 2 garlic cloves, 2 teaspoons crushed red pepper flakes** and ½ **cup extra-virgin olive oil** in a mortar with pestle or a sturdy bowl with a wooden spoon and pound to break up the herb leaves and garlic. Continue to pound the ingredients until they form a textured, uneven paste. Season to taste with **sea salt** and **freshly ground black pepper**. Refrigerate in an airtight container until ready to serve or for up to 4 days. Bring the chimichurri to room temperature before serving.

MINT GREMOLATA / Makes about 1 cup

Italian gremolata is traditionally a bright mix of chopped parsley, lemon and garlic. Here, the addition of mint gives the sauce more spunk. Serve with Grilled Racks of Lamb (page 134).

Place **2 cups fresh mint leaves, ½ bunch fresh parsley leaves, grated zest and juice of 1 lemon, 2 garlic cloves smashed and chopped, 1 slice sourdough bread** (crust removed, cut into small cubes) and **3 tablespoons extra-virgin olive oil** in the bowl of a food processor or the jar of a blender fitted with a metal blade. Pulse 6 to 8 times until the ingredients are chopped but not smooth, stopping to scrape down the sides of the bowl several times, 30 seconds to 1 minute. Transfer to a small bowl. Season with **sea salt** and **freshly ground black pepper** to taste. Refrigerate in an airtight container until ready to serve or for up to 4 days. Bring the gremolata to room temperature before serving.

RED ONION AND HORSERADISH GREMOLATA / Makes about 1 cup

Arugula, red onion and horseradish bring gusto to an already lively sauce. I particularly like this gremolata with a Slow-Roasted Leg of Lamb (page 161).

Combine **1 bunch parsley leaves, 1 cup arugula, grated zest and juice of 1 lemon, 2 tablespoons freshly grated horseradish root** (or 1 tablespoon prepared horseradish), **1 tablespoon red wine vinegar, 2 garlic cloves smashed and minced, 2 slices sourdough bread** (crust removed, cut into small cubes) and **2 tablespoons extra-virgin olive oil** in the bowl of a food processor or the jar of a blender fitted with a metal blade. Pulse 6 to 8 times until the ingredients are finely chopped but not smooth, stopping to scrape down the sides of the bowl several times, 30 seconds to 1 minute. Transfer to a small bowl. Stir in **½ minced red onion** and season to taste with **sea salt** and **freshly ground black pepper**. Refrigerate in an airtight container until ready to serve or for up to 4 days. Bring the gremolata to room temperature before serving.

BUTTERMILK YOGURT SAUCE WITH VARIATIONS / Makes about 1½ cups

This sauce has a strong foundation—yogurt, buttermilk, lemon juice and zest—for building extra flavor. Below are some of my favorite add-ins.

Mix **1 cup Greek yogurt** with **¼ cup well-shaken buttermilk, 1 tablespoon fresh lemon juice and grated zest of ½ lemon**. Stir to combine and season to taste with **sea salt** and **freshly ground black pepper**. Refrigerate in an airtight container until ready to serve or for up to 4 days. Just before serving, drizzle with **extra-virgin olive oil** and sprinkle with additional **pepper**.

In the Kitchen

VARIATIONS FOR BUTTERMILK YOGURT SAUCE

- **Herb:** add **½ cup chopped fresh herbs** such as basil, parsley, cilantro, dill or a combination.
- **South of the Border:** add **¼ cup finely chopped cilantro, 1 teaspoon ground cumin, 1 to 2 chipotle peppers in adobo sauce, diced**, and substitute **lime** for the lemon juice and zest.
- **Curry:** add **2 teaspoons curry powder** and **1 tablespoon sweet chutney**, such as Major Grey's.
- **Harissa:** stir in **2 tablespoons harissa** and **1 tablespoon chopped cilantro**.

VIETNAMESE CHILI SAUCE
Makes about 1 cup

A little sweet with a hint of heat, I particularly love this sauce mixed into a bowl of Basmati Rice with Green Peas, Edamame and Fresh Herbs (page 258).

Combine **¼ cup rice wine vinegar, grated zest and juice of 1 orange, 2 tablespoons fish sauce, 1 thinly sliced red Thai chile pepper, 1 tablespoon soy sauce, 1 teaspoon honey, 1 minced scallion, 1 (1-inch) piece grated fresh ginger, 2 tablespoons chopped fresh cilantro, 2 garlic cloves smashed and chopped, ½ teaspoon crushed red pepper** flakes and **sea salt** and **freshly ground black pepper** to taste in a small bowl and stir to mix. Refrigerate in an airtight container until ready to serve or for up to 4 days.

ROUILLE / Makes about 1½ cups

French for "rust," *rouille* is a Provençal pick-me-up traditionally made with chiles. Try this somewhat subtler version on crostini with fresh mozzarella, or spooned onto grilled steak or chicken.

Place **2 teaspoons crushed red pepper flakes, 1 cup fresh basil leaves, 4 garlic cloves smashed and minced, 1 thick slice of rustic bread** (sourdough, baguette or Italian, soaked in water and squeezed dry) and **1 roasted red bell pepper peeled, cored and seeded** (or 1 jarred roasted red bell pepper) in the bowl of a food processor and pulse several times to mix. Slowly add ¼ **cup olive oil** with the motor running and puree until thick and smooth. Season with **sea salt** and **freshly ground black pepper** to taste. Refrigerate in an airtight container until ready to serve or for up to 4 days.

AVOCADO CREMA / Makes about 1½ cups

Part guacamole, part sour cream, I never seem to make enough of this sauce. It's the first to go anytime I create a smattering of fixings for chili, tacos or tostadas (see Chile-Braised Pork Shoulder with Taco Fixings, page 130).

Place **2 ripe avocados peeled, pits removed and roughly chopped, 1 jalapeño pepper seeded and minced, 2 scallions chopped,** ¼ **cup Mexican crema** (substitute: Greek yogurt or sour cream), **juice of 1 lime, 2 tablespoons olive oil, a handful of cilantro leaves** and **sea salt** and **freshly ground black pepper** to taste in the bowl of a food processor or the jar of a blender fitted with a metal blade. Pulse 10 to 12 times to mix, stopping to scrape down the bowl several times, and then puree until the cream is smooth. Refrigerate in an airtight container until ready to serve or for up to 2 days.

BASIL PESTO WITH VARIATIONS
Makes about 2 cups

For fragrant pesto that takes linguine or grilled chicken to new heights, there's no need to look further than basil—until the garden sprouts over. Then any tender green or herb is game, from collards and kale to spinach, arugula and parsley.

Place **2 handfuls fresh basil leaves** (about 2 cups, firmly packed), **1 bunch fresh parsley leaves, 2 garlic cloves smashed and minced** and the **juice of 1 lemon** in the bowl of a food processor fitted with a metal blade. Pulse several times to roughly chop. With the motor running, pour ¼ **cup extra-virgin olive oil** in a slow, steady stream. Stop to scrape down the sides of the bowl several times while adding the oil. Add ½ **cup pine nuts, 3 ounces grated Parmesan cheese** (about 1 cup) and **sea salt** and **freshly ground black pepper** to taste and puree until smooth, about 1 minute. Refrigerate in an airtight container until ready to serve or for up to 4 days.

In the Kitchen

VARIATIONS FOR PESTO There's a pesto for every season. To make, leave the parsley, garlic, olive oil, salt and pepper the same as the recipe above, but mix up your greens, nuts and cheese.

- **Spring:** Arugula, Asiago and walnuts
- **Summer:** Mint, pecans and Pecorino
- **Fall:** Cilantro, pecans and dry Jack
- **Winter:** Kale, almonds and Parmesan; add a jalapeño pepper for extra kick

FOUR BREADY THINGS
FOR SOPPING UP SAUCE

TO SOAK IN EVERY LAST DROP, you don't have to bake your own bread. Just dress up what you already have or can grab at the store before dinner.

GRILLED OR TOASTED CORNBREAD SLICES

My grandmother rejuvenated day-old cornbread by toasting it in a cast-iron skillet with loads of butter. For breakfast, she also poured on local molasses. At Foster's, we use crisp cornbread as a vehicle for poached eggs or sautéed vegetables.

Cut **each slice of cornbread** in half crosswise, smear each side with **unsalted butter,** sprinkle with **sea salt** and **freshly ground black pepper** to taste and place buttered side down in a hot cast-iron skillet or grill pan over medium heat. Cook until lightly toasted and warm, about 2 minutes per side.

RUSTIC TOAST WITH OLIVE OIL AND SEA SALT

I like to sear thick slices of bread on my stovetop. But you can also toast directly on the racks of a preheated 400°F oven for 10 to 12 minutes. I often alternate methods, depending on what else I'm cooking—Tuscan Bean, Cabbage and Sausage Soup (page 97) on the range, or Judy's Lasagna (page 181) in the oven below.

Heat a grill pan or cast-iron skillet over medium-high heat until hot, about 2 minutes. While the pan is heating, brush **slices of rustic whole grain or sourdough bread** with **olive oil** on both sides. Sprinkle one side of each slice of bread with **salt** and **freshly ground black pepper** to taste. Place the bread on the grill pan and grill until lightly toasted, 2 to 3 minutes per side. Serve warm.

HERB AND GARLIC FLATBREAD

To gussy up supermarket pita or naan, a few fresh herbs do wonders.

Brush both sides of **pitas or naan** lightly with **olive oil** and place on a hot grill or grill pan until slightly crisp, about 2 minutes. Flip the bread over and sprinkle the other side with **chopped fresh herbs** such as parsley, rosemary or oregano and let the bottom side toast until crispy, about 2 minutes. Remove from the heat, drizzle with **olive oil** and sprinkle with **sea salt** and **freshly ground black pepper** to taste.

FLAME-TOASTED TORTILLAS

To prep, tortillas just need a little bit of heat—preferably from a gas stovetop or grill. A few seconds will do, so don't leave unattended.

Place **tortillas,** one by one, directly on the heat and toast until each is slightly charred in places and becomes pliable, moving over the flame often, 30 seconds to 1 minute per side. Wrap in a warm, clean dishcloth while heating others. If you have an electric stove, use a cast-iron skillet and heat until hot. Toast the tortilla in the skillet, 1 to 2 minutes per side. You can also toast directly on a grill rack if you already have the grill fired up.

CHAPTER 5

ONE-POT MEALS

ONE-POT MEALS

IN MANY WAYS, MY GRANDMOTHER, who we adoringly called Granny Foster, couldn't have cooked more differently than I. She had an arsenal of about 20 recipes (I never went to her house to find her trying something new), whereas (as this books attests) I have more than 150. Her kitchen tools were minimal; she used a teacup as a half-cup measure and a mug for a one-cup. On the other hand, I have home and professional kitchens full of gadgetry. But it's my grandmother from whom I learned the most. She grounded my cooking—in her backyard, teeming with vegetables; in her cupboard, put-up with pickles; and in her well-worn skillet, all she really needed for turning out crisp fried chicken and fork-tender pot roast.

The recipes that follow are far from Granny Foster's. What would she have thought of Grouper Pot Roast with Caramelized Onions and Oven-Roasted Tomatoes (page 150)? The recipe forgoes her traditional roast for fish dressed in fresh herbs; beyond that, we didn't catch grouper in western Tennessee. Similarly, there's Thai-Style Pot Roast with Fat Noodles (page 164). For Granny Foster, the right cut of meat is there, but so are chiles, cilantro and a stub of ginger. Or what about 20ish Garlic Cloves Chicken (page 153)—a dish centered on a bulb Granny Foster used in moderation, if ever. I like to think she would have sat down at the table for all of these entrees. She'd never turn down a hot meal with family or friends. At her welcome, I was known to invite at least five of mine over for dinner each Sunday. And I know she'd have smiled at my skillet, all that I'd need to prepare those meals and every other in this chapter.

As I learned from my grandmother, there's something a bit magical to one-pot cooking—to placing everything you need in a single dish, letting each ingredient flavor its neighbor. A Slow-Roasted Leg of Lamb (page 161) lends its pungency to fingerling potatoes and carrots, and a Pan-Roasted Spatchcock Chicken with Lentils and Roasted Tomatoes (page 154) cooks slowly together, absorbing the whole bird's broth. It's largely no-fuss cooking. Most of these dishes are placed in an oven and left alone to stew or braise, carving out time for other things. My grandmother would have snapped beans. I'd probably use the time to set the table, but for these recipes, the skillet—and the meal it contains—is the centerpiece.

Grouper Pot Roast with Caramelized Onions and Oven-Roasted Tomatoes

I OFTEN MAKE THIS ROAST WHEN MY SISTER, JUDY, VISITS because she pines for fresh fish in landlocked Tennessee, where she lives. With caramelized onions and roasted tomatoes, it has the same depth and complex flavors that make a pot roast like our mother made irresistible but with the lighter quality of fish. I use grouper because it's readily available in North Carolina, but rely on what's in season near you, as long as it is sturdy (about 1 inch thick). Halibut and cod also work well. **Serves 6 to 8**

3 tablespoons olive oil

1 onion, thinly sliced

2 sprigs fresh thyme

Sea salt and freshly ground black pepper

1 tablespoon unsalted butter

1 (2½- to 3-pound) skinless grouper fillet (about 1 inch thick)

½ pint (1 cup) cherry tomatoes, cut in half

1 cup dry white wine

¼ cup chopped fresh parsley

8 fresh basil leaves, thinly sliced

1. Preheat the oven to 375°F.

2. Heat 2 tablespoons of the olive oil in a large, ovenproof nonstick skillet over medium-high heat until sizzling hot. Add the onion and thyme, season with salt and pepper to taste and reduce the heat to low. Cook, stirring often, until caramelized, about 20 minutes. Remove from the skillet, discarding the thyme sprigs, and set aside.

3. Add the butter and remaining olive oil to the skillet in which the onions were cooked and heat until sizzling hot over medium-high heat. Season both sides of the fish with salt and pepper to taste and slide into the skillet flesh side down. Scatter the tomatoes around the edges of the skillet and fish. Reduce the heat to medium and cook the fish, undisturbed, until it becomes golden in places and lifts easily from the pan, about 4 minutes (longer if it's sticking). Gently stir the tomatoes occasionally so they cook on all sides. Flip the fish over and turn off the heat. Add the wine and scrape up any bits stuck to the skillet around the fish. Spoon the onions on top of and around the fish.

4. Place the fish in the oven and bake until flaky but not dry, 12 to 15 minutes. Transfer the fish to a platter and spoon the tomatoes, onions and broth over it. Sprinkle with parsley and basil and serve warm.

In the Kitchen

NONSTICK METHODS There's no need for special pans. To prevent meats from sticking, simply heat your vessel until it is sizzling hot—meaning, you can actually hear a sizzle when the protein hits the pan. After adding, let it cook for 4 to 5 minutes, resisting the urge to flip. If it sticks, it's not ready to turn. You'll know it's ready once it releases easily—same if you are using a grill or grill pan.

Weeknight Chicken Cooked in Wine

DON'T LET LAST WEEKEND'S WINE GO TO WASTE; use it to flavor this brothy baked chicken. Any dry vino will do. Admittedly, following New Year's or other celebrations, I've even been known to add a cup of withering Champagne. **Serves 4 to 6**

1 (3½- to 4-pound) chicken, cut into 8 pieces (see Cutting Up a Chicken, below)

Sea salt and freshly ground black pepper

1 tablespoon olive oil

1 tablespoon unsalted butter

1 onion, thinly sliced

2 celery stalks, thinly sliced

3 carrots, cut into 1-inch chunks

2 garlic cloves, smashed and thinly sliced

4 sprigs fresh thyme

2 sprigs fresh rosemary

1 cup dry red or white wine

1 cup low-sodium chicken broth

3 handfuls baby spinach or kale

¼ cup chopped fresh parsley

1. Preheat the oven to 325°F.

2. Rinse the chicken, pat dry and remove any excess skin or fat. Season all over with salt and pepper.

3. Heat the oil and butter in a large ovenproof skillet or Dutch oven over medium-high heat until sizzling hot. Add the chicken, in batches if needed, being careful not to overcrowd the skillet. Cook until light brown, about 5 minutes per side. Transfer to a plate and set aside.

4. Reduce the heat to medium, add the onion, celery and carrots to the same skillet and cook, stirring, until the vegetables are tender and golden, about 5 minutes. Add the garlic, thyme and rosemary and cook, stirring, about 1 minute more. Add the wine, scraping up any brown bits from the bottom of the pan, and cook until it reduces slightly, about 1 minute. Add the broth and bring to a simmer.

5. Return the chicken and any juices that have collected on the plate to the broth and place in the oven to roast uncovered, about 45 minutes, basting the chicken with the broth several times as it cooks.

6. Remove from the oven and transfer the chicken and vegetables to a platter. Cover loosely with foil to keep warm until ready to serve.

7. Place the skillet over medium heat and stir in the spinach, stirring often just until it wilts. Season with salt and pepper to taste and add parsley. Serve warm with the sauce and spinach spooned over the chicken.

In the Kitchen

CUTTING UP A CHICKEN A chicken cut into 8 pieces yields 4 breast pieces (2 breasts cut crosswise with wings attached), 2 legs and 2 thighs. Cutting the breast in half crosswise makes for more even cooking and size of pieces. Just discard the backbone.

20ish Garlic Cloves Chicken

DON'T COUNT, DON'T PEEL. For the 40-cloves chicken popularized by James Beard, an ample supply of garlic does the trick. Left in their papery shells, the cloves are subdued and lend an air of sweetness to the braised chicken. I tend to throw in 20 ... ish. **Serves 4 to 6**

1 (3½- to 4-pound) chicken

Sea salt and freshly ground black pepper

1 tablespoon olive oil

1 tablespoon unsalted butter

1 lemon, cut in half

1 onion, thinly sliced

3 celery stalks, thinly sliced

20 (more or less) garlic cloves, peeled or unpeeled, smashed

½ cup dry vermouth

2 to 3 cups low-sodium chicken broth

2 tablespoons chopped fresh tarragon (substitute: 2 teaspoons dried)

Rustic Toast with Olive Oil and Sea Salt (page 145)

1. Preheat the oven to 350°F.

2. Rinse the chicken, pat dry and remove any excess skin or fat. Season all over with salt and pepper and set aside.

3. Heat the oil and butter in a large Dutch oven or ovenproof pot with a tight-fitting lid over medium heat until sizzling hot. Place the chicken breast side down and cook until golden brown, about 5 minutes. Flip the chicken on its back and add the lemon halves cut side down, continuing to cook until both are golden brown, about 5 minutes more. Remove the chicken and lemon from the pot and set aside.

4. Add the onion and celery to the same pot and cook, stirring, until soft, about 5 minutes. Add the garlic and cook, stirring, 1 minute more. Add the vermouth and cook, scraping up any brown bits from the bottom of the pan, until the liquid is reduced by half, about 1 minute. Add 2 cups of the broth and bring to a low simmer.

5. Return the chicken to the pot, squeeze the lemon over the chicken and add the lemon halves. Add the remaining broth, if necessary, to cover about two-thirds of the chicken with liquid. Add the tarragon and stir to mix. Cover the pot tightly and place in the oven, undisturbed, about 1 hour and 15 minutes.

6. Remove from the oven and let sit, loosely covered, before serving, about 10 minutes. Remove the chicken from the pot, cut into pieces and place back in the liquid. Serve warm right from the pot with Rustic Toast with Olive Oil and Sea Salt (page 145) to dip into the sauce. You can also smear the garlic onto the bread.

In the Kitchen

SMASH YOUR GARLIC You'll notice in most of my recipes that I suggest smashing garlic before mincing or chopping. That's because simply pressing down on a clove with the side of a knife makes removing its papery peel a cinch. It also releases more flavor from the garlic clove.

On the Menu

SERVE WITH Bookend the 20ish Garlic Cloves Chicken with a bowl of Grilled Romaine Caesar with Rustic Crunchy Croutons (page 213) and a wedge of Coconut Cream Pie (page 292).

Pan-Roasted Spatchcock Chicken with Lentils and Roasted Tomatoes

SPLIT, FLATTENED AND LAID ATOP A BED OF LENTILS, the whole bird lends its savory juices to everything in the skillet below for an essential one-pot dinner. **Serves 4 to 6**

8 Roma tomatoes, cored and cut in half

2 tablespoons olive oil

1 (3½- to 4-pound) chicken

Sea salt and freshly ground black pepper

2 tablespoons chopped fresh tarragon

1 lemon, cut in half

3 shallots, quartered

3 garlic cloves, smashed

3 cups low-sodium chicken broth

1 cup dry white wine

2 tablespoons white wine vinegar

1 cup French lentils, rinsed and drained

4 tablespoons unsalted butter

2 tablespoons chopped fresh parsley

1. Preheat the oven to 400°F.

2. Toss the tomatoes with 1 tablespoon of the olive oil and season with salt and pepper to taste. Spread in an even layer on a rimmed baking sheet and place in the oven to roast until slightly caramelized around the edges, about 25 minutes. Remove from the oven and set aside.

3. Rinse the chicken, pat dry and remove any excess skin or fat. Place the chicken breast side down and pop the thighs from the backbone by pressing down at the joint. Using kitchen shears, cut along both sides of the backbone and remove it. Press down on the breastbone to crack it and flatten the chicken. Season all over with tarragon and salt and pepper.

4. Heat the remaining olive oil in a large ovenproof skillet over medium heat until sizzling hot. Place the chicken breast side down, arranging the legs and wings so the chicken lies flat at a roughly even thickness. Squeeze half the lemon over the chicken and cook, undisturbed, until the skin is light brown and crispy, 10 to 12 minutes. Flip the chicken skin side up, squeeze the remaining lemon half over the chicken and continue to cook until golden on the backside of the legs, about 10 minutes more. Remove from the skillet and set aside.

5. Add the shallots to the same skillet and cook, stirring, about 3 minutes. Add the garlic and continue to cook, stirring, 1 minute more. Add the broth, wine and vinegar and stir the liquid, scraping up all the brown bits from the bottom of the pan. Add the lentils, tomatoes and any juice collected in the pan, and stir to mix. Season with salt and pepper to taste.

6. Place the chicken on top of the lentils and put in the oven to cook until the juices run clear from the thighs or the internal temperature is 170°F and the lentils are tender, about 45 minutes. (Check several times during the cooking process to make sure there is still liquid in the pan for the lentils to cook; if needed, add more broth, about ½ cup at a time.)

7. Remove from the oven and place the chicken on a platter. Cover loosely with foil to keep warm, and let rest about 10 minutes.

8. Add the butter and parsley to the skillet and stir to melt the butter. Cut the chicken into pieces and place back in the skillet. Serve warm with lentils, tomatoes and shallots spooned around.

Ginger Chicken Stew

AS IT SIMMERS, THIS STEW FILLS THE KITCHEN WITH GINGER'S WARM AROMA. Complement it with something fresh. I prefer a bowl of steamed bok choy or Napa cabbage and a simple salad—sliced or julienned cucumbers and radishes tossed with rice wine vinegar and a sprinkle of sugar. **Serves 6 to 8**

8 boneless, skinless chicken thighs (about 2 pounds)

1 tablespoon curry powder

Sea salt and freshly ground black pepper

2 tablespoons sugar

2 tablespoons olive oil

1 red onion, thinly sliced

2 Thai chile peppers, thinly sliced

2 teaspoons crushed red pepper flakes

1 teaspoon coriander seeds

1 teaspoon yellow mustard seeds

1 (4-inch) piece ginger, peeled and julienned

2 garlic cloves, smashed and thinly sliced

1 cup dry white wine

2 cups low-sodium chicken broth

4 wide strips zest and juice of 1 orange

1 bunch fresh cilantro

2 tablespoons rice wine vinegar

1 teaspoon tamari or low-sodium soy sauce

Lime wedges

1. Rinse the chicken, pat dry and season all over with the curry powder, salt and black pepper and set aside.

2. Place the sugar in a large saucepan or Dutch oven over medium-high heat and cook, undisturbed, until the edges turn amber and start to bubble, about 3 minutes. Once the edges start to brown, stir the sugar until it dissolves and begins to caramelize. Carefully add 1 cup of water and stir until the caramel dissolves. Remove from the pan and set aside.

3. Heat 1 tablespoon of the olive oil over medium heat in the same pan until sizzling hot. Add the onion and cook, stirring, until the onion is translucent, about 5 minutes. Add the chiles, red pepper flakes, coriander seeds, mustard seeds and ginger and cook, stirring constantly, until the seeds begin to pop and become aromatic, about 1 minute. Remove from the pan and set aside.

4. Add the remaining olive oil to the pan and heat until sizzling hot. Add the chicken and cook until golden brown, about 4 minutes per side. Add the garlic and cook, stirring, about 1 minute more.

5. Add the wine, scraping up any brown bits from the bottom of the pan, and reduce the heat to low. Add the onion, spices and caramel water back to the pan with the chicken. Add the broth, orange strips and juice, half the cilantro (including stems), vinegar and soy sauce. Season with salt and pepper to taste. Reduce heat to low, cover and simmer until the chicken is tender and cooked through, about 20 minutes.

6. Remove the pot from the heat, chop the remaining cilantro leaves and garnish the stew just before serving. Serve warm with lime wedges to squeeze into the soup.

Fork-Tender Pork Ragù

THERE ARE DOZENS OF TAKES ON ITALIAN RAGÙ—a meaty sauce that, at its most basic, includes minced beef, diced onions, spiced tomatoes and a splash of red wine. Perhaps it's the Southerner in me, but my preferred version calls for pork, slowly braised and served over a bowl of thick noodles. **Makes about 2 quarts / Serves 6 to 8**

2 tablespoons olive oil

2½ pounds boneless pork shoulder or butt, cubed

Sea salt and freshly ground black pepper

1 onion, diced

2 carrots, grated

2 celery stalks, diced

4 garlic cloves, smashed and minced

1 cup dry red wine

1 tablespoon balsamic vinegar

1 (28-ounce) can crushed tomatoes

4 cups low-sodium chicken broth

2 tablespoons tomato paste

2 tablespoons Worcestershire sauce

2 teaspoons dried basil

1 teaspoon dried oregano

1 teaspoon crushed red pepper flakes

4 bay leaves

2 sprigs fresh rosemary

2 sprigs fresh thyme

2 sprigs fresh parsley

¼ cup chopped fresh parsley

8 fresh basil leaves, thinly sliced

1 tablespoon chopped fresh marjoram or oregano

1 pound pasta, cooked

Grated Parmesan

1. Heat the olive oil in a large saucepan or Dutch oven over medium-high heat until sizzling hot. Season the pork all over with salt and black pepper. Add the pork and onion to the pot and cook, stirring, until the pork is light brown all over, about 10 minutes. Remove from the pot and set aside.

2. Add the carrots and celery to the same pot, stirring often, until the vegetables are tender, about 5 minutes. Add the garlic and continue to cook, stirring, 1 minute more.

3. Add the wine and vinegar and cook, scraping up the brown bits from the bottom of the pot, until reduced slightly, about 2 minutes.

4. Return the pork and onion to the pot and stir to combine. Add the tomatoes, broth, tomato paste, Worcestershire sauce, dried basil, dried oregano and red pepper flakes and stir to mix. Tie the bay leaves and herb sprigs in a bundle with kitchen twine and add to the pot.

5. Season with salt and black pepper to taste and reduce the heat to a low simmer, partially covered and stirring occasionally, about 2 hours and 30 minutes. (Alternatively, place in a preheated 325°F oven to cook, tightly covered.) Add a little water or broth as needed, until the sauce is thick and the pork is tender.

6. Remove from the heat, remove the bay leaf bundle and stir in the fresh parsley, fresh basil and fresh marjoram. Serve warm over freshly cooked tagliatelle or pappardelle with freshly grated Parmesan cheese sprinkled on top.

In the Kitchen

MAKE AHEAD This is one of those recipes that gets better after it sits for a day. So make ahead of time to have on hand for a weeknight dinner. Or pop in the freezer until ready to serve.

Everyday Bolognese

I APPROACH BOLOGNESE AS I DO SOUP: make a lot at one time. The classic beef and tomato ragù freezes well and knows no end—from a topping for spaghetti to a base for wilted greens.

Makes about 2½ quarts / Serves 6 to 8

2 tablespoons olive oil

2 onions, diced

2 carrots, grated

4 garlic cloves, smashed and minced

2 pounds ground beef

Sea salt and freshly ground black pepper

2 teaspoons dried oregano

2 teaspoons dried marjoram

2 teaspoons dried basil

1 cup dry red wine

2 tablespoons balsamic vinegar

2 (28-ounce) cans crushed tomatoes

2 tablespoons tomato paste

2 cups low-sodium chicken or vegetable broth

6 fresh basil leaves, thinly sliced

2 tablespoons chopped fresh oregano or marjoram

1. Heat the olive oil in a large saucepan over medium-high heat until sizzling hot and add the onions. Reduce the heat to medium and cook, stirring, until the onions are cooked through, about 5 minutes. Add the carrots and continue to cook, stirring, until tender, 2 to 3 minutes longer. Add the garlic and continue to cook, stirring often, 1 minute more.

2. Add the beef, breaking it up as it cooks, and season with salt and pepper to taste. Add the dried oregano, dried marjoram and dried basil and cook, stirring, until the beef is cooked on the outside but still slightly pink inside, 4 to 5 minutes more.

3. Add the wine and balsamic vinegar and cook to reduce slightly, scraping up any brown bits from the bottom of the skillet, about 2 minutes. Add the tomatoes and tomato paste and stir to combine. Stir in the broth and bring to a low boil. Reduce the heat to a simmer, partially cover and cook, stirring occasionally, until the sauce thickens and the flavors meld, about 1 hour. Remove from the heat and stir in the fresh basil and oregano before serving. Serve warm or refrigerate in an airtight container until ready to serve.

In the Kitchen

VARIATION Today, it's more common to see Bolognese in Bologna, Italy, without milk. But traditionally, it was added to enrich the texture. To make your own velvety version, simply stir **1 cup whole milk** into the sauce at the end of cooking.

On the Menu

GOOD WITH You need not hail from Bologna to use Bolognese every day—or often, at least. The sauce has dozens of applications:

- Layered between noodles in my sister Judy's Lasagna (page 181)
- Served on a thick slice of Rustic Toast with Olive Oil and Sea Salt (page 145)
- Atop baked potatoes with grated Pecorino cheese and scallions
- Paired with Creamy Polenta (page 269)

Slow-Roasted Leg of Lamb

TENDER, SLOW-COOKED LAMB TAKES CENTER STAGE IN THIS DISH, but its backups sing well, too: fingerling potatoes and carrots stewed in an earthy broth. Rivaling the flavor is the dish's aesthetic. It's hard to match the stature of the bone-in braised lamb, slightly charred and speckled with parsley. **Serves 6 to 8**

1 (4½- to 5-pound) bone-in leg of lamb

Sea salt and freshly ground black pepper

1 bunch fresh parsley, chopped

¼ cup olive oil

6 garlic cloves, smashed and chopped

2 tablespoons chopped fresh rosemary

Zest and juice of 1 lemon

1 onion, quartered

4 sprigs fresh rosemary

4 sprigs fresh thyme

1 cup low-sodium chicken broth

1 cup dry red or white wine

2 pounds fingerling potatoes

1 bunch small carrots, trimmed and scrubbed

On the Menu

SERVE WITH For additional flavor, try also serving one of the following with the lamb:

- Bright Pounded Mint Chimichurri (page 140)
- Biting Red Onion and Horseradish Gremolata (page 142)
- Fresh Watermelon Arugula Tabbouleh with Feta (page 214)

1. Preheat the oven to 325°F.

2. Trim any excess fat from the lamb, season generously with salt and pepper and let sit until it reaches room temperature, about 1 hour.

3. Place the parsley, olive oil, garlic, chopped rosemary, and lemon zest and juice in a bowl and stir to combine.

4. Place the onion and rosemary and thyme sprigs in a large roasting pan and spread in an even layer. Place the lamb on top of the onion and herb sprigs and rub the parsley mixture all over the outside of the lamb. Add the broth and wine to the pan and cover tightly with foil.

5. Place in the oven to roast, undisturbed, about 2 hours and 30 minutes. Remove from the oven, uncover and add the potatoes and carrots to the bottom of the pan.

6. Increase the oven temperature to 400°F.

7. Return the lamb to the oven and continue to cook until the lamb is golden brown and very tender, another 25 to 30 minutes. Remove from the oven and place the lamb on a large platter or cutting board and cover loosely with foil to keep warm as it rests before slicing, about 30 minutes.

8. While the lamb is resting, return the potatoes and carrots back to the oven to continue to cook until tender and slightly golden around the edges, 20 to 30 minutes longer.

9. Slice the lamb (or pull into chunks) and place on a platter with the vegetables served on the side and some of the pan liquid spooned over and around the lamb. Season with salt and pepper to taste. Discard the herb sprigs and serve the remainder of the pan drippings on the side.

Spicy Meatballs in Everyday Marinara

STUDDED WITH FRESH HERBS, THESE BAKED MEATBALLS are not just for noodles (though delicate capellini makes for a failproof combination). Try them over spicy wilted greens topped with fresh mozzarella or grated Parmesan cheese; on an open-faced sandwich with peppers, melted mozzarella and arugula; or atop Creamy Polenta (page 269) . With a hint of mint, they're also apt for skewers; just skip the marinara and pair with Harissa Buttermilk Yogurt Sauce (page 142) or Vietnamese Chile Sauce (page 142). **Serves 4 to 6**

1½ pounds ground beef

½ pound ground pork

¾ cup fresh breadcrumbs

½ cup grated Parmesan cheese

2 large eggs

½ onion, grated

2 garlic cloves, smashed and minced

1 tablespoon Worcestershire sauce

2 tablespoons chopped fresh oregano

2 tablespoons chopped fresh parsley

1 tablespoon chopped fresh mint

1 teaspoon sea salt

½ teaspoon freshly ground black pepper

¼ teaspoon crushed red pepper flakes

2 tablespoons olive oil

Everyday Marinara (recipe follows)

1. Place the beef, pork, breadcrumbs and Parmesan in a large bowl. In a separate bowl, combine the eggs, onion, garlic, Worcestershire, oregano, parsley, mint, salt, black pepper and red pepper flakes and whisk to mix thoroughly. Add the egg mixture to the meat mixture with your hands or a wooden spoon and thoroughly combine; do not overmix.

2. Roll the mixture into about 20 (2-inch) balls and place on a rimmed baking sheet. Refrigerate to chill until firm, about 1 hour.

3. When ready to cook, preheat the oven to 375°F.

4. Brush the top of each meatball lightly with the olive oil. Place in the oven to cook until the juices run clear, about 15 minutes. (Alternatively, heat the olive oil in a large nonstick skillet over medium-high heat until sizzling hot. Add the meatballs in batches and brown on all sides, cooking about 12 minutes total.) Drop into a simmering pot of Everyday Marinara (recipe follows) and serve warm with extra sauce spooned over the top.

EVERYDAY MARINARA

MAKES ABOUT 4 CUPS

Heat **2 tablespoons of olive oil** in a large saucepan over medium-high heat until sizzling hot. Add **1 diced onion** and reduce the heat to medium. Cook, stirring, until the onion is soft and slightly golden, about 5 minutes. Add **2 minced garlic cloves** and cook, stirring, 1 minute more. Add **2 tablespoons balsamic vinegar** and stir until it bubbles and reduces by half. Add **1 cup dry red wine** and cook, stirring, until it reduces slightly. Stir in **1 (28-ounce) can crushed tomatoes, 2 teaspoons dried oregano** and **1 teaspoon dried basil**. Season with **kosher salt and black pepper to taste** and stir to mix. Reduce the heat to low and simmer until the sauce thickens, about 30 minutes. Remove from the heat and stir in ¼ **cup fresh basil, oregano** or **marjoram** (or a **combination of the three**).

Thai-Style Pot Roast with Fat Noodles

FOR CARAMELIZED POTATOES, ONIONS AND CARROTS WITH FORK-TENDER BEEF—a traditional pot roast—you don't need me. You need your grandmother, an aunt or that dependable neighbor. They have it down and cloaked in memory. What I can offer is this chuck roast, freshened up with lemongrass, ginger, orange and cilantro. It won't replace what you already know, but it won't disappoint either. **Serves 6 to 8**

2 tablespoons canola oil

1 (3- to 3½-pound) beef chuck roast

Sea salt and freshly ground black pepper

1 red onion, thinly sliced

6 carrots, cut into 1-inch chunks

1 lemongrass stalk, trimmed of tough outer leaves, pounded and thinly sliced

4 garlic cloves, smashed and thinly sliced

2 Thai chile peppers, thinly sliced with seeds

1 (1-inch) piece ginger, peeled and thinly sliced

1 cup dry red wine

Wide strips zest and juice of 1 orange

1 bunch fresh cilantro, divided

2 tablespoons tamari or low-sodium soy sauce

1 cinnamon stick

2 tablespoons light brown sugar

1 pound wide egg noodles

Olive oil

1 cup shredded unsweetened coconut flakes, toasted

1. Preheat the oven to 325°F.

2. Heat the oil in a large ovenproof skillet or Dutch oven over medium-high heat until sizzling hot. Season the beef generously all over with salt and pepper and sear until golden brown on both sides, about 5 minutes per side. Remove the beef from the skillet and set aside.

3. Reduce the heat to medium. In the same skillet, add the onion, carrots and lemongrass and cook, stirring, until the vegetables are tender, about 5 minutes. Add the garlic, chile peppers and ginger and cook, stirring, until aromatic, about 1 minute more.

4. Add the wine, scraping up any brown bits from the bottom of the pan. Add the orange strips and juice, half the bunch of cilantro (including stems), soy sauce and 2 cups water and bring to a low boil. Add the cinnamon stick and brown sugar and stir to combine.

5. Return the beef to the pot and add enough water to cover about two-thirds of the way up the side of the roast. Cover tightly and place in the oven to cook, undisturbed, until the meat is fork-tender and the sauce is slightly thickened, 2 hours 30 minutes to 3 hours. Remove from the oven and skim the fat from the top of the sauce. (The beef can be cooked up to 2 days in advance and refrigerated until ready to serve. Skim the fat off the top before reheating.) Set aside.

6. Cook the noodles according to package directions, drain and toss with a drizzle of olive oil. Chop half of the remaining cilantro (leaves only) and stir into the beef sauce. Pull the stems from the remaining cilantro and discard, reserving the leaves for garnish. Divide the noodles into individual serving bowls and spoon the beef, vegetables and sauce over the noodles. Top with cilantro leaves and toasted coconut and serve warm.

Pork Tenderloin Fricassee

FRICASSEE MOST COMMONLY FINDS CHICKEN stewing in a delicate cream. But for our Family Dinners at the Market, we often opt for pork, which tenderizes as it absorbs the silky sauce.

Serves 4 to 6

2 (1½-pound) pork tenderloins

1 tablespoon fresh thyme leaves

Sea salt and freshly ground black pepper

2 tablespoons unsalted butter

2 tablespoons olive oil

1 onion, diced

1 carrot, diced

1 celery stalk, diced

1 tablespoon all-purpose flour

1 cup dry white wine

1 cup low-sodium chicken broth

2 tablespoons Dijon mustard

¼ cup heavy cream

3 tablespoons chopped fresh parsley

Juice of ½ lemon

8 ounces cremini (baby bella) mushrooms, trimmed and cut in half

1. Preheat the oven to 375°F.

2. Rinse the pork, pat dry and remove the silver skin from the top of each loin. Season all over with the thyme and salt and pepper.

3. Melt 1 tablespoon of the butter with 1 tablespoon of the olive oil in a large ovenproof skillet over medium-high heat until sizzling hot. Add the pork and cook until golden brown, 4 to 5 minutes per side. Transfer to a plate and set aside.

4. Reduce the heat to medium, add the onion, carrot and celery to the same pan and sauté, stirring occasionally, until the vegetables are soft, about 5 minutes. Add the flour and cook, stirring, about 2 minutes more.

5. Add the wine and scrape the bottom of the skillet to loosen the brown bits. Cook until the liquid thickens slightly, about 1 minute. Add the broth and mustard and stir to combine, bringing to a low boil.

6. Return the pork and any liquid that has collected on the plate to the skillet. Spoon the sauce over each pork loin and place in the oven to roast, basting with the sauce several times while cooking, 15 to 20 minutes. Test for doneness with an internal thermometer inserted in the thickest part of the loin; when ready, it should read 145°F (for medium) or 160°F (for medium-well). The pork will continue to cook while resting.

7. Remove the pork from the sauce and cover loosely with foil to keep warm as it rests before slicing, about 10 minutes.

8. While the pork is resting, stir the cream, parsley and lemon juice into the sauce and season with salt and black pepper to taste.

9. Heat the remaining butter and olive oil in a large skillet over medium-high heat until sizzling hot and add the mushrooms. Sauté, stirring often, until golden around the edges, about 3 minutes. Return the pork to the sauce, spread the mushrooms over the top and serve warm with the sauce spooned over and around.

CHAPTER 6

CASSEROLES

CASSEROLES

GROWN-UP MAC AND CHEESE   172

KALE AND COLLARD GREENS GRATIN   174

ROASTED WINTER SQUASH CASSEROLE
    WITH FRESH RICOTTA   175

SLOPPY JOES TOPPED
    WITH CHEDDAR CORNBREAD   177

SCALLOPED POTATOES   179

JUDY'S LASAGNA   181

MUSHROOM AND SPINACH LASAGNA   182
    Pesto Cream Sauce

TURKEY MOUSSAKA   184

CHICKEN SPAGHETTI   188

SPINACH AND CHEESE ENCHILADAS   189

NOT YOUR MOM'S CHICKEN POT PIE   190

CHICKEN TINGA TORTILLA PIE   193
    Enchilada Sauce

SHORT RIB COTTAGE PIE   195

LAMB SHANK SHEPHERD'S PIE   196

ALTHOUGH I LOVED EATING THEM, I didn't grow up in a big casserole family—there were just four of us to feed, and we often ate fresh from my grandmother's garden—but my sister married into one. Her husband, Pat, is from a house of seven boys and one girl, so his mother (Bobbie of Bobbie's Cheese Dip fame; page 32) prepared heaping dishes. We've cooked that way for our Market family since the beginning with Chicken Spaghetti (page 188), my mother's favorite, and Judy's Lasagna (page 181), perfected under the tutelage of Pat and Bobbie, at the helm. Those casseroles and others have become some of our most sought-after fare. On weekends, it's not uncommon to find Duke students eating a plate of Grown-Up Mac and Cheese (page 172)—already warm and ready at the counter—while waiting on a Grits Bowl Your Way (page 74) for brunch. Our regular customers frequently call to see what casserole we have on the menu that day, prepared to order whole pans.

As is customary for casseroles, many in this chapter call on cheese (in addition to being a great binder, it undeniably adds a layer of comfort). But other ingredients often veer from the ordinary or expected. Mashed rutabagas sweeten the topping for Lamb Shank Shepherd's Pie (page 196) and lamb is swapped to make a lighter Turkey Moussaka (page 184). Celery root gets whipped into our Short Rib Cottage Pie (page 195) and noodles are sworn off for strands of spaghetti squash in our Roasted Winter Squash Casserole with Fresh Ricotta (page 175).

Surveying the recipes that follow, I guess you could say that, like my sister, I married into a casserole family of sorts, too. In the community we've built at the Market, a holiday wouldn't be complete without festive Scalloped Potatoes (page 179), nor a weeknight right without Sloppy Joes Topped with Cheddar Cornbread (page 177). I wouldn't have it any other way. Please pass the Mac and Cheese.

Grown-Up Mac and Cheese

WHEN I MAKE MACARONI AND CHEESE, WHICH IS OFTEN—we keep a version on the menu most days at the Market—I like to use pasta shells that really hold the sauce (if childhood tells us anything, isn't that the point?). Contenders include orecchiette, ziti, penne, ditalini, conchiglie and, of course, classic elbow noodles. **Makes one (9 x 13 x 2-inch) casserole / Serves 8 to 10**

1 pound orecchiette

1 tablespoon olive oil

8 tablespoons (1 stick) unsalted butter

6 tablespoons all-purpose flour

5 cups milk

2 cups (8 ounces) grated sharp Cheddar cheese

2 cups (8 ounces) grated Gruyère cheese

1 (5-ounce) package baby spinach

1 tablespoon hot sauce

1 teaspoon kosher salt

½ teaspoon ground cayenne pepper

½ teaspoon freshly ground black pepper

1 cup heavy cream

1 cup fresh breadcrumbs

1. Preheat the oven to 350°F. Lightly butter a 9 x 13 x 2-inch baking dish.

2. Prepare the pasta, cooking 2 to 3 minutes less than package directions, until al dente. Drain and toss in a colander with the olive oil and set aside to continue draining.

3. Heat the butter in a large skillet over medium heat until melted. Add the flour and cook, stirring constantly as it begins to foam, being careful not to let it brown, about 2 minutes. Whisk in the milk about ½ cup at a time and bring to a low boil, whisking constantly. Reduce the heat to simmer and cook until thick, about 10 minutes. Combine the Cheddar and Gruyère in a bowl and toss to mix. Remove from the heat and slowly stir in 3 cups of the cheese mixture until it melts.

4. Stir in the spinach, hot sauce, salt, cayenne pepper and black pepper until the spinach is wilted.

5. Add the pasta to the cheese sauce, season with additional salt and pepper to taste, if desired, and toss to coat the pasta. Place half the pasta into the prepared baking dish and sprinkle with half the remaining cheese mixture. Repeat with the remaining pasta, scraping all the cheese sauce from the skillet. Add remaining cheese mixture and pour the cream over the casserole.

6. Sprinkle the breadcrumbs evenly over the top, cover with foil and place in the oven to bake until bubbling around the edges, about 30 minutes. Remove from the oven, uncover and continue to bake until golden brown on top, 10 to 15 minutes more. Let stand about 10 minutes before serving warm.

In the Kitchen

KIDS' MAC AND CHEESE I'll admit, of all the versions of macaroni and cheese we serve at the Market, my favorite is that made simply with elbow noodles and Cheddar. It takes me back to the blue boxes of my youth, which were as much about pride as they were about dinner. My mother allowed me to make Kraft Macaroni & Cheese on my own whenever she had to work late. For a take on that standard without the powdered cheese, eliminate Gruyère, spinach and hot sauce from the Grown-Up recipe and double the Cheddar.

Kale and Collard Greens Gratin

WE OFFERED CREAMED SPINACH ON OUR HOLIDAY MENU FOR YEARS but now prefer this sturdier variation. Where spinach wilts and gives under the influence of creamy Gruyère, kale and collards hold their own, retaining their biting textures and flavors.

Makes one (9 x 9 x 2-inch) casserole / Serves 6 to 8

1 tablespoon olive oil

4 tablespoons (½ stick) unsalted butter

1 onion, thinly sliced

1 ounce country ham or prosciutto, chopped

2 garlic cloves, smashed and minced

1 bunch kale, stems removed and roughly chopped

1 bunch collard greens, stems removed and roughly chopped

¼ teaspoon crushed red pepper flakes

Sea salt and freshly ground black pepper

1 cup heavy cream

½ cup low-sodium chicken or vegetable broth

¼ cup chopped fresh parsley

2 teaspoons chopped fresh thyme

1 cup (4 ounces) grated Swiss or Gruyère cheese

1 cup fresh breadcrumbs

1. Preheat the oven to 350°F. Generously butter a 9 x 9 x 2-inch baking dish.

2. Melt the olive oil with 1 tablespoon of the butter in a large skillet over medium heat until sizzling hot. Add the onion and cook, stirring, until soft, about 3 minutes. Add the ham and continue to cook, just until the ham is crispy, about 3 minutes more. Add the garlic and cook, stirring, about 1 minute more.

3. Add the kale, collards and red pepper flakes, season with salt and black pepper to taste and cook, stirring, until just wilted, about 3 minutes. Add the cream and broth and continue to cook until the greens are tender and the sauce is reduced and slightly thick, about 10 minutes.

4. Spread the greens mixture evenly over the bottom of the prepared baking dish and season with parsley, thyme and additional salt and pepper to taste, if desired. Sprinkle the cheese evenly over the greens. Top with the breadcrumbs and dot with the remaining butter, melted.

5. Cover the baking dish with foil and place it in the oven to bake, about 30 minutes. Remove the foil and continue to bake until the top is golden brown and the juices in the gratin are bubbling around the edges, 15 to 20 minutes more. Remove from the oven and let sit about 10 minutes before serving. Serve warm.

In the Kitchen

MIXING GREENS You can make this, as we used to do, with straight-up spinach. Or you can incorporate a variety of greens including beet, turnip, mustard, swiss chard and tatsoi. Almost any braising leaf works well. But if using spinach or other tender varieties, you will need about twice as much, as they tend to cook down more.

Roasted Winter Squash Casserole with Fresh Ricotta

A ROASTED SPAGHETTI SQUASH YIELDS A HEAP OF LONG, LOVELY TENDRILS. But what it has in looks it lacks in taste, falling on the blander side of autumn's yield. In this dish, butternut squash lends its cousin a touch of sweetness. **Makes one (9 x 9 x 2-inch) casserole / Serves 6 to 8**

4 tablespoons (½ stick) unsalted butter

1 large spaghetti squash, cut in half lengthwise and seeded

1 butternut squash, cut in half lengthwise and seeded

1 pint cherry tomatoes

2 tablespoons olive oil

1 tablespoon balsamic vinegar

1 cup (3 ounces) grated Parmesan cheese

½ cup ricotta cheese

1 tablespoon chopped fresh rosemary

Sea salt and freshly ground black pepper

1. Preheat the oven to 400°F. Grease a 9 x 9 x 2-inch baking dish with 1 tablespoon of the butter.

2. Place the squash cut side down on a large rimmed baking sheet. Toss the tomatoes with 1 tablespoon of the olive oil and vinegar and place on the baking sheet with the squash. Add about ½ cup water and place in the oven to roast until the squash is tender to the touch and the tomatoes are caramelized around the edges, about 45 minutes. Remove the squash and tomatoes from the oven, and allow the squash to cool enough to handle.

3. Reduce the oven temperature to 350°F.

4. Take a fork and shred the spaghetti squash by running the fork down the inside of the squash, from the outside edge to the center. The squash will shred apart like spaghetti. Place in a large bowl. Scoop the flesh from the butternut squash and add to the bowl.

5. Add the tomatoes, remaining olive oil, half the Parmesan cheese, ricotta cheese, remaining butter and rosemary. Season with salt and pepper to taste and stir to mix. Spoon into the prepared dish and sprinkle with the remaining Parmesan cheese.

6. Place in the oven to bake until bubbling around the edges and slightly golden on top, 30 to 35 minutes. Serve warm.

On the Menu

VARIATION Spaghetti squash—like its noodle moniker—is a good vehicle for other vegetables or sauces. After roasting, try topping it with Everyday Bolognese (page 160), Fork-Tender Pork Ragù (page 158) or Spicy Meatballs in Marinara (page 163). For a simple side dish, drizzle with extra-virgin olive oil and sprinkle with grated Parmesan cheese, sea salt and freshly ground black pepper.

Sloppy Joes Topped with Cheddar Cornbread

CONFINED BY A CASSEROLE DISH AND A CRISP LAYER OF CORNBREAD, this appearance by Sloppy Joe isn't such a mess. For an easy weeknight dinner that's especially good for kids (or the young at heart), make the filling and serve on grilled sourdough or soft rolls.

Makes one (9 x 13 x 2-inch) casserole / Serves 8 to 10

FILLING

1 tablespoon canola oil

1 onion, diced

2 pounds ground beef

1 teaspoon chili powder

½ teaspoon garlic powder

Sea salt and freshly ground black pepper

1 jalapeño pepper, cored, seeded and diced

2 garlic cloves, smashed and minced

1 cup ketchup

1 cup sweet chili sauce

2 tablespoons Worcestershire sauce

2 tablespoons balsamic vinegar

1 teaspoon hot sauce

½ teaspoon crushed red pepper flakes

1 bunch cilantro, chopped

continues »

FILLING

1. Heat the oil in a large skillet over medium heat until sizzling hot. Add the onion and cook, stirring frequently, about 5 minutes.

2. Add the beef to the skillet, breaking it up as it cooks, and season with chili powder, garlic powder and salt and pepper to taste. Cook, stirring frequently, until the meat is cooked through, about 10 minutes. Drain off the fat from the skillet and add the jalapeño and garlic. Cook, stirring, about 2 minutes more.

3. Add the ketchup, chili sauce, Worcestershire sauce, vinegar, hot sauce and red pepper flakes. Stir in ½ cup water, reduce the heat to low and cook, stirring often, until the sauce thickens, about 20 minutes. If the mixture begins to get too dry, add a little more water.

4. While the mixture is cooking, preheat the oven to 400°F.

5. Remove from the heat and stir in the cilantro. Pour into a 9 x 13 x 2-inch baking dish and set aside.

continues »

TOPPING

1 cup yellow cornmeal

1 cup all-purpose flour

2 tablespoons sugar

1 teaspoon baking powder

½ teaspoon kosher salt

1 cup well-shaken buttermilk

1 (14¾-ounce) can creamed corn

2 large eggs, lightly beaten

1 tablespoon vegetable oil

1 jalapeño pepper, cored, seeded and minced

1 cup (4 ounces) grated Cheddar cheese

Avocado Crema (page 143)

TOPPING

1. Combine the cornmeal, flour, sugar, baking powder and salt in a large bowl and stir to mix thoroughly.

2. Add the buttermilk, corn, eggs, oil, jalapeño and cheese and stir just to combine.

3. Spread over the top of the Sloppy Joe filling and place in the oven to bake until the cornbread is golden brown and the filling is bubbling around the edges, and a wooden skewer inserted in the center comes out clean, about 35 minutes. (If the top is getting too brown, cover with foil.) Remove from the oven and let sit about 10 minutes before serving. Serve warm with a dollop of Avocado Crema (page 143) on the side.

In the Kitchen

CREAMED CORN For homemade creamed corn in place of the canned variety, use 2 cups of corn and increase the buttermilk by ½ cup.

On the Menu

SERVE WITH This is a meal in itself. All you need is a salad and a little something sweet. Serve with Spring Chopped Vegetables Salad with Seasonal Variations (page 211) and Chocolate Chess Pie (page 294).

Scalloped Potatoes

THIN POTATOES AND HEAVY CREAM STRIKE A BALANCE in this tried-and
We offer it on all of our holiday menus at the Market. It's festive. It's comforting.
everything. **Makes one (9 x 13 x 2-inch) casserole / Serves 8 to 12**

4 tablespoons (½ stick) unsalted butter, softened

4 pounds Yukon Gold potatoes (about 6 medium), peeled and very thinly sliced

½ cup chopped fresh parsley

2 tablespoons fresh thyme leaves

Sea salt and freshly ground black pepper

2 pounds sweet potatoes (about 3 medium), peeled and very thinly sliced

1¼ cups heavy cream

¾ cup half-and-half

1 cup (4 ounces) grated Swiss or Gruyère cheese

1. Preheat the oven to 350°F. Generously butter a 9 x 13 x 2-inch baking dish.

2. Arrange one-third of the Yukon Gold potato slices evenly over the bottom of the prepared baking dish and season with the parsley, thyme and salt and pepper to taste. Dot with about 2 tablespoons of the butter. Arrange half the sweet potatoes over the Yukon Gold potatoes and season with parsley and thyme and additional salt and pepper to taste. Repeat the process, ending with a layer of Yukon Gold potatoes. Press the top layer of potatoes down firmly with the palm of your hand or a spatula to press the layers together.

3. Pour the cream and half-and-half over the potatoes. Cover with foil and place in the oven to bake, undisturbed, about 40 minutes.

4. Remove from the oven. Remove the foil and sprinkle with the cheese. Return the potatoes to the oven until the cheese is golden brown and the juices in the gratin are bubbling, 15 to 20 minutes longer. Remove from the oven and let sit, loosely covered with foil to keep warm, about 15 minutes before serving. Slice into squares or wedges and serve warm.

In the Kitchen

MANDOLIN TO THINLY SLICE VEGETABLES When I have to slice a lot of something very thin and even, I prefer to use a mandolin over a knife. A hand-held mandolin is inexpensive, and easy to use and clean. You can place a mandolin right over the bowl where you want whatever it is that you're slicing.

Judy's Lasagna

PER OUR CUSTOMERS' CONSTANT REQUESTS, we placed my sister's lasagna recipe on Foster's website years ago to great fanfare. It's been one of our most viewed pages ever since. As one person commented on the site, "This is my all-time favorite lasagna recipe!" It's ours, too.

Makes one (9 x 13 x 2-inch) casserole / Serves 8 to 10

10 to 12 lasagna noodles

1 tablespoon olive oil

1 (16-ounce) container cottage cheese

1 (8-ounce) container whole-milk ricotta cheese

2 large eggs

10 fresh basil leaves, thinly sliced

1 tablespoon chopped fresh oregano

Kosher salt and freshly ground black pepper

Everyday Bolognese (page 160)

4 cups shredded mozzarella cheese or Italian cheese blend

1 cup (3 ounces) grated Parmesan cheese

1. Preheat the oven to 350°F. Lightly grease a 9 x 13 x 2-inch baking dish.

2. Bring a large pot of water to a boil and add salt. Prepare the lasagna noodles, cooking 2 to 3 minutes less than package directions, until al dente and pliable. Drain and rinse the noodles, toss with olive oil and set aside to continue draining.

3. Combine the cottage cheese, ricotta cheese, eggs, basil and oregano, season with salt and pepper to taste and stir to mix.

4. Layer the lasagna in the prepared dish starting with the Everyday Bolognese sauce, using about 3 cups. Place half the noodles over the sauce and sprinkle with half the mozzarella. Top with another 3 cups of sauce, the remaining noodles and the cottage cheese mixture.

5. Cover with the remaining mozzarella, remaining sauce and Parmesan.

6. Cover with foil and place in the oven to bake until heated through, 50 to 60 minutes. Remove from the oven, uncover and place back in the oven and continue to bake until slightly brown on top, about 15 minutes more.

7. Remove from the oven and let sit, loosely covered with foil to keep warm, about 30 minutes before serving. Serve warm with extra Parmesan cheese for sprinkling on top.

In the Kitchen

MAKING LASAGNA Lasagna is admittedly better if made the day before, and it also freezes well. If removing from the refrigerator or freezer, let it come to room temperature before cooking or it will require more cooking time. The sauce can also be made in advance and frozen. If making the lasagna the same day you plan to serve it, factor in enough time to let it rest. This will help the layers stay together and make the lasagna easier to serve.

Mushroom and Spinach Lasagna

FOR TRUE COMFORT, LAYER UP WITH THIS VEGETARIAN LASAGNA no matter the season. We regularly fold mushrooms and spinach into a creamy pesto sauce, but in winter we also turn to butternut squash and kale, and in summer ratatouille with Everyday Marinara (page 163).

Makes one (9 x 13 x 2-inch) casserole / Serves 8 to 10

10 to 12 lasagna noodles

3 tablespoons olive oil

1 onion, diced

2 garlic cloves, smashed and minced

1 pound wild mushrooms (a mixture of oyster, cremini, shiitake and chanterelle), thinly sliced

Sea salt and freshly ground black pepper

3 (10-ounce) bags baby spinach

3 cups whole milk ricotta cheese

8 ounces soft goat cheese, crumbled

1½ cups (4½ ounces) grated Parmesan cheese

3 large eggs

½ cup chopped fresh basil

1 teaspoon dried oregano

1 teaspoon dried marjoram

Pesto Cream Sauce (page 183)

2 cups (8 ounces) grated mozzarella cheese

1. Preheat oven to 350°F. Lightly oil a 9 x 13 x 2-inch baking dish and set aside.

2. Bring a large pot of water to a boil and add salt. Prepare the lasagna noodles, cooking 2 to 3 minutes less than package directions, until al dente and pliable. Drain and rinse the noodles, toss with 1 tablespoon of the olive oil and set aside to continue draining.

3. Heat 1 tablespoon of the olive oil in a large skillet over medium heat until sizzling hot. Add the onion and cook, stirring, until tender, about 5 minutes. Add the garlic and cook, stirring, about 1 minute more.

4. Add half the mushrooms, season with salt and pepper to taste and cook, stirring, until golden brown. Transfer the mushroom mixture to a bowl and set aside. Repeat the process with the remaining olive oil and mushrooms.

5. Add the spinach to the same skillet and cook, stirring, just until spinach is wilted, about 1 minute longer. Remove from the heat. When cool enough to handle, squeeze any excess water from the spinach and add to the mushroom mixture. Stir to mix and set aside until ready to use.

6. Combine the ricotta, goat cheese, ½ cup of the Parmesan, eggs, half the basil, oregano and marjoram. Season with salt and pepper to taste and stir to mix, and set aside until ready to use.

7. Layer the ingredients as follows: place about 1 cup of the Pesto Cream Sauce on the bottom of the prepared baking dish. Arrange half the mushroom-spinach mixture on top of the sauce and top with a layer of noodles. Scatter with half the mozzarella. Spread another layer of sauce and mushroom-spinach mixture and top with a layer of noodles. Spread the ricotta mixture over the noodles and scatter with the remaining mozzarella. Add sauce and top with the remaining Parmesan cheese.

8. Cover with foil and bake about 35 minutes. Remove the foil and continue to bake until the edges are bubbling and the top is golden brown, 10 to 15 minutes longer. Let rest about 30 minutes before serving warm.

PESTO CREAM SAUCE

6 tablespoons unsalted butter

¼ cup all-purpose flour

4 cups milk

Sea salt and freshly ground black pepper

¼ cup Basil Pesto (page 143)

1. Melt the butter in a small, heavy saucepan over low heat.

2. Whisk the flour into the melted butter and cook, whisking constantly, until the flour is cooked, about 2 minutes, being careful not to brown.

3. In a slow, steady stream, whisk the milk into the flour and butter. Season with salt and pepper to taste and bring to a low boil. Reduce the heat to low, whisking frequently, until the mixture thickens and coats the back of a spoon, 4 to 5 minutes. Stir in the Basil Pesto and set aside until ready to use.

In the Kitchen

LAYERING LASAGNA To make firm lasagna that retains it layers, always undercook the noodles, then drain and toss them with a small amount of olive oil. Use a few eggs to help bind the cheese mixture. And don't oversauce—this will make the lasagna runny, causing it not to set properly. To finish, always let it rest at least 30 minutes before cutting.

CHICKEN LASAGNA For more protein, add **4 cups cooked chopped chicken** with the Pesto Cream Sauce. You might also try the recipe with fresh spinach noodles, which are striking in appearance and can save time. Using fresh sheets of any pasta means you don't have to cook it before adding it to the lasagna.

Turkey Moussaka

I LOVE CLASSIC GREEK MOUSSAKA: baked layers of eggplant, tomatoes, minced meat and béchamel sauce. But I find the traditional use of lamb too rich for the mix, so I often opt for ground turkey, which has plenty of depth, especially when spiced with cinnamon, nutmeg, ginger and allspice. **Makes one (9 x 13 x 2-inch) casserole / Serves 8 to 10**

2 tablespoons olive oil

1 onion, diced

2 garlic cloves, smashed and minced

2 pounds ground turkey

Sea salt and freshly ground black pepper

1 teaspoon ground cinnamon

2 bay leaves

1 teaspoon dried basil

½ teaspoon crushed red pepper flakes

½ teaspoon freshly grated nutmeg

½ teaspoon ground ginger

¼ teaspoon ground allspice

1 (28-ounce) can crushed tomatoes

3 tablespoons tomato paste

1 tablespoon balsamic vinegar

6 tablespoons unsalted butter

½ cup all-purpose flour

3 cups milk

3 eggs yolks, lightly beaten

½ cup nonfat Greek yogurt

continues »

1. Heat the olive oil in a large skillet over medium-high heat until sizzling hot. Add the onion and reduce the heat to medium and cook, stirring, until the onion is soft, about 5 minutes. Add the garlic and continue to cook, stirring, 1 minute more.

2. Add the turkey and season with salt and black pepper to taste, stirring to break up the meat as it cooks. Add the cinnamon, bay leaves, basil, red pepper flakes, half the nutmeg, ginger and allspice and cook, stirring, until the turkey is cooked through, about 5 minutes.

3. Add the tomatoes, tomato paste and vinegar and stir to combine. Reduce the heat to low and simmer until slightly thick, about 30 minutes. Remove from the heat and set aside.

4. While the meat sauce is simmering, make the béchamel sauce: melt the butter in a saucepan over medium heat, whisk in the flour and cook until smooth and pale in color, about 2 minutes. Add the milk in a slow, steady stream, whisking constantly, until all is incorporated. Bring to a low boil, reduce the heat to low and cook, whisking often, until thick and slightly reduced, about 10 minutes. Season with salt and black pepper to taste and remaining nutmeg. Remove from the heat and let cool slightly.

5. In a small bowl whisk together the egg yolks and yogurt. Whisk this into the milk mixture until smooth, and set the béchamel sauce aside.

continues »

1 cup canola or vegetable oil (or enough to cover the bottom of the pan)

2 eggplants, peeled and sliced lengthwise ¼ inch thick

3 Yukon Gold potatoes, thinly sliced

1 cup (4 ounces) grated Gruyère cheese (substitute: Swiss)

6. Heat just enough canola oil in a large skillet to cover the bottom of the pan about ⅛ inch deep over medium-high heat until sizzling hot. Working in batches, cook the eggplant until golden brown on both sides, about 2 minutes per side, adding more oil as needed. Transfer to a paper towel to drain.

7. Add the potatoes to the same skillet, working in batches, and cook, just until tender but not cooked through, about 2 minutes per side. Remove from the skillet and drain on a paper towel.

8. Preheat the oven to 350°F.

9. Layer the ingredients as follows: spread 1 cup of the béchamel sauce on the bottom of a 9 x 13 x 2-inch baking dish. Sprinkle with half of the cheese. Spread the potatoes over the cheese and top with half the eggplant slices. Pour the meat sauce over the eggplant and top with the remaining eggplant and the béchamel sauce and sprinkle with the remaining cheese.

10. Cover with foil and bake about 30 minutes. Remove the foil and continue to bake until golden brown and bubbling around the edges, about 15 minutes more. Remove from the oven and let sit about 30 minutes before serving. Serve warm.

Chicken Spaghetti

MY SISTER AND I ARGUE ABOUT WHICH JUNIOR LEAGUE COOKBOOK introduced us to this casserole (I stand my ground that it was Louisiana's spiral-bound *River Road Recipes* from 1959). What we agree on is that, regardless of where we found it, we're never letting it go.

Makes one (9 x 13 x 2-inch) casserole / Serves 8 to 10

1 (3½- to 4-pound) chicken

8 ounces spaghetti

2 tablespoons olive oil

3 tablespoons unsalted butter

1 onion, chopped

8 ounces button mushrooms, thinly sliced

1 green or red bell pepper, cored, seeded and diced

2 jalapeño peppers, cored, seeded and minced

4 celery stalks, chopped

¼ cup all-purpose flour

3 cups chicken broth (or reserved cooking liquid from chicken)

1 (14-ounce) can diced tomatoes

1 cup (4 ounces) grated mozzarella cheese

1 cup (4 ounces) grated fontina cheese

½ cup (2 ounces) grated Asiago cheese

1 tablespoon chopped fresh parsley

1 teaspoon crushed red pepper flakes

2 teaspoons kosher salt

½ teaspoon freshly ground black pepper

1 cup (3 ounces) grated Parmesan cheese

1. Rinse the chicken, pat dry and remove any excess skin or fat. Place in a large pot with enough water to cover by about 3 inches. Bring to a low boil, reduce heat to low and simmer until the juices run clear when pierced in the thickest part of the thigh, about 45 minutes. Remove the chicken from the broth (reserving 3 cups of the broth) and let cool enough to handle. Pull the meat from the chicken in large chunks, discarding the skin and bones; there should be about 4 cups cooked shredded meat.

2. Preheat the oven to 350°F. Lightly grease a 9 x 13 x 2-inch baking dish and set aside.

3. Bring a large pot of water to boil and add salt. Prepare the spaghetti, cooking 2 to 3 minutes less than package directions, until al dente. Drain and toss in a colander with 1 tablespoon of the olive oil and set aside to continue draining.

4. Melt the butter and remaining olive oil over medium-high heat in a large skillet until sizzling hot. Reduce the heat to medium, add the onion and mushrooms and cook, stirring, until golden brown, about 5 minutes. Add the bell pepper, jalapeños and celery and cook, stirring, until the vegetables are soft, about 5 minutes more. Add the flour and reduce heat to low. Cook, stirring constantly, about 2 minutes longer.

5. Slowly stir in the chicken broth or reserved cooking liquid, stirring constantly, until the liquid comes to a boil. Reduce the heat to simmer and cook, stirring occasionally, until thick enough to coat the back of spoon, about 5 minutes.

6. Add the tomatoes, mozzarella, fontina, Asiago, parsley, red pepper flakes, salt and black pepper and remove from the heat. Stir until the cheese melts.

7. Add the chicken and spaghetti to the sauce mixture and toss just to blend; do not overmix or the spaghetti will break apart. Pour the mixture into the prepared baking dish.

8. Cover with foil and bake until bubbling around the edges, 25 to 30 minutes. Remove the foil, top with the Parmesan and continue to bake until golden brown, 10 to 15 minutes more. Let sit about 10 minutes before serving warm with extra cheese to sprinkle on top.

Spinach and Cheese Enchiladas

THESE ARE A GREAT WEEKNIGHT MEAL. The sauce can be made in advance and the enchiladas require very little prep work—simply wilting spinach and layering cheese.

Makes one (9 x 13 x 2-inch) casserole / Serves 6 to 8

2 tablespoons olive oil

2 onions, diced

4 garlic cloves, smashed and minced

1 (10-ounce) bag baby spinach

4 cups Enchilada Sauce (page 194)

1 tablespoon ground cumin

2 teaspoons dried oregano

1 teaspoon dried marjoram

½ teaspoon crushed red pepper flakes

Sea salt and freshly ground black pepper

12 corn tortillas

⅓ cup vegetable oil

2 cups (8 ounces) grated pepper Jack cheese

1 cup (4 ounces) grated sharp Cheddar cheese

½ cup chopped cilantro

2 limes, cut into wedges

On the Menu

SERVE WITH Add flavor by the dollop: make your own Avocado Crema (page 143) or Summer Tomato Salsa (page 34) to serve on top.

1. Preheat the oven to 375°F. Lightly grease a 9 x 13 x 2-inch baking dish and set aside.

2. Heat the olive oil in a large skillet over medium heat until sizzling hot. Add half of the onions and cook, stirring, until soft, about 5 minutes. Add the garlic and cook, stirring, about 1 minute longer. Add the spinach and cook, stirring often, just until the spinach wilts, about 2 minutes. Remove the spinach mixture from the skillet and set aside.

3. Place the Enchilada Sauce in the same skillet and add the cumin, oregano, marjoram and red pepper flakes, season with salt and pepper to taste and stir to mix. Reduce the heat to simmer and cook, stirring often, until heated through, about 10 minutes. Remove from the heat and set aside.

4. Place the tortillas on 2 rimmed baking sheets and brush each tortilla lightly with the vegetable oil. Place in the oven to bake until just pliable and slightly crisp around the edges, about 5 minutes. Remove from the oven and dip, one by one, into the sauce to coat on both sides. Place back on the baking sheet.

5. Spread about 2 cups of the sauce on the bottom of the prepared dish.

6. Mix the pepper Jack and Cheddar together in a bowl and sprinkle the tortillas, one at a time, with about ¼ cup of the cheese mixture and a small portion of the spinach. Roll each tortilla up and place in the prepared baking dish, seam side down. Repeat the process with the remaining tortillas, spinach and cheese. Spoon the remaining sauce down the middle of the enchiladas and sprinkle with the remaining onion.

7. Place in the oven to bake until heated through and the cheese melts, 15 to 20 minutes. Serve warm topped with chopped cilantro, fresh cilantro leaves and wedges of lime to squeeze over the top.

Not Your Mom's Chicken Pot Pie

DON'T REPLACE YOUR MOTHER'S POT PIE (personally, I know I never could); add a new one to your repertoire. You can't have too many when crisp, cool days roll in. Here, trusty peas and carrots are set aside for roasted butternut squash, sautéed kale and a medley of mushrooms. After Thanksgiving, when sweet potatoes are abundant, I often make this with leftover turkey.

Makes one (9 x 13 x 2-inch) casserole / Serves 6 to 8

½ **butternut squash, peeled, seeded and cut into 1-inch cubes**

2 **tablespoons olive oil**

6 **tablespoons (¾ stick) cold unsalted butter**

Sea salt and freshly ground black pepper

2 **shallots, minced**

8 **ounces wild mushrooms (a mixture of oyster, cremini, shiitake and chanterelle), thinly sliced**

¼ **cup all-purpose flour**

4 **cups low-sodium chicken broth**

4 **cups cooked shredded chicken, from a rotisserie chicken (or see How to Cook a Whole Chicken, below)**

1 **tablespoon fresh thyme leaves**

1 **(5-ounce) package baby spinach or kale**

Sweet Potato Sorghum Biscuits dough (page 63)

2 **tablespoons unsalted butter, melted**

1. Preheat the oven to 400°F. Lightly grease a 9 x 13 x 2-inch baking dish or 12-inch ovenproof skillet.

2. Toss the squash with 1 tablespoon of the olive oil and 1 tablespoon of the chilled butter, season with salt and pepper to taste and spread evenly on a rimmed baking sheet.

3. Bake until tender and golden brown, about 30 minutes. Remove from the oven and set aside.

4. Reduce the oven temperature to 350°F.

5. Melt 2 tablespoons of the butter with the remaining olive oil in a large skillet over medium heat until sizzling hot. Add the shallots and mushrooms and cook, stirring often, until light brown, 5 to 6 minutes.

6. Add the remaining butter and stir until it melts. Add the flour and cook, stirring often, until light brown, about 2 minutes longer. Slowly whisk in the broth and bring to a low boil, whisking constantly.

7. Add the chicken, squash and thyme, season with salt and pepper to taste and stir to mix. Reduce the heat and simmer until thick and creamy, 10 to 15 minutes. Stir in the spinach just until wilted. Remove from the heat and scoop into the prepared dish. Set aside.

8. Roll the biscuit dough on a lightly floured surface as directed and cut into 12 biscuits. Place the biscuits over the top of the filling and brush the tops with the melted butter.

9. Bake until the biscuits are cooked through and golden brown and the sauce is bubbling around the edges, 25 to 30 minutes. (If the biscuits are browning too quickly, cover loosely with foil). Serve warm.

In the Kitchen

HOW TO COOK A WHOLE CHICKEN There's not much as simple and satisfying as a whole-cooked chicken. To achieve a succulent, golden bird, simply rub it with olive oil, salt and pepper and place in a preheated 400°F oven for about 1 hour. For a tender stewed chicken that yields a delicate, savory stock, rinse the chicken, pat dry and remove any excess skin or fat. Place the whole chicken in a large pot with enough water to cover by about 3 inches. Bring to a low boil, reduce heat to low and simmer until the juices run clear when pierced in the thickest part of the thigh, about 45 minutes.

Chicken Tinga Tortilla Pie

MY TAKE ON TINGA—stewed chicken in tomato sauce that is popular in Puebla, Mexico—forgoes smoky chiles in lieu of a mashed sweet potato. I find that it makes a smooth base for tender poached chicken. And jalapeños and red pepper flakes add all the heat I need.

Makes one (9 x 13 x 2-inch) casserole / Serves 6 to 8

1 (3½ to 4 pound) chicken

Sea salt and freshly ground black pepper

2 cups Enchilada Sauce (page 194)

2 jalapeño peppers, seeded, minced and chopped

2 garlic cloves, smashed and minced

12 corn tortillas

⅓ cup vegetable oil

½ cup light sour cream

1 cup jarred salsa verde, plus more for serving

½ cup crumbled queso fresco

½ cup chopped fresh cilantro

1½ cups (6 ounces) grated pepper Jack cheese

1½ cups (6 ounces) grated sharp Cheddar cheese

Avocado Crema (page 143), for serving

1. Preheat the oven to 350°F.

2. Rinse the chicken, pat dry and remove any excess skin or fat. Place the chicken in a large pot with enough water to cover by about 3 inches. Season with salt to taste and bring to a low boil. Reduce the heat to simmer, cover and cook until the juices run clear in the thickest part of the thigh when pierced with the tip of a small knife, about 45 minutes. Remove from the pot (reserving ½ cup of the liquid) and let cool enough to handle. Pull the meat from the chicken, discarding the skin and bones.

3. Place the chicken back in the pot with ½ cup of the cooking liquid, the Enchilada Sauce, jalapeños and garlic. Season with salt and pepper to taste and simmer until slightly thick, about 20 minutes.

4. While the sauce is simmering, place the tortillas on 2 rimmed baking sheets and brush lightly with the oil. Place in the oven to bake until crisp and golden brown, about 10 minutes.

5. In a small bowl, stir together the sour cream, salsa, queso fresco and cilantro.

6. Layer the ingredients as follows: arrange half the tortillas in the bottom of a 9 x 13 x 2-inch baking dish. Spread half the chicken mixture over the top. Spoon half the sour cream mixture over the chicken and sprinkle with half the pepper Jack and Cheddar. Repeat the process with the remaining ingredients, ending with the pepper Jack and Cheddar.

7. Cover and place in the oven to bake until the mixture is bubbling around the edges, about 30 minutes. Uncover and continue to bake until the top is golden brown, 10 to 15 minutes more. Serve warm topped with additional salsa or Avocado Crema (page 143), if desired.

In the Kitchen

CHICKEN TINGA TOSTADAS I often make chicken tinga (following steps 1, 2 and 3) to serve on crispy tortillas (step 4) for tostadas. It's a bit lighter than the tortilla pie. Top with a sprinkle of cheese, Summer Tomato Salsa (page 34), Avocado Crema (page 143) or sliced avocado and mixed greens.

ENCHILADA SAUCE

MAKES ABOUT 6 CUPS

1 sweet potato

2 tablespoons olive oil

1 onion, diced

4 garlic cloves, smashed and minced

1 cup dry white wine

1 (28-ounce) can crushed tomatoes

¼ cup Worcestershire sauce

Juice of 1 orange

Juice of 1 lime

1 tablespoon chili powder

1 tablespoon ground cumin

1 teaspoon crushed red pepper flakes

1 teaspoon kosher salt

½ teaspoon freshly ground black pepper

1. Preheat the oven to 400°F.

2. Place the sweet potato in the oven and bake until soft when pierced with a knife, about 40 minutes. Remove from the oven and cut in half lengthwise to cool slightly. Remove the skin from the potato while still warm and set the potato aside.

3. While the potato is cooking, heat the olive oil in a saucepan over medium heat until sizzling hot. Add the onion and cook, stirring, until soft, about 5 minutes. Add the garlic and cook 1 minute longer. Add the wine and let reduce slightly, about 1 minute.

4. Add the tomatoes, Worcestershire sauce, orange juice, lime juice, chili powder, cumin, red pepper flakes, salt and black pepper and reduce the heat to low. Simmer about 20 minutes, stirring occasionally, until the mixture is slightly thick.

5. Add the sweet potato to the sauce and remove from the heat to cool slightly. Puree with an immersion blender or in a food processor or blender until smooth. Refrigerate until ready to use, for up to 5 days.

On the Menu

SERVE WITH Beyond tortillas, Enchilada Sauce goes well atop eggs, such as Six Original Egg Scrambles (page 62) and grilled chicken or steak with Creamy Polenta (page 269). For breakfast, I also serve it on Chorizo Sweet Potato Hash (page 83).

Short Rib Cottage Pie

COMBINED WITH YUKON GOLDS, mashed celery root provides a light yet pungent cap on this hearty pie. In place of short ribs, you can substitute ground chuck, which browns faster. Or, if you want to stick with short ribs, which are laden with flavorful fat, ask your butcher to grind them for you. **Makes one (9 x 13 x 2-inch) casserole / Serves 10 to 12**

2½ pounds boneless short ribs, cut into 1-inch chunks

Sea salt and freshly ground black pepper

3 tablespoons olive oil

1 cup dry red wine

2½ pounds Yukon Gold potatoes, peeled and cut into large chunks

1 large celery root, peeled and cut into large chunks

8 tablespoons (1 stick) unsalted butter

8 ounces wild mushrooms (a mixture of oyster, cremini, shiitake and chanterelles), thinly sliced (substitute: button mushrooms)

1 onion, diced

3 garlic cloves, smashed and minced

2 tablespoons all-purpose flour

1½ cups reserved cooking liquid from short ribs, or low-sodium beef broth

2 tablespoons tomato paste

2 tablespoons Worcestershire sauce

2 tablespoons chopped fresh rosemary

2 tablespoons chopped fresh parsley

1. Preheat the oven to 325°F.

2. Season the short ribs all over with salt and pepper to taste. Heat 1 tablespoon of the olive oil in a large ovenproof skillet over medium-high heat. Add the ribs and brown, about 5 minutes per side. Add the wine and reduce slightly, scraping up any brown bits from the bottom of the pan. Add enough water to cover the ribs by about two-thirds, cover tightly and place in the oven to cook until fork-tender, about 2 hours. Remove from the oven and strain the liquid from the pan, reserving the liquid and skimming the fat from the top. Set the beef aside. (This can be done up to 2 days in advance. Store refrigerated in the liquid. The fat will rise to the top, and you can easily skim it off.)

3. While the beef is cooking, boil the potatoes and celery root in a large pot of boiling water until soft, about 20 minutes. Drain and mash with 6 tablespoons of the butter and season with salt and pepper to taste. Set aside.

4. Increase the oven temperature to 400°F.

5. Heat the remaining olive oil and butter in a large skillet over medium-high heat until sizzling hot. Add the mushrooms and sauté until golden brown, about 2 minutes. Remove from the skillet and set aside.

6. Add the onion to the same skillet, reduce the heat to medium and cook, stirring, until soft, about 5 minutes. Add the garlic and continue to cook, stirring, 1 minute more. Add the beef and flour to the skillet and cook, stirring, about 2 minutes. Add the reserved cooking liquid and scrape up any brown bits from the bottom of the pan.

7. Stir in the tomato paste, Worcestershire, rosemary and parsley and reduce the heat to simmer until slightly thick, about 5 minutes.

8. Transfer beef mixture to a 9 x 13 x 2-inch baking dish. Dollop mashed vegetables over the top. Bake until juices are bubbling around the edges and top is golden, about 20 minutes. Let stand 5 minutes before serving warm.

Lamb Shank Shepherd's Pie

THIS RECIPE IS TRUE TO ITS TITLE with a shepherd's requisite lamb. But in place of more common versions that rely on ground meat, this calls for tender stewed shanks. For best results, make the stew a day in advance and the topping the day you plan to serve the pie.

Makes one (9 x 13 x 2-inch) casserole / Serves 8 to 10

LAMB

2 tablespoons olive oil

4 lamb shanks (3 to 3½ pounds)

Kosher salt and freshly ground black pepper

1 onion, quartered

6 sprigs fresh thyme or rosemary

1 cup dry red wine

PIE

8 tablespoons (1 stick) unsalted butter

2 tablespoons olive oil

1 onion, thinly sliced

¼ cup all-purpose flour

1 cup dry red wine

2 cups reserved cooking liquid from lamb or low-sodium beef or chicken broth

1 tablespoon tomato paste

1 tablespoon fresh thyme leaves

2 tablespoons chopped fresh parsley

4 carrots, cut into ½-inch chunks

1 (10-ounce) bag frozen green peas

continues »

LAMB

1. Preheat the oven to 350°F.

2. Heat the olive oil in a large Dutch oven or a deep ovenproof skillet with a lid over medium-high heat until sizzling hot. Season the lamb generously with the salt and pepper to taste and place in the skillet and cook until brown, about 5 minutes per side. Remove from the skillet and set aside.

3. Reduce the heat to medium, add the onion to the same skillet and cook, stirring, until the onion is tender and light brown, about 5 minutes. Add the thyme and wine and scrape up any brown bits from the bottom of the pan.

4. Return the lamb to the pan and add enough water to cover about two-thirds of the way up the lamb, and bring the liquid to a low boil. Cover the pan tightly and place in the oven, undisturbed, until the lamb is fork-tender, about 2½ hours.

5. Remove the pan from the oven. Remove the lamb from the liquid (reserving the liquid) to cool slightly. Pull the lamb off the bones in large chunks. You should have about 4 cups of cooked meat. (This can be done several days in advance. Store refrigerated in the liquid. The fat will rise to the top and you can skim it off after it has cooled completely.)

PIE

1. Heat 2 tablespoons of the butter and olive oil in a large skillet over medium-high heat until sizzling hot. Reduce the heat to medium and add the onion and cook, stirring often, until soft, about 5 minutes. Sprinkle the flour over the onion and continue to cook, stirring, another 2 minutes.

continues »

Kosher salt and freshly ground black pepper

2 pounds rutabagas, peeled and cut into large chunks (substitute: sweet potatoes or butternut squash)

2 pounds Yukon Gold potatoes (about 4 or 5), peeled and cut into large chunks

1 tablespoon chopped fresh rosemary

Ground paprika

2. Slowly add the wine and scrape up brown bits from the bottom of the pan. Whisk in the broth or reserved cooking liquid about ½ cup at a time and bring to a low boil, whisking constantly. Stir in the tomato paste to mix. Reduce the heat to simmer and cook until slightly thick, about 10 minutes. Add the lamb, thyme, parsley, carrots and peas and continue to cook until the carrots are tender, about 20 minutes. Season with salt and pepper to taste.

3. Preheat the oven to 400°F. Lightly grease a 9 x 13 x 2-inch baking dish and set aside.

4. While the filling is cooking, place the rutabagas and potatoes in a large pot of boiling water and cook until tender, about 25 minutes. Drain; add the remaining butter, season with salt and pepper to taste and mash until smooth.

5. Pour the filling into the prepared baking dish and spoon the potato mixture on top in serving sizes. Sprinkle with rosemary and paprika and place in the oven until golden brown on top and bubbling around the edges, 25 to 30 minutes. Serve warm, scooping out a portion of the potatoes and lamb for each serving.

In the Kitchen

VARIATION For a quicker option, replace the lamb shanks with 2 pounds of ground lamb or ground beef, sautéed until light brown with the onion in Pie, step 1. Or, if time is on your side, slowly stew beef just as you would the lamb.

CHAPTER 7

SALADS

SALADS

FRESH MOZZARELLA TOMATO SALAD
WITH TORN PESTO CROUTONS 204

SOUTHERN MIXED SWEET POTATOES
SALAD WITH CAPER VINAIGRETTE 208
Caper Vinaigrette

MY BIG FAT TUSCAN SALAD 209
Herb Italian Vinaigrette

SPRING CHOPPED VEGETABLES SALAD
WITH SEASONAL VARIATIONS 211
Green Goddess Vinaigrette

GRILLED ROMAINE CAESAR WITH RUSTIC
CRUNCHY CROUTONS 213
Tangy Caesar Dressing

WATERMELON ARUGULA TABBOULEH
WITH FETA AND MINT 214

ROASTED RED PEPPER PANZANELLA
WITH ARUGULA AND
GOAT CHEESE 217

ROASTED BUTTERNUT SQUASH
AND WHITE BEAN SALAD
WITH CRISPY PROSCIUTTO 218
Rosemary Vinaigrette

CARROT, BEET, APPLE
AND RAISIN SLAW 220
Citrus Vinaigrette

TANGY CABBAGE AND KALE SLAW 223
Grainy Vinaigrette

HEIRLOOM AND SHELL BEAN
SALAD 224
Sherry Vinaigrette

CURRIED LENTIL SALAD 226
Curry Vinaigrette

KALE SALAD WITH TANGERINES,
AVOCADO AND CRISPY COUNTRY
HAM 229
Peter's Coffee Mug Dressing

BLT SALAD WITH ARUGULA,
AVOCADO AND CORN 230
Fresh Summer Herb Vinaigrette

CITRUS WINTER AMBROSIA
WITH FLAKY COCONUT 233

ROASTED CHICKEN AND BREAD SALAD
WITH PAN JUICE VINAIGRETTE 235
Pan Juice Vinaigrette

TARRAGON CHICKEN SALAD
WITH GRAPES, APPLES AND
BIBB LETTUCE 236
Tarragon Mayonnaise

WHILE PETER AND I WERE STILL LIVING IN CONNECTICUT,
we rented a place in North Carolina between Chapel Hill and Pittsboro and
brought our horses down to ride. I fell in love with the area right away, but what
sealed the deal was a roadside stand. Near the intersection of Highway 15-
501 and Mount Moriah Road, I met my dear friend Betsy Hitt, who was selling
every variety of pumpkin you could imagine and who told me about the vibrant
Carrboro Farmers' Market. (It had some 90 vendors over the course of 1989,
the year Peter and I moved South.) With access to an abundance of local farms
and produce, I knew I could open the kind of shop I admired up North—those like
Hay Day and Balducci's with fresh prepared salads and really fine baked goods—
in a region I loved and called home. You could say that fresh vegetables and
salads helped launch the Market.

The first to make an appearance on Foster's menu was Tarragon Chicken
Salad with Grapes, Apples and Bibb Lettuce (page 236), a dish I inherited from
my time at Soho Charcuterie in New York. There (as I wrote in the introduction
to Soups, page 87), my job was to survey the walk-in cooler and incorporate any
seasonal produce into soups or salads to limit food waste. I still do that daily—at
Foster's and at home. In fact, my inspiration for Kale Salad with Tangerines,
Avocado and Crispy Country Ham (page 229) came from doing just that (see
also Pork Tenderloin with Olives and Tangerines, page 128).

I draw the bulk of my ideas, however, from local fields and markets. In
autumn, rugged greens yield Tangy Cabbage and Kale Slaw (page 223). In winter,
hearty gourds mean Roasted Butternut Squash and White Bean Salad with
Crispy Prosciutto (page 218). Warmer days invite Spring Chopped Vegetables
Salad (page 211). And summer days call for Watermelon Arugula Tabbouleh with
Feta and Mint (page 214). Then it's back to fall, which means back to the drawing
(cutting) board.

Fresh Mozzarella Tomato Salad with Torn Pesto Croutons

I CAN'T GET ENOUGH FRESH BASIL IN SUMMER (Peter can; see below), so I often bake pesto croutons, which provide extra herbs and crunch. I love this salad on its own or spread across a bed arugula. And I'll put the croutons on any fresh mix of greens. **Serves 4 to 6**

½ cup **Basil Pesto (page 143)**

¼ cup **extra-virgin olive oil**

½ **day-old baguette or Italian bread, cut or torn into 1-inch pieces**

Sea salt and freshly ground black pepper

2 **large heirloom tomatoes, cored and sliced**

8 ounces **fresh mozzarella cheese, thinly sliced**

12 **fresh basil leaves, torn into pieces or thinly sliced**

1. Preheat the oven to 400°F.

2. Place the pesto in a large bowl and stir in 2 tablespoons of the olive oil to combine. Add the bread and toss to coat evenly. Season with salt and pepper to taste and spread on a rimmed baking sheet in an even layer.

3. Bake until crispy and golden brown around the edges, about 10 minutes. Remove from the oven and set aside to cool.

4. Arrange the tomatoes and mozzarella on a large platter, drizzle with the remaining olive oil, sprinkle with basil, season to taste with salt and pepper and top with the croutons. This salad is best served room temperature.

In the Kitchen

MAKE AHEAD The croutons can be made several days in advance, completely cooled and stored in a resealable plastic bag or airtight container at room temperature until ready to use. The pesto can also be made in advance and refrigerated until ready to use. Doing so makes this salad easy to assemble right before serving. Just slice the tomatoes and mozzarella, arrange the ingredients and drizzle with olive oil.

On the Lawn

PETER'S BASIL PARABLE Peter and I spent our first 20 years in North Carolina living on a farm, where we initially set aside acreage to grow vegetables and flowers for the Market. We didn't keep at it for long (to read how the flowers turned out, see the Introduction, page 10), in part because of basil. Against the advice of my cousins at Lyon Farms in Creedmoor, North Carolina, Peter planted rows and rows of the herb early in the season before leaving town on a work trip. Of course, a cold snap came, so Peter found himself up one night tending to the irrigation. I say one night because that's all it lasted. Peter let it freeze and gave up farming.

Southern Mixed Sweet Potatoes Salad with Caper Vinaigrette

I'LL EMBRACE THE KNICK AND NOB OF ANY SWEET POTATO—from copper-skinned Jewels to blushing Covingtons, to rich-hued Garnets. For this salad, use multiple varieties. I sometimes toss in Yukon Golds and fingerlings, too. **Serves 6 to 8**

3 pounds mixed sweet potatoes, cut into 1-inch chunks

2 tablespoons olive oil

2 tablespoons fresh thyme leaves

Sea salt and freshly ground black pepper

2 celery stalks (with leaves), chopped

2 scallions, minced

¼ cup chopped fresh parsley

½ cup Caper Vinaigrette (recipe follows)

1. Preheat the oven to 400°F.

2. Place the potatoes on a rimmed baking sheet, drizzle with olive oil, sprinkle with thyme and season with salt and pepper to taste. Toss to coat evenly and spread in a single layer.

3. Place in the oven to roast until the potatoes are just tender and golden around the edges, about 30 minutes. Remove from the oven and allow to cool.

4. Toss the potatoes in a large bowl with the celery, scallions, parsley and vinaigrette and season with additional salt and pepper to taste, if desired. Serve at room temperature or refrigerate until ready to use.

In the Kitchen

ROASTING VEGETABLES When roasting, spread vegetables in a single layer, allowing them to get slightly golden around the edges and begin to caramelize. This brings out the natural sugars in the vegetables and makes them more flavorful. If you crowd and pile them on a baking sheet, they will merely steam and soften.

CAPER VINAIGRETTE

MAKES ABOUT 1 CUP

Stir ¼ **cup capers, roughly chopped;** ¼ **cup red wine vinegar; 1 tablespoon Dijon mustard;** ½ **teaspoon crushed red pepper flakes; 2 scallions (white part only), trimmed and minced;** and **1 tablespoon chopped fresh parsley** together in a small bowl. Add ½ **cup extra-virgin olive oil** in a thin, steady stream, whisking constantly, until all is incorporated. Season with **sea salt** and **freshly ground black pepper** to taste and store refrigerated in an airtight container until ready to use for up to 1 week.

My Big Fat Tuscan Salad

WE VISIT OTHER PLACES THROUGH MANY OF THE SALADS WE SERVE—Greece and the Southwest, among them. But my favorite destination is Italy through this Tuscan Salad, with bitter greens, sweet cured meats and nutty Pecorino and chickpeas. **Serves 6 to 8**

2 handfuls arugula

1 head radicchio, roughly chopped or torn into pieces

1 head romaine, roughly chopped or torn into pieces

1 cup fresh basil leaves

1 (15½-ounce) can chickpeas, drained and rinsed

1 pint cherry tomatoes, cut in half

1 cup pepperoncini peppers, cut in half

Herb Italian Vinaigrette (recipe follows)

Sea salt and freshly ground black pepper

6 ounces thinly sliced prosciutto

6 ounces thinly sliced salami

8 ounces fresh mozzarella cheese, cut into ¼-inch cubes

2 ounces Pecorino cheese, shaved or very thinly sliced (substitute: Parmesan)

1. Place the arugula, radicchio, romaine, basil, chickpeas, tomatoes and pepperoncini in a large bowl. Drizzle with half of the vinaigrette, season with salt and pepper to taste and toss to mix.

2. Arrange the greens on a large platter or divide among individual plates, lay the prosciutto and salami over the greens and top with the mozzarella and Pecorino. Drizzle the remaining vinaigrette over the salad or serve on the side. Season with additional salt and pepper to taste, if desired, and serve.

HERB ITALIAN VINAIGRETTE

MAKES ABOUT 1 CUP

Combine ¼ **cup red wine vinegar, 1 minced shallot, grated zest and juice of 1 lemon, 1 tablespoon chopped fresh oregano, 1 tablespoon chopped fresh marjoram, 6 thinly sliced basil leaves** and **2 minced garlic cloves** in a small bowl and stir to mix. Slowly whisk in ½ **cup extra-virgin olive oil** until all is incorporated. Season with **sea salt** and **freshly ground black pepper** to taste and pour over the salad or refrigerate in an airtight container until ready to use for up to 1 week. If you are making it in advance, stir in the fresh herbs just before using.

Spring Chopped Vegetables Salad with Seasonal Variations

I MAKE A VERSION OF THIS SALAD ALL YEAR LONG, but I prefer spring, when tender vegetables first start to appear. Then, asparagus and snap peas require just a minute to blanch, and chopped baby beets don't even need cooking. **Serves 6 to 8**

½ pound sugar snap peas, roughly chopped

1 bunch asparagus, trimmed and chopped

4 carrots, chopped

1 bunch radishes, trimmed and chopped

1 bunch small beets, trimmed (greens reserved), peeled and chopped

½ cup chopped fresh cilantro

Sea salt and freshly ground black pepper

Green Goddess Vinaigrette (recipe follows)

2 handfuls field greens, plus baby beet greens

1. Blanch the peas and asparagus by placing in a saucepan of salted boiling water until bright green and crisp-tender, about 1 minute. Remove from the water with a strainer and immediately place into ice-cold water until completely cooled. Place in a colander to drain thoroughly.

2. Place the peas, asparagus, carrots, radishes, beets and cilantro in a large bowl and season with salt and pepper to taste. Add half the vinaigrette and toss to mix, adding more if desired.

3. Place the greens on a large platter, spoon the vegetables over the top and serve with additional vinaigrette on the side.

In the Kitchen

SEASONAL VARIATIONS

Summer: Green beans, corn, summer squash, red bell peppers, heirloom cherry tomatoes, cucumbers and torn basil with Rosemary Vinaigrette (page 218)

Fall: Roasted winter squash, sweet potatoes, beets or turnips and roasted onions tossed with spinach and a maple vinaigrette

Winter: Roasted cauliflower, broccoli, Brussels sprouts, parsnips, rutabaga and beets tossed with Napa cabbage and balsamic vinaigrette

GREEN GODDESS VINAIGRETTE

MAKES ABOUT 1 CUP

Place **2 tablespoons chopped fresh cilantro, 2 tablespoons chopped fresh chives, 2 tablespoons chopped fresh dill, grated zest and juice of 1 lime, grated zest and juice of 1 lemon, 3 tablespoons white wine vinegar** and ½ **cup vegetable oil** in a container with a tight fitting-lid and shake to combine. Season with **sea salt** and **freshly ground black pepper** to taste. Store refrigerated in an airtight container until ready to serve for up to 1 week.

Grilled Romaine Caesar with Rustic Crunchy Croutons

I FIRST ENCOUNTERED A GRILLED CAESAR AT NANA'S, my friend Scott Howell's restaurant just down the Boulevard from the Market. As much as I love anything off the grill, I couldn't believe I had never thought to char romaine myself. The leaves become slightly sweet and smoky—an excellent companion for salty Caesar dressing. I now make this dish almost anytime I fire up my grill (and am not at Nana's with Peter for our weekly dinner). **Serves 6 to 8**

3 heads romaine, trimmed and cut in half lengthwise (cores left intact)

2 tablespoons olive oil

Sea salt and freshly ground black pepper

Tangy Caesar Dressing (recipe follows)

Rustic Crunchy Croutons (recipe follows)

2 ounces Parmesan cheese, shaved

1. About 30 minutes before ready to grill, build a fire in a gas or charcoal grill. If using a charcoal grill, let the coals burn to a gray ash with a slight red glow. If using a gas grill, preheat to medium. (Alternatively, heat a grill pan over medium-high heat.)

2. Lay the romaine halves cut side up on a baking sheet. Brush lightly with olive oil and season with salt and pepper to taste. Place the romaine, cut side down, on the grill and cook, only on one side, until the lettuce is slightly wilted and charred with grill marks but parts of it are still crunchy. (You may need to do this in batches, depending on the size of your grill.)

3. Remove the lettuce from the grill and place, cut side up, on a serving platter. Drizzle with half of the dressing, adding more as desired, and season with additional salt and pepper to taste. Scatter the croutons on top of the salad and sprinkle with shaved Parmesan. Serve warm or at room temperature.

TANGY CAESAR DRESSING

MAKES ABOUT 1 CUP

In a small bowl, whisk together **1 large egg, 1 tablespoon anchovy paste, the juice of 1 lemon, 1 teaspoon Worcestershire sauce** and **2 minced garlic cloves**. Slowly whisk in ½ **cup olive oil** until all is incorporated and the dressing is emulsified. Stir in ¼ **cup freshly grated Parmesan cheese** and season with **sea salt** and **freshly ground black pepper** to taste. Store refrigerated in an airtight container until ready to serve or for up to 4 days.

RUSTIC CRUNCHY CROUTONS

Preheat the oven to 400°F. Tear **half a loaf of rustic day-old bread or baguette into 1- to 2-inch pieces**. Toss the bread with **3 tablespoons olive oil** and season liberally with **sea salt** and **freshly ground black pepper**. Spread the bread pieces evenly on a rimmed baking sheet and toast in the oven until golden around the edges, about 10 minutes. Remove the croutons from the oven and set aside to cool to room temperature. Use right away or store in an airtight container at room temperature for up to several days.

Watermelon Arugula Tabbouleh with Feta and Mint

I GREW UP EATING SALT ON ICE-COLD WATERMELON, so this combination seemed only natural. The sweetness of the melon and the salty feta cheese make it one of my favorite summer treats. **Serves 6 to 8**

1 cup bulgur

Zest and juice of 1 lemon

Zest and juice of 1 lime

4 cups cubed watermelon

4 handfuls arugula or mixed baby greens

2 small Kirby cucumbers, chopped

1 cup (4 ounces) cubed feta cheese

2 tablespoons extra-virgin olive oil

2 tablespoons balsamic vinegar

2 tablespoons chopped fresh mint

2 tablespoons chopped fresh cilantro

2 tablespoons minced red onion

Sea salt and freshly ground black pepper

1. Combine the bulgur, lemon zest and juice, and lime zest and juice in a saucepan with just enough water to cover, about 1 cup, and bring to a low boil. Cover and let simmer until the liquid is absorbed, about 10 minutes. Remove from the heat and drain any excess liquid.

2. Place the bulgur, melon, arugula, cucumbers, feta, oil, vinegar, mint, cilantro and onion in a large bowl. Season with salt and pepper to taste and toss gently to mix. Serve or refrigerate in an airtight container until ready to serve.

In the Kitchen

DELICATE SALADS The secret to delicate salads like this is not to overmix. Simply place everything in a bowl, season with salt and pepper and mix only once. Otherwise, the melon and the arugula will start to break down and become watery and/or wilted.

Roasted Red Pepper Panzanella with Arugula and Goat Cheese

THIS IS THE PERFECT WAY TO USE PART OF A BAGUETTE left over from dinner the night before. The croutons can be cooked several days in advance, as can the peppers, making this a salad that's easy on time and resources. The only thing to go big on here is olive oil. Use the best you have, as it really makes a difference. **Serves 6 to 8**

½ day-old baguette or Italian bread, cut or torn into 1-inch pieces

Sea salt and freshly ground black pepper

⅓ cup extra-virgin olive oil

3 red, green or yellow bell peppers

2 beefsteak or heirloom tomatoes, cored and cut into wedges

2 tablespoons minced red onion

3 tablespoons red wine vinegar

1 cup fresh basil leaves, thinly sliced

6 handfuls arugula

½ cup (2 ounces) crumbled goat cheese

1. Preheat the oven to 400°F.

2. Put the bread in a large bowl, season with salt and pepper to taste and toss to mix. Drizzle with about 3 tablespoons of the olive oil and toss to coat. Spread evenly in a single layer on a rimmed baking sheet.

3. Place in the oven to toast until golden brown around the edges, about 10 minutes. Remove from the oven and set aside to cool.

4. While the bread is toasting, roast each pepper over an open flame of a gas stove using tongs or together under the broiler of the oven on a rimmed baking sheet, turning often, until charred all over, about 10 minutes. Place in a paper bag or a covered bowl to sweat and loosen the charred skin, about 10 minutes. Slip off the charred outside of the peppers and discard the stems and seeds. Resist putting the peppers under water; this dilutes the flavor. Scrape any small pieces of char left on the skin with a small knife. Slice the peppers into strips and place in the bowl the bread was tossed in.

5. Add the toasted bread, tomatoes, onion, vinegar, remaining olive oil and basil. Season with salt and pepper to taste and toss gently to combine. Let the salad stand so the juices soak in and flavor the bread, about 10 minutes. Just before serving, add the arugula and toss lightly to combine. Place the salad on a platter and top with the crumbled goat cheese and whole leaves or strips of fresh basil and serve room temperature.

In the Kitchen

VARIATIONS For a more traditional panzanella, eliminate the roasted peppers and add more tomatoes. For a Southern version, use warm cornbread croutons, fresh corn kernels, tomatoes and basil.

Roasted Butternut Squash and White Bean Salad with Crispy Prosciutto

FOR A SIMPLE DINNER, I OFTEN SPRINKLE ROSEMARY LEAVES over roasted butternut squash. This is the salad version, with warm Rosemary Vinaigrette (recipe follows) as a binder for squash, peppers, white beans, baby greens and thin, crisped prosciutto. **Serves 6 to 8**

1 butternut squash, peeled, seeded and cut into chunks

1 onion, thinly sliced

3 tablespoons olive oil

1 tablespoon chopped fresh rosemary

Sea salt and freshly ground black pepper

1 ounce prosciutto, thinly sliced

1 (15½-ounce) can navy or cannellini beans, drained and rinsed

2 handfuls baby spinach, arugula or field greens

8 pepperoncini peppers, sliced into rounds

¼ cup chopped fresh parsley

½ cup Rosemary Vinaigrette (recipe follows)

1. Preheat the oven to 400°F.

2. Place the squash and onion on a rimmed baking sheet and drizzle with 2 tablespoons of the olive oil. Sprinkle with the rosemary, season with salt and pepper to taste and toss to coat.

3. Place in the oven to roast until the squash is tender and golden around the edges, about 30 minutes. Remove from the oven and cool.

4. While the squash is cooking, heat the remaining olive oil in a skillet until sizzling hot, add the prosciutto and cook until crispy on both sides, about 1 minute. Remove and place on a paper towel to drain.

5. When the squash and onions are cool enough to handle, place in a large bowl with the beans. Add the greens, peppers, parsley and half the vinaigrette, season with salt and pepper to taste and toss to mix. Crumble the crispy prosciutto over the top and serve warm or room temperature with the additional vinaigrette on the side.

ROSEMARY VINAIGRETTE

MAKES ABOUT 1 CUP

Combine ⅓ **cup white wine vinegar, grated zest and juice of 1 lemon, 2 minced garlic cloves, 2 tablespoons chopped fresh parsley, 1 tablespoon chopped fresh rosemary** and **1 teaspoon ground paprika** in a small bowl and stir to mix thoroughly. Add ½ **cup extra-virgin olive oil** in a slow, steady stream until all is incorporated. Season with **sea salt** and **freshly ground black pepper** to taste and store refrigerated in an airtight container until ready to use for up to 1 week.

Carrot, Beet, Apple and Raisin Slaw

MOVE OVER MAYONNAISE. My take on traditional carrot and raisin salad is dressed in a tangy vinaigrette and gets more company—thinly sliced radishes, beets and apples, plus sprouts and cilantro for extra crunch. **Serves 6 to 8**

1 tart apple, cored and julienned

Juice of 1 lemon

3 carrots, julienned

2 golden or red beets, peeled and julienned

4 watermelon radishes, thinly sliced (substitute: any radish)

4 scallions, julienned

1 cup golden raisins

¼ cup chopped fresh cilantro

1 cup pea, radish or sunflower sprouts

Citrus Vinaigrette (recipe follows)

Sea salt and freshly ground pepper

1. As you julienne the apple, place in a large bowl and toss with lemon juice.

2. Add the carrots, beets, radishes, scallions, raisins, cilantro, sprouts and about half the vinaigrette to the bowl. Season with salt and pepper to taste and toss gently to mix. Serve with additional vinaigrette on the side to use as needed.

CITRUS VINAIGRETTE

MAKES ABOUT 1 CUP

Combine ¼ **cup rice wine vinegar, grated zest and juice of 1 orange, grated zest and juice of 1 lime, 2 tablespoons chopped fresh cilantro, ½ cup olive oil, sea salt** and **freshly ground black pepper** to taste in a jar and shake to combine. Season with additional **salt** and **pepper,** if desired. Refrigerate in an airtight container until ready to use for up to 1 week. If you are making it in advance, stir in the fresh herbs just before using.

Tangy Cabbage and Kale Slaw

THERE'S A SLAW FOR EVERY SEASON. With cool-loving greens and a tart, crisp apple, this belongs to none other than fall. **Serves 6 to 8**

¼ **head red cabbage, cored and very thinly sliced**

1 apple, cored and julienned

Juice of 1 lemon

1 bunch curly or lacinato kale, stems removed and roughly chopped

¼ **head green cabbage, cored and thinly sliced**

3 carrots, julienned

2 watermelon radishes, thinly sliced (substitute: any radish)

1 cup pea, sunflower or radish sprouts

½ **cup chopped fresh spring herbs, such as chives, mint, cilantro, parsley and dill**

Sea salt and freshly ground black pepper

Grainy Vinaigrette (recipe follows)

1. Soak the red cabbage in cold water for about 30 minutes; this will help retain its color and keep it from bleeding onto the other salad ingredients. Drain well and pat dry.

2. As you julienne the apple, place in a large bowl and toss with lemon juice.

3. Add the kale, green cabbage, red cabbage, carrots and radish to the bowl as you prep. (If making ahead, stop at this point and refrigerate until ready to use.) Just before serving, toss gently with the sprouts, herbs, salt and pepper to taste and vinaigrette to mix.

GRAINY VINAIGRETTE

MAKES ABOUT 1 CUP

Combine **1 tablespoon whole grain mustard**, grated zest and juice of **2 limes, 1 minced shallot, 2 tablespoons sherry vinegar, 1 tablespoon honey,** ½ **cup extra-virgin olive oil, sea salt** and **freshly ground black pepper** to taste in a glass jar with tight-fitting lid and shake to mix. This will keep refrigerated in an airtight container for up to 1 week.

Heirloom and Shell Bean Salad with Sherry Vinaigrette

LET THE FARMERS' MARKET BE YOUR GUIDE. Select a variety of fresh beans and peas to throw into this salad (as well as into resealable bags to freeze for winter months). You can also use canned or dried beans. I love to order dried heirloom offerings like Moros and Christmas Limas from Rancho Gordo of Napa, California. The only must for this recipe is to mix at least three varieties. **Serves 6 to 8**

½ cup dried scarlet runner beans

½ cup dried black calypso beans

½ cup dried cranberry beans

½ cup dried Florida butter beans

½ pound French green, Roma, pole or wax beans (or a combination)

Kosher salt

1 red bell pepper, cored, seeded and diced

1 jalapeño pepper, cored, seeded and diced

3 handfuls arugula

10 fresh mint leaves

10 fresh basil leaves, thinly sliced

Sherry Vinaigrette (recipe follows)

Sea salt and freshly ground black pepper

1. Rinse the dried beans and place in a large pot with enough water to cover by about 4 inches. Bring to a low boil and cook until just tender, but not mushy, about 1 hour. Drain, rinse and cool completely. Place in a large bowl.

2. Remove the stem end of the fresh beans. Bring a large pot of water to a boil, add salt and blanch each variety of fresh beans separately. To blanch, place the beans in the water until they turn bright green or yellow, about 1 minute. Remove from the water with a strainer and immediately place into ice-cold water until completely cooled. Drain thoroughly and place in a large bowl, season with salt and pepper to taste and toss to mix.

3. Add the red pepper, jalapeño, arugula, mint and basil and season with salt and pepper to taste. Pour the vinaigrette over the beans, toss to mix and serve or refrigerate in an airtight container until ready to serve.

In the Kitchen

VARIATION To make this salad with fresh beans and peas, replace the dried beans with **fresh and blanched butter beans, field peas, green peas or any type of pole beans, small French green beans, wax beans or green beans**. You will need about ½ pound of 3 to 5 different varieties.

SHERRY VINAIGRETTE

MAKES ABOUT 1 CUP

In a small bowl whisk together the **grated zest and juice of 1 lemon, 2 tablespoons sherry vinegar, 1 minced garlic clove, ¼ cup olive oil, ¼ cup vegetable oil, 2 tablespoons chopped fresh parsley, 10 thinly sliced basil leaves** and **sea salt** and **freshly ground pepper** to taste. Pour over the salad and sprinkle with additional **salt** and **pepper,** if desired. Refrigerate in an airtight container until ready to use for up to 1 week. If you are making it in advance, stir in the fresh herbs just before using.

Curried Lentil Salad

OF ALL THE VEGETABLE SALADS IN OUR COOLER DISPLAY, this one gets ordered the most. Lentils complement almost anything. With that in mind, I tend to put the called-for zucchini on rotation, opting for whatever is in season: tender, summer squash (which I usually slice thin and eat raw), quick blanched green beans and slow-roasted carrots, beets, sweet potatoes or butternut squash. **Serves 6 to 8**

1½ cups green lentils (preferably French Le Puy), picked through and rinsed

1 zucchini, cut into ¼-inch-thick slices lengthwise

1 red bell pepper, cut in half, cored and seeded

½ red onion, cut into ¼-inch-thick rounds

2 tablespoons olive oil

2 tablespoons balsamic vinegar

Sea salt and freshly ground black pepper

2 scallions, thinly sliced

¼ cup chopped fresh parsley

¼ cup chopped fresh cilantro

Curry Vinaigrette (recipe follows)

1. Place the lentils in a small saucepan with about 4 cups of water and bring to a boil. Reduce the heat to medium and cook until tender, 20 to 25 minutes. Drain and set aside.

2. While the lentils are cooking, toss the zucchini, pepper and onion with the olive oil and vinegar and season with salt and pepper to taste.

3. About 30 minutes before ready to grill, build a fire in a gas or charcoal grill. If using a charcoal grill, let the coals burn to a gray ash with a slight red glow. If using a gas grill, preheat to medium. (Alternatively, heat a grill pan to just below the smoking point.) Grill the vegetables just until slightly charred with grill marks and crisp-tender (a little crunchy, not completely cooked). Cool slightly, chop and place in the bowl with the lentils.

4. Add the scallions, parsley and cilantro to the lentils. Drizzle with half of the dressing, adding more as desired, and season with salt and pepper to taste. Toss gently to mix and serve at room temperature, or refrigerate until ready to serve.

CURRY VINAIGRETTE

MAKES ABOUT 1 CUP

Whisk together ¼ **cup white wine vinegar, grated zest and juice of 1 orange, 1 tablespoon honey, 1 tablespoon curry powder, 1 minced shallot, 1 tablespoon chopped fresh cilantro, sea salt** and **freshly ground black pepper** to taste in a small bowl. Slowly whisk in ¼ **cup canola oil** and ½ **cup extra-virgin olive oil** until all is incorporated. Toss with the salad or refrigerate in an airtight container until ready to use for up to 1 week.

Kale Salad with Tangerines, Avocado and Crispy Country Ham

WHENEVER I ASK PETER TO MAKE SALAD DRESSING, he reaches for a coffee mug instead of a bowl or jar, as I would do. He uses very little oil and whatever mustard he happens to pull from the refrigerator door: Dijon, yellow, honey or whole grain. His concoction is never quite the same, but it's always delicious, particularly on this salad. A heavy hand with mustard goes great with the thin, crisped country ham. **Serves 6 to 8**

Splash of olive oil

2 thin slices country ham

1 bunch curly purple or lacinato kale, stems removed and roughly chopped

3 tangerines, clementines or mandarin oranges, peeled and sliced into rounds

1 avocado, halved, pitted, skin removed and cubed

½ cup freshly grated Parmesan cheese

Sea salt and freshly ground black pepper

Peter's Coffee Mug Dressing (recipe follows)

1. Heat the olive oil in a cast-iron skillet until sizzling hot. Add the ham and cook until crispy on both sides, about 2 minutes. Remove and place on a paper towel to drain.

2. Place the kale in a large bowl and gently squeeze with paper towels to remove any excess water and slightly bruise. Add the ham, tangerines, avocado and Parmesan and season with salt and pepper to taste. Drizzle the dressing over the top, toss to coat the salad and serve.

PETER'S COFFEE MUG DRESSING

MAKES ABOUT ½ CUP

Put a **heaping tablespoon of mustard** in a coffee mug or small bowl and add **3 tablespoons vinegar** (white wine or rice wine). Using a fork, stir in an about ¼ **cup olive oil** to combine. Season with sea salt and freshly ground black pepper to taste. Toss with the salad or refrigerate in an airtight container until ready to serve for up to 1 week.

BLT Salad with Arugula, Avocado and Corn

START THE DAY WITH THIS SALAD. Crisp bacon makes it apt for brunch alongside Six Original Egg Scrambles (page 62), Crustless Quiche (page 76) or simple soft-boiled eggs with toast points. For lunch (after all, it is modeled after a BLT sandwich), pair it with Herb and Garlic Flatbread (page 145) or Grilled or Toasted Cornbread Slices (page 145). **Serves 6 to 8**

4 ears corn, shucked

2 avocados, halved, pitted, skin removed and cubed

4 handfuls arugula or mixed baby greens

2 tomatoes, cored and cut into wedges, or 1 pint cherry tomatoes, cut in half

10 fresh basil leaves, thinly sliced

½ cup Fresh Summer Herb Vinaigrette (recipe follows)

Sea salt and freshly ground black pepper

6 slices crisp cooked bacon, cut in half

1. Cut the kernels off the cobs into a large bowl. Place the corn in a skillet with ¼ cup water, bring to a low boil and immediately remove from the heat. Drain and cool.

2. When the corn is completely cool, place in a large bowl and add the avocados, arugula, tomatoes and basil. Drizzle half the vinaigrette over the salad, season with salt and pepper to taste and toss gently just to coat the vegetables, being careful not to overmix or mush the avocados. Arrange the bacon over the top of the salad and serve with the remaining vinaigrette on the side to drizzle over as needed.

FRESH SUMMER HERB VINAIGRETTE

MAKES ABOUT 1¼ CUPS

Combine ⅓ **cup red wine vinegar, 2 tablespoons Dijon mustard,** the **grated zest and juice of 1 lemon, 3 thinly sliced fresh basil leaves, 2 tablespoons chopped fresh chives** and **2 tablespoons chopped fresh parsley** in a small bowl and stir to mix. Whisk in ¾ **cup extra-virgin olive oil** in a slow, steady stream until all is incorporated. Refrigerate in an airtight container until ready to use for up to 1 week. If you are making it in advance, stir in the fresh herbs just before using.

Citrus Winter Ambrosia with Flaky Coconut

WHEN THE DAYS GROW DARK AND LONG, clementines and navel oranges stand in for the sun with their vibrant hues and healthy dose of vitamins. I like to cut them into pith-free segments for ambrosia, adding extra color and flavor with ruby red grapefruits, cara caras and blood oranges, and a touch of sweetness with dried cranberries and coconut. **Serves 8 to 10**

2 navel oranges

2 cara cara oranges

2 blood oranges

2 ruby red grapefruits

2 clementines

½ cup dried cranberries or cherries

½ cup sweetened flaked coconut

1 Meyer lemon

1. Peel the oranges, grapefruits and clementines with a sharp knife by first cutting off the top and the bottom of each piece of fruit so that it sits flat. Stand the fruit on a cutting board and cut away the skin and pith by going around the outside of the fruit from top to bottom with a knife.

2. Slice each piece into rounds or half-rounds, depending on the size. Remove any seeds and place on a large platter along with any juice that has collected on the board. Sprinkle the cranberries and coconut over the top. Zest the lemon over the salad, cut it in half and squeeze the juice over and serve, or cover and refrigerate until ready to serve.

On the Lawn

CITRUS Since we don't really grow oranges in North Carolina, this entry is more like "on the doorstep" than "on the lawn." For bulk orders of fruit or for hard-to-find varieties, I often look to L'Hoste Citrus of Plaquemines Parish, Louisiana (lhostecitrus.com), or Robert Is Here of Homestead, Florida (robertishere.com), both of which deliver.

Roasted Chicken and Bread Salad with Pan Juice Vinaigrette

CHICKEN DOES MOST OF THE WORK IN THIS SALAD. Its juices soak into homemade croutons as it cooks, and its fat lends flavor to a savory vinaigrette. In summer, add thick wedges of tomatoes and torn basil and in winter, any roasted squash or potato. **Serves 4 to 6**

½ day-old baguette, cut or torn into 1-inch pieces

¼ cup olive oil

Sea salt and freshly ground black pepper

2 tablespoons red wine vinegar

1 tablespoon unsalted butter, melted

Zest and juice of 1 lemon

½ cup dry white wine

2 tablespoons chopped fresh parsley

1 tablespoon chopped fresh rosemary

1 (3½- to 4-pound) chicken, cut up (see Cutting Up a Chicken, page 152)

2 heads Little Gem lettuce, torn into large leaves (substitute: Bibb)

4 to 5 fresh basil leaves, thinly sliced

Pan Juice Vinaigrette (recipe follows)

½ cup (1½ ounces) shaved Parmesan cheese

1. Preheat the oven to 400°F.

2. Toss the bread with 2 tablespoons of the olive oil and season with salt and pepper to taste. Spread evenly in a single layer on a rimmed baking sheet.

3. Mix the remaining olive oil, vinegar, butter, lemon zest and juice, wine, half the parsley and half the rosemary together in a small bowl to blend.

4. Rinse the chicken pieces, pat dry and remove any excess skin or fat. Place the chicken on top of the bread and drizzle all over with the oil-vinegar mixture. Season with salt and pepper to taste and place in the oven to roast until the juices run clear in the thickest part of the thigh when pierced with the tip of a small knife, about 45 minutes. While the chicken is roasting, stir the bread several times to prevent from getting too brown.

5. Remove the chicken from the oven and let cool enough to handle. Arrange the lettuce leaves on a large platter and top with the chicken and croutons. Sprinkle with the basil and remaining parsley and rosemary. Drizzle with the vinaigrette, season with salt and pepper to taste and serve warm topped with freshly shaved Parmesan.

PAN JUICE VINAIGRETTE

MAKES ABOUT ¾ CUP

While the chicken is cooling, carefully pour ¼ **cup pan drippings** into a small bowl. Stir in **2 tablespoons red wine vinegar** and **1 teaspoon Dijon mustard** and whisk in ¼ **cup extra-virgin olive oil**. Season with **sea salt** and **freshly ground black pepper** to taste and pour over the salad while warm.

Tarragon Chicken Salad with Grapes, Apples and Bibb Lettuce

THIS ISN'T JUST OUR MOST POPULAR SALAD AT THE MARKET. It's one of our most popular dishes (if not the very one). I first started making Tarragon Chicken Salad with Grapes, Apples and Bibb Lettuce at Soho Charcuterie and have had it on the Market's menu since we opened in 1990. It keeps well refrigerated for several days; just add the grapes and apples before you plan to serve it. **Serves 4 to 6**

6 cups cooked shredded chicken breast

3 celery stalks (leaves reserved), thinly sliced

1 cup red seedless grapes, cut in half

1 tart apple, cored and thinly sliced

1½ cups Tarragon Mayonnaise (recipe follows)

3 tablespoons chopped fresh parsley

Sea salt and freshly ground black pepper

2 heads Bibb lettuce, separated into leaves

1. Combine the chicken, celery, grapes, apple, mayonnaise and parsley in a large bowl, season with salt and pepper to taste and stir to mix thoroughly. Refrigerate until ready to serve.

2. When ready to serve, arrange the lettuce leaves on a platter or individual serving plates and top with the chicken salad. Garnish with parsley and celery leaves, if desired, and serve cold.

TARRAGON MAYONNAISE

MAKES ABOUT 1½ CUPS

Place **2 large eggs, 3 tablespoons tarragon vinegar,** the **juice of 1 lemon** and **½ cup fresh tarragon leaves** in the bowl of a food processor fitted with a metal blade. Process until well blended, stopping to scrape down the sides of the bowl several times. Add **1 cup canola or safflower oil** in a slow, steady stream down the feed tube with the motor running and process until all the oil is incorporated. The dressing should be thick and creamy. Add **1 minced shallot** and puree until smooth. Season with **sea salt** and **freshly ground black pepper** to taste. Refrigerate in an airtight container until ready to use for up to 5 days.

In the Kitchen

DRIED TARRAGON If fresh tarragon is not available, heat **1 tablespoon dried tarragon** in a small saucepan with the vinegar. Cool completely before proceeding. If you are lucky enough to find **tarragon leaves packed in brine,** as we used at Soho Charcuterie, use them instead of fresh leaves for more intense flavor.

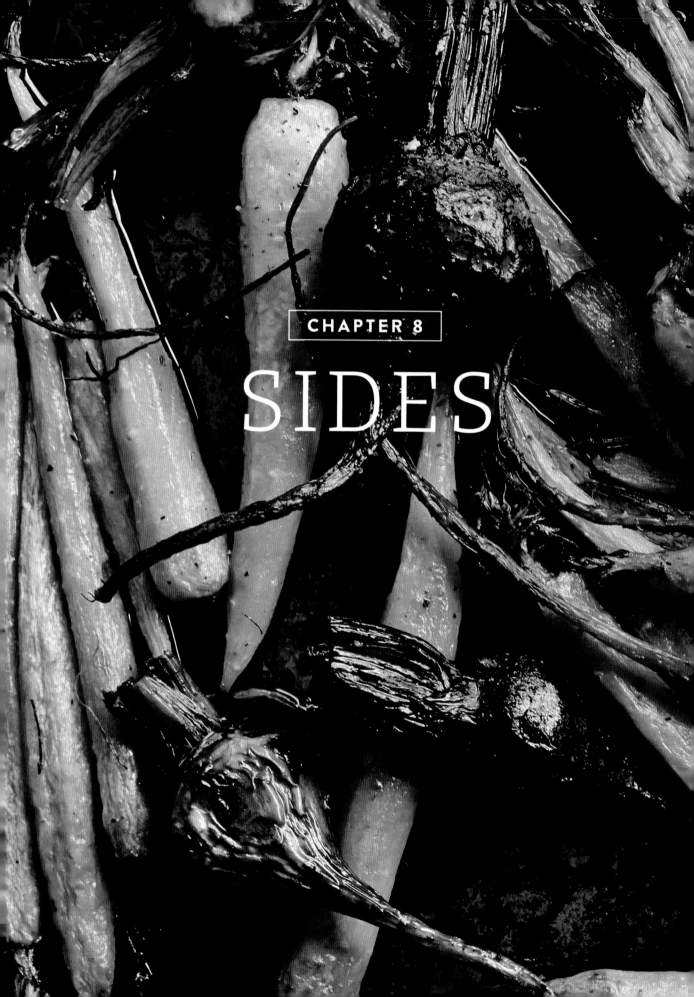

CHAPTER 8

SIDES

ALTHOUGH I GREW UP EATING AT TRADITIONAL meat-and-three restaurants, these days I am one of those folks who'd forgo the meat at the center for a plate of endless vegetables. I often judge an entrée order based on the sides that accompany it. With that in mind, I think of the dishes in this chapter as more central than secondary.

Creamy Polenta (page 269) and Mixed Mashed Potatoes (page 247) are foundations for a Big Platter of Roasted Vegetables (page 254) or Spicy Meatballs (page 163). Stuffed Portobellos (page 265) are vehicles for sides and sauces including sautéed spinach with Everyday Marinara (page 163) and Basmati Rice with Green Peas, Edamame and Fresh Herbs (page 258). And Twice-Baked Yukon Gold and Sweet Potatoes with Toppings (page 248) are the main event, to be eaten two-by-two.

When Peter is out of town and I'm dining on my own—or when we just want something simple—that's often what I eat: a sweet potato topped with nothing more than a squeeze of lime and a sprinkle of sea salt. Similarly, Fried Rice Pilaf with Quinoa and Crispy Lentils (page 256) speckled with extra vegetables will more than do. As you can probably imagine, I'm not one to be overwhelmed by summer's abundance of crops. I'm one that fires up the grill, piles more on the Big Platter of Grilled Vegetables (page 253) and makes room on my plate for another side. Or two. Or three, no meat.

Maque Choux

THERE'S ONLY ONE TIME TO MAKE THIS Cajun and Native American dish: summer, when corn is at its peak. To catch every drop after the kernels have been cut loose, use the back of a knife to scrape and release the cob's sweet juices. **Serves 6 to 8**

3 tablespoons unsalted butter

1 tablespoon olive oil

1 red bell pepper, cored, seeded and diced

1 red onion, diced

1 jalapeño pepper, cored, seeded and diced

8 ears corn, shucked

Pinch of sugar

Sea salt and freshly ground black pepper

6 fresh basil leaves, thinly sliced

1. Heat the butter and olive oil in a large skillet over medium heat until sizzling hot. Add the red bell pepper, onion and jalapeño and cook, stirring, until the onion is translucent, 3 to 4 minutes.

2. While the vegetables are cooking, remove the corn from the cobs and scrape the stripped cobs with the back of the knife to release the juice. Add the kernels and juice to the skillet. Season with sugar, salt and pepper to taste and cook, stirring, until the corn is tender, about 4 minutes. Remove from the heat and stir in the basil. Serve warm.

In the Kitchen

VARIATIONS I often bolster Maque Choux with chopped summer squash and vine-ripened tomatoes. To make it a meal, I toss in bacon, shrimp or crawfish and serve it over a Grits Bowl Your Way (page 74). It's also great inside an Easy Quesadilla (page 123) or spooned on top like a relish.

On the Menu

SERVE WITH Spicy Backyard Barbecue Chicken (page 123), Watermelon Arugula Tabbouleh with Feta and Fresh Mint (page 214) and Mixed Berry Pie with Crumb Topping (page 295).

Quick-Braised Spring Vegetables

BRAISING BRINGS OUT THE NATURAL FLAVORS AND COLORS of vibrant springtime vegetables. I make this with a mélange, depending on what I find at the farmers' market. When available, tender asparagus is always a great addition, as are spinach, baby bok choy or fingerling potatoes. **Serves 6 to 8**

1 bunch small carrots

1 bunch small turnips

1 bunch radishes

1 bunch small beets

2 tablespoons unsalted butter

2 tablespoons olive oil

Sea salt and freshly ground black pepper

½ cup low-sodium vegetable or chicken broth

Zest and juice of 1 orange

2 cups shelled fresh green peas

½ pound sugar snap peas

1 tablespoon chopped fresh tarragon

1 tablespoon chopped fresh chives

1. Trim the tops off the carrots, turnips, radishes and beets, leaving about ½ inch of the green stems attached; scrub or peel to clean.

2. Heat the butter and olive oil in a large skillet over medium heat until sizzling hot. Add the carrots, turnips, radishes and beets and season with salt and pepper to taste. Sauté the vegetables, stirring occasionally, until slightly brown around the edges, about 6 minutes.

3. Stir in the broth and orange zest and juice, cover the pan and cook just until tender, about 3 minutes. Add the green peas and snap peas. Season the vegetables with additional salt and pepper to taste, cover the pan and steam, stirring occasionally, until the peas turn bright green and are crisp-tender, about 2 minutes. Sprinkle with the tarragon and chives and serve warm.

On the Menu

SERVE WITH Grilled Slab of Salmon (page 112) or Moroccan-Rubbed Grilled Boneless Leg of Lamb (page 136) and Judy's Berry Trifle (page 302).

Sweet and Sour Cabbage

BALSAMIC VINEGAR ENHANCES THIS DISH in both flavor and color, and brown sugar creates the balance. Pair with Mixed Grilled Chicken Thighs and Sausages (page 122), Peter's Breakfast Potatoes (page 251) and a good stout beer. For lunch, I also like a sandwich of sweet and sour cabbage in a baguette with grilled sausage and a smear of spicy mustard. **Serves 6 to 8**

2 tablespoons olive oil

1 red onion, thinly sliced

½ head red cabbage, cored and thinly sliced

½ cup light brown sugar

½ cup balsamic vinegar

Sea salt and freshly ground black pepper

½ cup shaved blue cheese

2 tablespoons chopped fresh chives

1. Heat the olive oil in a large skillet over medium-high heat until sizzling hot. Add the onion and reduce the heat to medium. Cook, stirring, until the onion is translucent, about 5 minutes.

2. Add the cabbage, sugar and vinegar, season with salt and pepper to taste and stir to mix. Add ½ cup water, reduce the heat to low and cook, stirring often, until the liquid has evaporated and the cabbage is very tender and just beginning to caramelize, about 30 minutes. Serve warm topped with shaved blue cheese and chives.

MIXED MASHED POTATOES

THIS COMBINATION OF YUKON GOLDS AND SWEET POTATOES is good all around: beside Pickle-Brined Fried Chicken (page 120) or Market Meatloaf (page 110), on top of Short Rib Cottage Pie (page 195), under Slow-Roasted Leg of Lamb (page 161) and tucked into Stuffed Portobellos (page 265). **Serves 6 to 8**

Peel **2 pounds Yukon Gold or russet potatoes** and **1 pound sweet potatoes**. Cut any larger potatoes in half so that all are roughly the same size. Place the Yukon Golds or russets in a large saucepan and add cold water to cover by about 2 inches. Bring to a low boil over medium-high heat, cover, reduce the heat and simmer about 10 minutes. Add the sweet potatoes and more water if needed to keep covered by 2 inches and continue to simmer until the potatoes are tender when pierced with the tip of a small knife, about 20 minutes more.

Drain the potatoes and return to the saucepan while still warm. Remove from the heat, add **8 tablespoons (1 stick) unsalted butter,** cover and let sit until the butter melts. Add ½ **cup well-shaken buttermilk** and mash with a potato masher or whip with an electric beater until the potatoes are creamy and all the butter and buttermilk are incorporated. Season with **sea salt and freshly ground black pepper** to taste and stir to mix. Serve warm.

In the Kitchen

VARIATIONS It's hard to beat these mashed potatoes. We make hundreds of pounds of them each holiday season, when they snag the top seat on our catering menu. But sometimes we still like to change them up, mixing in other vegetables—celery root, butternut squash and parsnips among them—or fruit. Roasted pears and apples work well.

Twice-Baked Yukon Gold and Sweet Potatoes with Toppings

I LIKE TO SERVE THESE POTATOES AS I DO TACOS AND CHILI—with an expansive bar of toppings that guests can choose from. Combinations can be as light as lime juice and sea salt for a sweet potato, or as filling as chili, sour cream and cheddar for a Yukon Gold. Use small to medium potatoes so that folks can create several options. **Serves 6 to 8**

POTATOES

4 small Yukon Gold potatoes, scrubbed

4 small sweet potatoes, scrubbed

2 tablespoons olive oil

Sea salt and freshly ground black pepper

TOPPINGS

½ cup (2 ounces) grated Swiss cheese

½ cup (2 ounces) grated Cheddar cheese

½ cup light sour cream

½ cup Herb Buttermilk Yogurt Sauce (page 142)

8 tablespoons (1 stick) butter, softened

1. Preheat the oven to 400°F.

2. Place the potatoes on a rimmed baking sheet and pierce 3 to 4 times with a fork. Rub with the olive oil, sprinkle with sea salt and place in the oven to bake until the potatoes are tender when pierced with the tip of a small knife, about 45 minutes. Remove from the oven, slit each open about halfway down and push both ends together to create a pocket.

3. While the potatoes are cooking, place the toppings into small bowls.

4. About 15 minutes before ready to serve, have your guests fill the potatoes with the toppings of their choice and place back on the baking sheet. Sprinkle with salt and pepper to taste. Return potatoes to the oven until heated through and any added cheese melts, about 10 minutes.

In the Kitchen

VARIATIONS For twice-baked potatoes, I often turn to these combinations:

- Garlicky Sautéed Broccoli Florets with Bacon and Melted Blue Cheese
- Sweet Peas with Parmesan and Chives
- Roasted Red Peppers with Corn and Cheddar
- Fresh Lime Juice, Sea Salt and Olive Oil
- Crispy Country Ham with Grated Manchego Cheese

For a lower-calorie potato, substitute plain low-fat yogurt and a little olive oil for the butter and sour cream.

Peter's Breakfast Potatoes

IN LAKE PLACID, NEW YORK, WHERE PETER AND I FIRST MET and now spend many summer days, his vice is Hinerwadel's Salt Potatoes. The spuds are sold in 5-pound paper sacks with a 12-ounce box of salt, intended to boil together—a Central New York tradition that dates back to the late 1800s, fueled in part by salt marshes near Syracuse and Irish workers who sometimes lunched on potatoes. I encourage less salt but am admittedly a sucker for the sea-kissed skin that forms around the potatoes. For breakfast, Peter smashes, roasts and garnishes them with fragrant rosemary.   **Serves 6 to 8**

2 pounds small Yukon Gold or white potatoes

Kosher salt

¼ cup extra-virgin olive oil

Sea salt and freshly ground black pepper

1 tablespoon chopped fresh rosemary or parsley

Ketchup

1. Preheat the oven to 450°F.

2. Place the potatoes in a large pot of cold water and bring to a boil over high heat. Reduce the heat to a low boil, add kosher salt and cook until just soft when pierced with the tip of a small knife but not completely cooked through, 15 to 20 minutes. (You do not want them to be too soft.) Drain the potatoes and allow to cool enough to handle.

3. Pour half of the olive oil on a large rimmed baking sheet and spread evenly. When the potatoes are cool enough to handle, smash them flat on a cutting board, one at a time, with the heel of your hand or the bottom of a cup, then place on the prepared pan. Drizzle the tops of the potatoes with the remaining olive oil and sprinkle generously with sea salt and pepper to taste.

4. Place in the oven to roast until the undersides are golden brown, about 20 minutes. Remove from the oven, flip the potatoes over and continue to roast until the other side is golden brown and edges are crispy, 15 to 20 minutes more. Serve warm sprinkled with fresh rosemary or parsley and a side of ketchup to dip into.

On the Menu

SERVE WITH Beyond breakfast, Peter's Breakfast Potatoes are equally good for dinner alongside Grilled Racks of Lamb (page 134) or Market Meatloaf (page 110). Do as Peter would: also crack open an ice-cold Bud Light.

Big Platter of Grilled Vegetables

THERE'S NOWHERE I'D RATHER SPEND SUMMER'S LONG DAYS than outside: sitting under the shady eave of the Market's front porch, walking through Duke Forest with our dogs, Ruby and Olive, or standing on the patio over a smoldering grill. While Ruby and Olive hope for sausages, my inclination is a grill full of crisp, charred peppers, summer squash, zucchini and okra. **Serves 6 to 8**

1 pound fingerling potatoes (substitute: other small variety)

Pinch of kosher salt

2 small yellow summer squash, cut into 1-inch chunks

2 small zucchini, cut into 1-inch chunks

1 pint small okra, trimmed

8 to 10 red, yellow or orange mini sweet peppers

¼ cup olive oil

Juice of 1 lemon

2 tablespoons balsamic vinegar

Sea salt and freshly ground black pepper

12 fresh basil leaves, thinly sliced

1. Prepare a hot fire in a gas or charcoal grill. If using a charcoal grill, let the coals burn to a gray ash with a slight red glow and bank them on one side. If using a gas grill, preheat only one side to medium.

2. Place the potatoes in a pot of water to cover by about 2 inches. Bring to a boil. Add the kosher salt and reduce the heat to a low boil and simmer until tender but still firm and not fully cooked, about 15 minutes. Drain and place in a large bowl. Set aside.

3. Add the yellow squash, zucchini, okra, peppers, olive oil, lemon juice and vinegar to the bowl with the potatoes and toss to mix and coat the vegetables evenly. Season with sea salt and pepper to taste.

4. Place the vegetables on the grill to cook until slightly charred with grill marks but still crisp-tender, 3 to 4 minutes per side. The potatoes will take a little longer; keep turning until soft. Remove the vegetables from the grill and serve warm sprinkled with the fresh basil and additional salt and pepper, if needed.

On the Lawn

FOSTER'S FARMERS' MARKET When we first opened there wasn't yet a farmers' market in downtown Durham. Where better to start one, Peter and I ambitiously thought, than Foster's gravel parking lot. On Wednesdays, farmers like Ken Dawson of Maple Spring Gardens in Cedar Grove, Dan Graham of Graham Woodworking and Family Farm in Pittsboro, Mark Lyon of Lyon Farms in Creedmoor and a number of farmers from Granville County set up shop. For my part, I put a grill on the lawn and sold fresh grilled chickens and corn on the cob dressed with herbed butter. Those days were easily some of our best, spent among dear friends and an abundance of local food.

Big Platter of Roasted Vegetables

I COLLECT PLATTERS—McCarty from the Mississippi Delta, Seagrove from the North Carolina Piedmont and anything else that catches my eye—not just because of their stunning craftsmanship, but because of the ethos they embody. To me, they are signs of big, convivial gatherings with family and friends. In winter, I load the dishes up with sturdy potatoes, squash, carrots and peppers. And in summer, I serve a Big Platter of Grilled Vegetables (page 253). **Serves 6 to 8**

1 pound small potatoes (such as Red Thumbs, LaRettes or other small variety)

1 small butternut squash, peeled, seeded and cut into 1-inch chunks

¼ cup olive oil

2 tablespoons chopped fresh rosemary

1 tablespoon fresh thyme leaves

Sea salt and freshly ground black pepper

1 red onion, cut into wedges

1 bunch small carrots, trimmed and scrubbed

1 red bell pepper, cored, seeded and cut into 1-inch chunks

1. Preheat the oven to 400°F.

2. Place the potatoes and squash on a rimmed baking sheet with 2 tablespoons of the olive oil and half the herbs; season with salt and pepper to taste. Stir the vegetables to coat evenly and spread in a single layer.

3. Place the onion, carrots and pepper on a separate rimmed baking sheet, drizzle with the remaining olive oil and herbs, season with salt and pepper to taste and toss to coat evenly. Spread the vegetables in a single layer.

4. Place both pans in the oven to roast the vegetables, stirring several times while cooking, until the potatoes are soft when pierced with the tip of a knife and the edges are light brown, 30 to 40 minutes. The pan with the peppers will take a little less time. Remove from the oven, combine all the vegetables on a large platter and serve warm or at room temperature.

In the Kitchen

ROASTING FOR ALL SEASONS Almost any vegetable can be roasted. In fall, I use cauliflower, eggplant, turnips, beets and sweet potatoes. For winter, any varieties of winter squash and pumpkin are welcome. To usher in spring, I look for fennel, radishes and asparagus. And in summer, nothing tops fresh corn and cherry tomatoes. When roasting, just be sure to group together vegetables with similar cooking times.

MIX IT UP To add extra color and flavor—particularly to winter's squash and pumpkin—toss in a few handfuls of spinach when the vegetables come out of the oven, allowing it to wilt slightly. Roasted vegetables are great served over a bed of Creamy Polenta (page 269) and sprinkled with freshly grated Parmesan cheese or drizzled with Kale Pesto (page 143).

Fried Rice Pilaf
with Quinoa and Crispy Lentils

WE MAKE ENDLESS RICE SALADS AT FOSTER'S, adding everything from pea tendrils and sprouts to roasted vegetables and mixed greens. This dish—spiked with pan-fried lentils and rice, and studded with fresh vegetables and herbs—takes a hint from crispy Indian chaat. **Serves 6 to 8**

3 cups water

1 cup brown basmati rice

Kosher salt

½ cup quinoa

½ cup green lentils

3 tablespoons olive oil

2 carrots, chopped

½ teaspoon crushed red pepper flakes

Sea salt and freshly ground black pepper

1 red onion, thinly sliced

2 tablespoons balsamic vinegar

2 tablespoons thyme leaves

2 tablespoons unsalted butter

2 handfuls baby spinach or kale, roughly chopped

2 tablespoons chopped fresh cilantro

2 tablespoons chopped fresh mint

Herb Buttermilk Yogurt Sauce (page 142)

1. Bring the water to a boil, add rice and season with kosher salt. Reduce the heat, bring to a low boil, cover and cook over low heat 10 minutes. Add the quinoa, reduce the heat to simmer, cover and continue to cook until all the liquid has evaporated, about 20 minutes more. Remove from the heat and let sit until fluffy, about 5 minutes.

2. While the rice is cooking, place the lentils in a small saucepan with about 4 cups of water and bring to a boil. Reduce the heat to medium and cook until tender, 20 to 25 minutes. Drain and set aside.

3. Heat 2 tablespoons of the olive oil in a large skillet or wok over medium-high heat until sizzling hot. Add the lentils, carrots and red pepper flakes, season with salt and pepper to taste and cook, stirring occasionally, until crispy on the outside, about 5 minutes. Remove from the skillet, drain and set aside.

4. In the same skillet, add the remaining olive oil and the onion and reduce the heat to medium. Cook, stirring, until the onion is slightly crispy, about 5 minutes. Add the vinegar and thyme, season with salt and pepper to taste and continue to cook until all the liquid has evaporated and the onion is slightly caramelized, about 5 minutes more. Add the butter and melt until sizzling hot. Add the lentils, carrots, rice, quinoa and spinach and cook, stirring, until the rice is slightly crispy on the outside, about 3 minutes more.

5. Remove from the heat, add the cilantro and mint, season with additional salt and pepper to taste, if desired, and toss gently. Serve warm topped with a big spoonful of Herb Buttermilk Yogurt Sauce.

BASMATI RICE

FRIED RICE PILAF

Basmati Rice with Green Peas, Edamame and Fresh Herbs

HERE, BASMATI IS PUNCTUATED BY POPS OF GREEN PEAS, edamame and herbs. But my relationship with rice is more of a run-on sentence. Beyond basmati (and toothier brown basmati), I never stop experimenting with different varieties—sweet Carolina Gold, grainy Wehani or fragrant jasmine—and different vegetables or herbs to mix in, depending on what's in season or lingering on my shelves. At the Market, we stock yellow bags of heirloom Carolina Plantation, grown near South Carolina's Great Pee Dee River. **Serves 6 to 8**

1 tablespoon olive oil

1 tablespoon unsalted butter

1 onion, diced

1 cup white basmati rice

Sea salt

Zest and juice of 1 lemon

2 cups low-sodium vegetable or chicken broth

1 cup shelled fresh or frozen green peas

1 cup shelled fresh or frozen edamame

1 handful spinach or kale, roughly chopped

½ bunch chopped fresh parsley

2 tablespoons chopped fresh chives

Freshly ground black pepper

1. Heat the oil and butter in a saucepan over medium heat until sizzling hot. Add the onion and cook, stirring, until the onion is soft and translucent, 3 to 4 minutes.

2. Rinse the rice in a colander until the water runs clear. Drain and add to the saucepan. Add salt to taste and cook, stirring occasionally, until the rice slides around easily in the pan, 2 to 3 minutes. Add the lemon zest and juice and the broth and stir to mix, being sure to release any rice stuck to the bottom of the pan. Bring to a low boil, reduce the heat to low and simmer, covered, about 10 minutes.

3. Add the peas and edamame and continue to simmer, without stirring, until all the broth is absorbed and the peas are tender, about 10 minutes more. Add the spinach, without stirring.

4. Remove from the heat to let sit, covered, until the rice is fluffy and soft in texture and the spinach is slightly wilted, about 10 minutes. Add the parsley and chives and season to taste with salt and pepper. Stir gently to combine and fluff the rice and serve warm.

On the Menu

SERVE WITH Korean Barbecue Swordfish Kebabs (page 111) or Greek Lamb Kebabs (page 137), Kale Salad with Tangerines, Avocado and Crispy Country Ham (page 229) and Lemon Bars (page 286) for dessert.

Image on page 257

Winter Couscous with Curry-Roasted Cauliflower and Chickpeas

DURING FOSTER'S FIRST DAYS, WE HAD A SALAD MAKER from Lebanon named Dunia, who made couscous countless ways. Rather than cooking the couscous, she poured in very hot tap water and let it sit, covered, until all of the water was absorbed. It came out so light and fluffy every time that, since meeting Dunia, I've never cooked couscous on the stovetop again. Instead, I spend time thinking about what combination of vegetables, beans, nuts or dried fruits to add to the mix—one of my favorite fallbacks being this combination. **Serves 6 to 8**

1 head cauliflower, cut or broken into bite-size florets

1 (15-ounce) can chickpeas, drained and rinsed

3 tablespoons olive oil

2 tablespoons unsalted butter, melted

1 tablespoon sherry vinegar

1 tablespoon curry powder

1 tablespoon chopped fresh rosemary

Sea salt and freshly ground black pepper

1 cup couscous

Zest and juice of 1 lemon

½ bunch chopped fresh parsley

¼ cup chopped fresh mint

Zest and juice of 1 lime

1. Preheat the oven to 400°F.

2. Place the cauliflower and chickpeas in a large bowl. In a separate small bowl, combine 2 tablespoons of the olive oil, butter, vinegar, curry and rosemary and stir to mix. Pour over the cauliflower and chickpeas, season with salt and pepper to taste and toss to coat evenly.

3. Spread in a single layer on a large rimmed baking sheet and place in the oven to roast, stirring the vegetables midway through, until light brown around the edges, 25 to 30 minutes. Remove from the oven and set aside to cool slightly.

4. While the vegetables are cooking, place the couscous and lemon zest and juice in the same bowl the vegetables were tossed in and add just enough hot water to barely cover, about ½ cup. Cover tightly with plastic wrap and let sit until all the water is absorbed, about 10 minutes. Fluff the couscous using 2 forks and season with salt and pepper to taste.

5. Add the cauliflower mixture, parsley and mint to the bowl with the couscous. Drizzle the remaining olive oil over the top, add the lime zest and juice and toss to mix. Season with additional salt and pepper to taste, if desired, and serve warm or refrigerate until ready to serve.

On the Menu

SERVE WITH Chicken Piccata (page 125) or Pork Tenderloin with Olives and Tangerines (page 128) and Coconut Macaroons Dipped in Chocolate (page 284) for dessert.

Farro with Roasted Squash, Cauliflower and Curly Kale

AS GRAINS GO, FARRO RETAINS ITS TEXTURE and delightfully nutty flavor. Here it stands up to hearty, sweet roasted squash and cauliflower better than some of its delicate counterparts, including couscous and quinoa. **Serves 6 to 8**

1 butternut squash, peeled, seeded and cut into small cubes

1 head cauliflower, cut or broken into small florets

3 tablespoons unsalted butter, melted

2 tablespoons olive oil

2 tablespoons chopped fresh rosemary

Sea salt and freshly ground black pepper

1 cup farro (substitute: barley)

1 bunch curly kale, stems removed and torn into pieces

Zest and juice of 1 lemon

2 tablespoons chopped fresh parsley

1. Preheat the oven to 400°F.

2. Place the squash and cauliflower on a rimmed baking sheet. Combine the butter, olive oil and rosemary in a small bowl and drizzle over the vegetables, stirring to coat evenly. Spread in a single layer and season with salt and pepper to taste.

3. Place in the oven to roast, stirring midway, until tender and light brown around the edges, 30 to 35 minutes.

4. While the vegetables are cooking, place the farro in a large saucepan with enough water to cover by about 2 inches (approximately 4 cups depending on the size of your pan). Bring to a boil and season with salt. Reduce the heat to a low boil and cook until tender, 20 to 25 minutes. Drain and place in a large bowl and cover to keep warm.

5. Remove the vegetables from the oven and place in the bowl with the farro, scraping any of the oil mixture from the bottom of the pan into the bowl. Add the kale, lemon zest and juice and parsley and season with additional salt and pepper to taste, if desired. Toss gently, just to slightly wilt the kale, and serve warm or at room temperature.

On the Menu

SERVE WITH 20ish Garlic Cloves Chicken (page 153) or Pork Tenderloin Fricassee (page 166) and Brown Sugar Apple Crisp (page 301) for dessert.

Roasted Beets and Carrots with Sprouts, Spicy Pumpkin Seeds and Harissa Yogurt

SWEET ROASTED BEETS AND CARROTS ARE HARD TO TRUMP, but they can be topped. I prefer to add crisp sprouts, fresh herbs, Spicy Pumpkins Seeds (recipe below), a dash of orange juice and a dab of Harissa Buttermilk Yogurt Sauce (page 142). **Serves 6 to 8**

1 bunch small beets

1 bunch small carrots

Juice of 1 orange

2 tablespoons olive oil

Salt and freshly ground black pepper

½ cup Harissa Buttermilk Yogurt Sauce (page 142)

½ cup pea, radish or sunflower sprouts

¼ cup Spicy Pumpkin Seeds (recipe follows)

½ cup fresh cilantro leaves

¼ cup fresh mint leaves

1. Preheat the oven to 400°F.

2. Trim the tops off and peel or scrub the beets and carrots, leaving about ½ inch of the green stems attached. Place on a rimmed baking sheet. (If using a combination of red and golden beets, separate them to prevent the reds from bleeding into the goldens.) Pour the orange juice and olive oil over the vegetables, season with salt and pepper to taste and stir to coat.

3. Place in the oven to roast until tender when pierced with the tip of a knife, about 30 minutes. Remove the vegetables from the oven and arrange on a platter or individual plates. Serve with the Harissa Buttermilk Yogurt Sauce drizzled over the top or in a bowl to dip into. Sprinkle with sprouts, pumpkin seeds, cilantro and mint.

In the Kitchen

GO WITH THE GREENS It is better to buy beets and carrots in bunches with their tops still intact; they'll be the freshest. If you are lucky enough to get these at your farmers' market or local grocery, don't toss the greens. Trim them and sauté with a little butter or olive oil, garlic, salt and freshly ground black pepper. Serve over Creamy Polenta (page 269) or as a bed for Everyday Marinara (page 163) with freshly grated Parmesan cheese.

SPICY PUMPKIN SEEDS Pumpkin seeds can project as much personality as the jack-o'-lantern from which they came. I lean toward hot, adding **crushed red pepper flakes** or a **Szechuan spice blend** (Whole Foods stocks a particularly good mix packed with garlic, chiles and sesame seeds). For a milder option, try dried **rosemary, thyme** or **oregano**. To make, toss seeds with **olive oil** and preferred spices, then roast on a lined baking sheet at 325°F until golden brown, about 20 minutes.

Curry-Roasted Sweet Potatoes and Eggplant

IN MY TRAVELS, WHETHER ON FOOT OR THROUGH READING, I am constantly inspired and look for ways to translate what I've learned from other people and places to Foster's Market. One such inspiration is *Plenty: Vibrant Vegetable Recipes from London's Ottolenghi*. I continually turn to Yotam Ottolenghi's cookbook for its push toward bold flavors and unexpected combinations, like this mix of curry and eggplant served with mint chimichurri, which takes a cue from that text.

Serves 6 to 8

4 small sweet potatoes, cut into wedges

1 eggplant, peeled and cut into wedges

¼ cup olive oil

2 tablespoons fresh thyme leaves

1 tablespoon curry powder

2 garlic cloves, smashed and minced

Sea salt and freshly ground black pepper

½ cup Pounded Mint Chimichurri (page 140) or Harissa Buttermilk Yogurt Sauce (page 142)

1. Preheat the oven to 400°F.

2. Place the sweet potatoes and eggplant on a large rimmed baking sheet. Combine the olive oil, thyme, curry powder and garlic in a small bowl and pour over the vegetables, turning to coat evenly with the mixture.

3. Spread sweet potatoes and eggplant in a single layer and season with salt and pepper to taste.

4. Place in the oven to roast until the vegetables are just tender and golden brown around the edges, 25 to 30 minutes. Remove from the oven and serve warm drizzled with the Pounded Mint Chimichurri or dipped into the Harissa Buttermilk Yogurt Sauce.

On the Menu

SERVE WITH For dinner, Moroccan-Rubbed Grilled Boneless Leg of Lamb (page 136) and Tangy Cabbage and Kale Slaw (page 223) make for excellent pairings. For dessert, tart tangerines and dark chocolate provide a perfect ending.

Stuffed Portobellos

PORTOBELLOS ARE MORE THAN SUITABLE STUFFERS. Their bowl-like shape holds ample fillings, which their spongy texture takes in. Here, a pile of Mixed Mashed Potatoes (page 247) makes for a soft and savory center. **Serves 4 to 6**

¼ **cup olive oil**

2 **tablespoons balsamic vinegar**

6 **small to medium portobello mushrooms, cleaned and stems removed**

1 **teaspoon sea salt**

½ **teaspoon freshly ground black pepper**

½ **recipe Mixed Mashed Potatoes (page 247)**

½ **cup grated Parmesan cheese**

2 **scallions, trimmed and thinly sliced**

1. Preheat the oven to 400°F.

2. Mix the olive oil and vinegar together in a small bowl. Place the mushrooms on a rimmed baking sheet, brush with the olive oil mixture inside and out and season with salt and pepper to taste.

3. Place the mushrooms in the oven to roast until just tender and not completely cooked, about 10 minutes.

4. Remove from the oven and fill each cap with about ½ cup of the potato mixture. Sprinkle the tops with the cheese and scallions and place back in the oven to bake until the potato mixture is heated through and slightly golden on top, 10 to 15 minutes. Remove from the oven and serve warm.

On the Menu

OTHER STUFFINGS For a light, springy stuffing, try Basmati Rice with Green Peas, Edamame and Fresh Herbs (page 258). Or to make your mushrooms more of a meal, stuff with sautéed spinach topped with Everyday Marinara (page 163), or Creamy Polenta (page 269) topped with Everyday Marinara (page 163).

Simple Herb Spaghetti with Greens, Pesto and Parmesan

WHEN THE LARDER IS EMPTY, I turn to my lawn and windowsill. There, bright green herbs sprout from all manner of pots and buckets, ready to be plucked and thrown into spaghetti—a simple staple I always keep on hand. It's a no-fuss meal that's full of flavor, which can be bulked up with Spicy Meatballs (page 163) or grilled sausages ... when the larder's not empty. **Serves 6 to 8**

Kosher salt

12 ounces spaghetti (substitute: capellini)

3 tablespoons olive oil

½ cup Kale or Basil Pesto (page 143)

Zest and juice of 1 lemon

4 handfuls spring greens (such as arugula, baby lettuce, spinach or a mixture)

10 fresh basil leaves

¼ cup fresh parsley leaves

¼ cup fresh cilantro leaves

¼ cup fresh chopped chives

1 cup finely grated Parmesan cheese

Sea salt and freshly ground black pepper

1. Bring a large pot of water to a boil and generously add kosher salt. Cook the pasta according to package directions, stirring occasionally, until al dente. Drain, rinse, toss with a drizzle of olive oil and set aside.

2. While the pasta is cooking, add the pesto to a large bowl and stir in the lemon zest and juice. Slowly whisk in the remaining olive oil until all is incorporated.

3. Add the pasta, greens, basil, parsley, cilantro, chives and Parmesan to the bowl with the pesto and season with sea salt and pepper to taste. Toss gently to mix. Garnish with additional herbs and Parmesan and serve warm or room temperature.

On the Menu

SERVE WITH Chicken Piccata (page 125) or Sweet and Sticky Baby Back Ribs (page 133), or top with Pork Ragù. For dessert: Meyer Lemon Coconut Pound Cake (page 312) with lightly sweetened whipped cream.

On the Menu

TOP WITH When it comes to polenta, pile it on. My standbys include:

- Sautéed Wild Mushrooms
- Sautéed Garlicky Greens
- Everyday Marinara (page 163) or Everyday Bolognese (page 160)
- Big Platter of Roasted Vegetables (page 254)

Creamy Polenta

MORE THAN ITS ACTUAL RELATIVE, GRITS, I think of rice as polenta's closest kin. I use the two almost interchangeably as a bed for herbs and vegetables, and a dependable dinner companion. I offer some suggestions below. **Serves 4 to 6**

4 cups water

2 teaspoons kosher salt

1 cup polenta (not quick-cooking)

1 cup milk

4 tablespoons (½ stick) unsalted butter

1 cup (3 ounces) grated Parmesan cheese

¼ teaspoon crushed red pepper flakes

Sea salt and freshly ground black pepper

1 tablespoon chopped fresh parsley

1. Bring the water to a boil in a large saucepan over high heat. Add the salt and reduce the heat to a low boil. Slowly add the polenta in a steady stream, whisking constantly. Reduce the heat to simmer and cook, stirring frequently, until thick and creamy, 15 to 20 minutes. Stir in the milk and continue to cook until the grains are tender and most of the milk is absorbed but still creamy, 5 to 10 minutes more.

2. Remove from the heat and stir in the butter, cheese, red pepper flakes and salt and black pepper to taste, stirring until the butter and cheese have melted. The polenta should be loose and creamy. If it becomes too stiff, add a little more milk, about ¼ cup at a time. Serve warm with additional cheese on top if desired.

On the Shelves

POLENTA VS. GRITS At the Market, we offer polenta by Carolina Grits & Co. from Rocky Mount, North Carolina. We also stock their stone-ground grits, which raises a question I often end up discussing: What's the difference between Italian polenta and Southern grits? Polenta can have a coarser texture. It's also traditionally milled from a different variety of corn. But what I hear most often from customers and friends—and what I find hilarious but still I sometimes inadvertently adhere to—is that grits are for breakfast and polenta is for dinner. (Some go on to argue that grits are allowed to make the transition to evening, whereas polenta should not start the day.)

SWEETS

OUR SWEETS ARE OFTEN WHAT BRING PEOPLE through the Market's front door. They're iconic—what people know about us before ever having stepped foot inside. One day, I watched a new customer bend down to peer into the cakes display case and hit her head while exclaiming with excitement. Her reaction admittedly hit me over the head, too. We've been baking a wide range of cookies, bars, pies, cobblers, crisps, puddings and cakes for so long (since day one, really), that I sometimes take it all for granted. But sweets hold impressive real estate in the Market.

Enter the door and you walk straight toward a display of Whoppers (page 280) and Foster's Brownies (page 289). Keep going and the case curves around to a cooler stocked with Coconut Cake with Cream Cheese Frosting (page 311), Vanilla Cake with Milk Chocolate Frosting (page 308), Double Chocolate Cake (page 305) and a rotating cast of pies. Farther down the island you'll find Say's Bread Pudding (page 298) and in another refrigerated display, Lemon or Pecan Bars (page 286) and more. We have about 20 different types of desserts each day, which change according to the season.

In spring, we're excited to see strawberries for strawberry shortcake. In summer, we look forward to fresh peach pies. And in fall, we can't wait to turn pumpkins and sweet potatoes into savory desserts. Then we usher in the holiday season, when we make hundreds of pies for take-out orders and family gatherings—our extended family, both old and new.

After 25 years, it's refreshing to see our expansive spread still admired in the eyes our customers, who ask for a slice of Chocolate Chess Pie (page 294) before ordering a Grits Bowl (page 74). In that way, this chapter is not the end of this book, really. It's a chance to have a cookie before turning back to breakfast, and a chance to look forward to the food and folks and stories ahead.

Chocolate Chunk Cookies

CHUNKS TRUMP CHIPS IN THIS ICONIC COOKIE RECIPE, forming large pockets of warm chocolate. The better quality chocolate you use, the better quality cookies you'll get. Before baking, just be sure you have milk on hand, as these demand an ice-cold glass.

Makes about 2½ dozen (2-inch) cookies

½ **pound (2 sticks) unsalted butter, softened**

1 cup light brown sugar

1 cup granulated sugar

2 large eggs

2 teaspoons pure vanilla extract

3 cups all-purpose flour

1 teaspoons baking soda

1 teaspoon ground cinnamon

¼ **teaspoon kosher salt**

6 ounces semisweet chocolate, chopped

6 ounces bittersweet chocolate, chopped

1 cup roughly chopped walnuts or pecans

1. Preheat the oven to 375°F. Lightly grease 2 baking sheets with vegetable oil or spray or line with parchment paper and set aside.

2. Cream the butter, brown sugar and granulated sugar in a large bowl with an electric mixer on high speed until light and fluffy, stopping to scrape down the sides of the bowl several times. Add the eggs, one at a time, beating well and scraping down the sides of the bowl after each addition. Add the vanilla and mix thoroughly.

3. In a separate large bowl, combine the flour, baking soda, cinnamon and salt and stir to mix.

4. Add the flour mixture to the butter mixture and stir just until blended well. Stir in the chocolate and walnuts to distribute evenly throughout the dough.

5. Scoop the dough using a ¼-cup measure or ice-cream scoop onto the prepared baking sheets, spaced about 2 inches apart. Press the cookies to about ¼ inch thick with the palm of your hand or the back of a spatula.

6. Bake 12 to 14 minutes for soft, chewy cookies or 15 to 17 minutes for crunchy cookies. Remove from the oven and let cool on the baking sheets about 5 minutes before transferring to a baking rack to cool completely. Serve warm or let cool completely before storing in an airtight container until ready to serve.

On the Shelves

CHOCOLATE BARS In the Triangle, we're fortunate to have two local chocolate bar makers: Escazu and Videri, both of Raleigh. When baking small batches of cookies, I like to chop up fine bars, such as Escazu's Roasted Cocoa Nibs, Videri's Dark Chocolate with Sea Salt, Scharffen Berger's Sea Salt Bark or Valrhona's Caramelia with Crunchy Pearls.

Martha's Peanut Butter–Chocolate Chip Oatmeal Cookies

THERE'S NO NEED TO CHOOSE A FAVORITE COOKIE. Simply combine three of the very best. We learned this trick from the *Martha Stewart's Cookies* book in 2008 and have been making a version ever since. **Makes about 3 dozen (3-inch) cookies**

½ **pound (2 sticks) unsalted butter, softened**

½ **cup creamy natural peanut butter**

1 **cup light brown sugar**

1 **cup granulated sugar**

2 **large eggs**

2 **teaspoons pure vanilla extract**

3 **cups old-fashioned rolled oats**

¾ **cup all-purpose or whole-wheat flour**

1 **teaspoon baking powder**

1 **teaspoon ground cinnamon**

½ **teaspoon kosher salt**

2 **cups semisweet chocolate chips**

2 **cups salted whole peanuts**

1. Preheat the oven to 375°F. Lightly grease 2 baking sheets with vegetable oil or spray or line with parchment paper and set aside.

2. Cream the butter, peanut butter, brown sugar and granulated sugar in a large bowl with an electric mixer on high speed until light and fluffy, stopping to scrape down the side of the bowl several times. Add the eggs, one at a time, beating well and scraping down the sides of the bowl after each addition. Add the vanilla and mix thoroughly.

3. In a separate large bowl, combine the oats, flour, baking powder, cinnamon and salt and stir to mix.

4. Add the flour mixture to the butter mixture and stir just until blended well. Stir in the chocolate chips and peanuts to distribute evenly throughout the dough.

5. Scoop the dough using a ¼-cup measure or ice-cream scoop onto the prepared baking sheets, spaced about 2 inches apart. Press the cookies to about ¼ inch thick with the palm of your hand or the back of a spatula.

6. Bake 12 to 14 minutes for soft, chewy cookies or 15 to 16 minutes for crunchy cookies. Remove from the oven and let cool on the baking sheets about 5 minutes before transferring to a baking rack to cool completely. Serve warm or let cool completely and store in an airtight container until ready to serve.

Oatmeal Golden Raisin Cookies

THE OATS ARE OLD-FASHIONED but the cookies are contemporary—or at least a little different from the norm, with plump golden raisins in place of standard purples. Take these along on a picnic or deck them out, sandwiching ice cream between two, for a great end to a summer day.

Makes about 2 dozen (2½- to 3-inch) cookies

½ **pound (2 sticks) unsalted butter, softened**

1 cup light brown sugar

1 cup granulated sugar

2 large eggs

1 teaspoon pure vanilla extract

3 cups old-fashioned rolled oats

1½ cups all-purpose flour

1 teaspoon baking powder

1 teaspoon ground cinnamon

½ **teaspoon freshly grated nutmeg**

½ **teaspoon kosher salt**

2 cups golden raisins

1. Preheat the oven to 375°F. Lightly grease 2 baking sheets with vegetable oil or spray or line with parchment paper and set aside.

2. Cream the butter, brown sugar and granulated sugar in a large bowl with an electric mixer on high speed until light and fluffy, stopping to scrape down the sides of the bowl several times. Add the eggs, one at a time, beating well and scraping down the sides of the bowl after each addition. Add the vanilla and mix thoroughly.

3. In a separate large bowl, combine the oats, flour, baking powder, cinnamon, nutmeg and salt and stir to mix.

4. Add the flour mixture to the egg mixture and stir just until the dry ingredients are moist and blended. Add the raisins and stir to distribute evenly throughout the dough.

5. Scoop the dough using a ¼-cup measure or ice-cream scoop onto the prepared baking sheets, spaced about 2 inches apart. Press the cookies to about ¼ inch thick with the palm of your hand or the back of a spatula.

6. Bake 13 to 14 minutes for soft, chewy cookies or 15 to 16 minutes for crunchy cookies. Remove from the oven and let cool on the baking sheets about 5 minutes before transferring to a baking rack to cool completely. Serve warm or let cool completely and store in an airtight container until ready to serve.

Whoppers (GLUTEN FREE)

YOU COULD USE A SMALLER SCOOP TO SLIM DOWN these jumbo cookies. But as I've learned over the years (we've made these since day one, inspired by a recipe at Soho Charcuterie in New York), you'll simply end up eating two. **Makes about 2 dozen (2½- to 3-inch) cookies**

4 cups semisweet chocolate chips

8 tablespoons (1 stick) unsalted butter

3 large eggs

¾ cup sugar

2 teaspoons pure vanilla extract

⅓ cup gluten-free flour

1 teaspoon baking powder

½ teaspoon kosher salt

4 cups roughly chopped walnuts

1. Preheat the oven to 350°F degrees. Lightly grease 2 baking sheets with vegetable oil or spray or line with parchment paper and set aside.

2. Melt 2 cups of the chocolate and butter in a heatproof bowl of a double boiler over low heat until just melted, stirring occasionally. (You can do this in the microwave but be careful not to overheat. Remove as soon as the chocolate has melted, about 3 minutes.) Stir to blend the chocolate and butter and set aside.

3. In a large bowl, whisk the eggs, sugar and vanilla until thick and creamy. In a separate bowl, stir together the flour, baking powder and salt to mix.

4. Add the chocolate mixture to the egg mixture and stir to combine. Add the flour mixture and stir just until the dry ingredients are moist. Fold in the remaining chocolate and walnuts and stir to mix. The batter will be very moist, similar to the consistency of cake batter.

5. Scoop the batter using a ¼-cup measure or ice-cream scoop or by the heaping tablespoon and drop onto the prepared baking sheets, spaced about 3 inches apart. Bake right away before the chocolate begins to cool and harden.

6. Bake 15 to 17 minutes, rotating the baking sheets halfway through the cooking time. The cookies will still be very gooey inside and soft. Do not overcook or the cooled cookies will be dry. Cool about 20 minutes on the baking sheets before gently transferring to a baking rack to cool completely. Serve warm or let cool completely and store in an airtight container until ready to serve.

In the Kitchen

GLUTEN-FREE FLOUR There is a nice range of gluten-free flours available, including chickpea, millet and buckwheat. For baking, I generally use a blend. This recipe calls for such a small amount that any of these should do, depending on what you have. If you are not bothered by gluten, all-purpose flour also works here.

Almond Butter Sandwich Cookies

GO NUTS. That's what we've done since Big Spoon Roasters started production down the street from us in Durham. Their line of hand-crafted nut butters—from almond ginger to chai spice to peanut cocoa—inspires cookies well beyond plain old peanut butter (which, for the record, we also adore). **Makes about 1 dozen (3-inch) cookies**

8 tablespoons (1 stick) unsalted butter, softened

½ cup creamy almond butter

½ cup light brown sugar

½ cup granulated sugar, plus 2 tablespoons for sprinkling on top

1 large egg

1 teaspoon pure vanilla extract

1½ cups all-purpose flour

1 teaspoon baking powder

½ teaspoon freshly grated nutmeg

½ teaspoon kosher salt

1 tablespoon sea salt

Creamy Almond Butter Filling (recipe follows)

1 cup sliced blanched almonds, roughly chopped

1. Cream the butter, almond butter, brown sugar and ½ cup of the granulated sugar in a large bowl with an electric mixer, stopping to scrape down the bowl several times, or wooden spoon by hand until smooth. Add the egg and vanilla and mix to combine.

2. In a separate bowl, combine the flour, baking powder, nutmeg and kosher salt and stir to mix.

3. Slowly add the flour mixture to the almond butter mixture and blend until the dry ingredients are incorporated.

4. Roll the dough into a log about 2 inches wide by 10 inches long, wrap in plastic wrap and place in the refrigerator for about 1 hour to chill.

5. When ready to bake, preheat the oven to 350°F. Lightly grease 2 baking sheets with vegetable oil or spray or line with parchment paper and set aside.

6. Remove the dough from the refrigerator. Slice into rounds about ¼ inch thick and place onto the prepared baking sheets, spaced about 2 inches apart. Sprinkle with the remaining sugar and sea salt.

7. Bake 12 to 14 minutes, until golden brown around the edges. Remove from the oven and let cool on the baking sheets about 5 minutes before transferring to a baking rack to cool completely.

8. After the cookies have cooled completely, spread about 1 heaping tablespoon of the filling onto the flat side of 12 cookies and top each with another cookie, flat side down, to make a sandwich. Place the almonds on a small plate and roll the creamy edges of the cookie into the almonds to adhere to the sides.

CREAMY ALMOND BUTTER FILLING

Cream together **6 ounces soft cream cheese, ½ cup creamy almond butter, ½ cup sliced blanched almonds, 4 tablespoons (½ stick) soft unsalted butter, ¼ cup confectioners' sugar and ½ teaspoon kosher salt** in a large bowl with an electric mixer or wooden spoon by hand until thoroughly blended. Refrigerate until ready to use or spread onto the center of the almond butter sandwich cookies while soft. If you refrigerate the butter, remove it about 1 hour before spreading to soften.

Coconut Macaroons Dipped in Chocolate (GLUTEN FREE)

THESE COCONUT CLUSTERS ARE WELL ROUNDED, balancing a chewy interior with a crisp, golden crust, and sweetened flaked coconut with a semisweet chocolate topping.

Makes about 1½ dozen (2½- to 3-inch) cookies

4 large egg whites

1 cup sugar

1 tablespoon honey

1 teaspoon pure vanilla extract

3 cups sweetened flaked coconut

1 cup almond flour

1 teaspoon kosher salt

6 ounces semisweet chocolate

1. Combine the egg whites, sugar, honey and vanilla in a heatproof bowl of a double boiler. Cook, stirring constantly, until the sugar dissolves and the mixture looks opaque or milky in color, 6 to 8 minutes.

2. Combine the coconut, almond flour and salt in a separate bowl and stir to mix.

3. Remove the egg white mixture from the heat and stir in the coconut mixture. Cover and refrigerate until firm, at least 1 hour or overnight.

4. When ready to bake, preheat the oven to 325°F. Lightly grease 2 baking sheets with vegetable oil or spray or line with parchment paper and set aside.

5. Remove the batter from the refrigerator and scoop with a ¼-cup measure or ice-cream scoop or by the heaping tablespoon and drop onto the prepared baking sheets, spaced about 2 inches apart.

6. Bake 15 to 20 minutes, until golden brown around the edges but still soft and creamy in the center. Cool 5 to 10 minutes on the baking sheets before transferring to a baking rack to cool completely.

7. While the cookies are cooling, melt the chocolate in a double boiler or in the microwave. Dip the cookies halfway into the melted chocolate and place on a rack until the chocolate hardens, 15 to 20 minutes. Store in an airtight container until ready to serve.

Lemon or Pecan Bars

SAY WHAT YOU WILL: lemon bars or lemon squares, pee-cans or pah-cahns. They all mean something tasty in the recipes that follow. Simply make the crust and choose your filling. I often serve both at parties. **Makes about 1 dozen (3-inch) bars**

CRUST

½ **cup confectioners' sugar**

½ **pound (2 sticks) unsalted butter, softened**

2¼ **cups all-purpose flour**

½ **teaspoon kosher salt**

LEMON FILLING

3 **cups granulated sugar**

¼ **cup all-purpose flour**

½ **teaspoon baking powder**

½ **teaspoon kosher salt**

7 **large eggs, lightly beaten**

Zest and juice of 5 lemons

¼ **cup confectioners' sugar**

PECAN FILLING

6 **large eggs**

2 **cups granulated sugar**

2 **cups dark corn syrup**

4 **tablespoons (½ stick) unsalted butter, melted**

1 **tablespoon pure vanilla extract**

3 **cups roughly chopped pecans**

CRUST

1. Preheat the oven to 350°F. Lightly grease the sides of a 9 x 13 x 2-inch baking pan, line the bottom with parchment paper and set aside.

2. Cream the confectioners' sugar and butter in a large bowl with an electric mixer until combined.

3. Place the flour and salt in a separate bowl and stir to combine. Add the flour mixture to the butter mixture and mix until the dough begins to clump together.

4. With lightly floured hands, form the dough into a soft ball. Flatten the dough and press evenly into the bottom of the prepared pan. The dough will be about ¼ inch thick.

5. Bake 20 to 25 minutes, until light brown around the edges but not quite done. Remove from the oven and set aside to cool.

LEMON FILLING

1. Combine the granulated sugar, flour, baking powder and salt in a bowl and set aside.

2. Mix the eggs and lemon zest and juice in a separate bowl and whisk until smooth and well blended. Sift the flour mixture into the egg mixture and stir until well blended.

3. Pour the filling on top of the crust and return to the oven to bake until set, 30 to 35 minutes. Remove from the oven and let cool. Refrigerate for several hours or overnight before cutting.

4. Trim the edges and cut into bars. For smaller bars, cut each bar in half down the center or on the diagonal. Dust with confectioner's sugar just before serving.

PECAN FILLING

1. Whisk the eggs and sugar in a bowl until well blended. Add the corn syrup, butter and vanilla and stir to mix. Fold in the pecans to combine.

2. Pour the filling on top of the crust and return to the oven to bake until the filling is firm around the edges, 50 to 55 minutes. The center will be slightly loose. Remove from the oven, let cool and refrigerate several hours or overnight before cutting. Trim the edges and cut into bars. For a smaller bar, cut each bar in half down the center or on the diagonal.

Foster's Brownies

THIS IS THE BROWNIE RECIPE I RELIED ON when I catered in Connecticut because they always turned out well, even in huge quantities. And the thing about brownies is that next to having a reliable recipe, the best thing to have is lots of them. **Makes about 1 dozen (3-inch) brownies**

1½ cups all-purpose flour

⅔ cup unsweetened cocoa

1 teaspoon baking powder

1 teaspoon kosher salt

4 large eggs

2 cups sugar

½ pound (2 sticks) unsalted butter, melted

1 tablespoon plus 2 teaspoons pure vanilla extract

2 cups semisweet chocolate chips

1 cup roughly chopped walnuts

1. Preheat the oven to 325°F. Lightly grease and flour a 9 x 13 x 2-inch baking dish and set aside.

2. Sift together the flour, cocoa, baking powder and salt in a bowl and stir to mix.

3. In a separate bowl, mix the eggs, sugar, butter and vanilla until well blended.

4. Add the flour mixture to the butter mixture and combine just until the dry ingredients are moistened, being careful not to overmix. Fold in the chocolate chips and walnuts and stir to blend.

5. Spread the batter evenly into the prepared pan. Bake 30 to 35 minutes, until the brownies are firm to the touch. They will be slightly soft in the center when tested with a wooden skewer. Remove from the oven and let cool completely before cutting. Trim the edges, cut into squares and serve.

On the Menu

ICE CREAM BUFFET WITH MIX-INS When I serve these brownies, I have several sauces and flavors of ice cream for guests to choose from, along with different sweet and salty things to sprinkle on top. Some of my favorites are:
- Vanilla ice cream
- Rocky Road ice cream
- Hot fudge sauce
- Dulce de leche sauce
- Sea salt, salted peanuts or caramel corn

Everyday Pie Dough

MY SISTER MAKES DOUGH WITH SHORTENING, and I make dough with butter, but the best result for everyday baking is when we meet in the middle. With a mix of both fats, this recipe makes a sturdy and pliable crust with a buttery flavor. **Makes one (9-inch) shell**

2 cups all-purpose flour

1 teaspoon sugar

½ teaspoon kosher salt

8 tablespoons (1 stick) cold unsalted butter, cut into small pieces

3 tablespoons vegetable shortening

1 large egg, lightly beaten

1 teaspoon distilled white vinegar

¼ cup ice water, plus more if needed

1. Place the flour, sugar and salt in the bowl of a food processor fitted with a metal blade and pulse several times to mix.

2. Add the butter and shortening and pulse until the mixture resembles coarse meal.

3. Combine the egg and vinegar in a small bowl and stir to mix. Add the egg mixture to the flour mixture and pulse to combine. Add the ¼ cup ice water and pulse until the dough begins to clump together, adding 1 to 2 more tablespoons if needed.

4. Turn the dough onto a lightly floured piece of plastic wrap or wax paper and knead several times until it comes together. Form into a flat round and wrap with the plastic wrap or wax paper and refrigerate until firm enough to roll, at least 30 minutes or overnight. The dough can be made up to 3 days in advance and refrigerated until ready to use.

5. Roll the dough on a lightly floured surface into a 12-inch circle, about ⅛ inch thick. Place into a 9-inch pie plate or pan with the edges draping over slightly. Prick the bottom of the crust five or six times with a fork. Fold the edge under, creating a thick lip around the pie. Use your fingers or a fork to crimp or press the edge of the pie. Refrigerate at least 1 hour or until ready to use. (To prepare a prebaked crust, see Know-How, below).

Know-How

PREBAKING A PIE SHELL The recipes in this chapter using Everyday Pie Dough call for either an unbaked or prebaked crust. To prepare a prebaked crust, preheat the oven to 425°F. Line the bottom of the chilled shell with parchment paper or aluminum foil. Pour in ceramic pie weights, dried beans or dried coffee beans to fill (so the shell will not shrink as it bakes). Bake 10 to 15 minutes, until the dough is no longer translucent but not yet golden brown. Remove the parchment paper and pie weights; continue baking 6 to 8 minutes more, until the crust is golden brown and flaky. Remove from the oven and let cool.

Coconut Cream Pie

CHANGE IT UP. Use a meringue or whipped cream topping (I prefer whipped cream if I'm not going to serve the pie the same day I make it) or toss in bananas. **Makes one (9-inch) pie / Serves 8 to 10**

PIE

3 cups half-and-half

¼ cup cornstarch, sifted

4 large eggs

¾ cup granulated sugar

½ teaspoon kosher salt

1 vanilla bean

2 cups sweetened flaked coconut

3 tablespoons unsalted butter

1 prebaked (9-inch) Everyday Pie Dough (page 290)

MERINGUE

4 egg whites

¼ teaspoon cream of tartar

Pinch of kosher salt

¼ cup confectioners' sugar

½ cup sweetened flaked coconut, toasted

In the Kitchen

BANANA CREAM PIE This recipe makes a great base for a banana cream pie. I like a combination of both the banana and coconut. To make, simply peel and slice 3 bananas and fold or layer into the custard at the end of step 2.

PIE

1. Combine ½ cup of the half-and-half and the cornstarch in a large bowl and whisk to blend. Add the eggs and mix thoroughly.

2. Place the remaining half-and-half, sugar and salt in a saucepan. Split the vanilla bean in half lengthwise with a small knife. Use the back of the knife to scrape loose the seeds and place in the pot with the pod. Bring to a low boil over medium heat, stirring occasionally, until the sugar dissolves. Whisk 1 cup of the sugar mixture into the egg mixture to temper the eggs. Whisking constantly, pour the egg mixture back into the saucepan with the sugar mixture and cook over low heat, continuing to whisk constantly, until thick, about 5 minutes. Remove from the heat and stir in the coconut and butter. Let cool slightly and discard the vanilla bean.

3. Pour the filling into the cooled pie shell and refrigerate at least 4 hours or overnight, until firm.

MERINGUE

1. Preheat the oven to 375°F.

2. Place the egg whites, cream of tartar and salt in a glass or metal bowl and beat with an electric mixer on medium-high speed until soft peaks form. Increase the speed to high and beat until they turn opaque and add the confectioners' sugar, a little at a time, and continue beating until the whites are shiny and form stiff peaks. (Stiff peaks will keep their shape when you lift the beaters out of the whites.) Do not beat the whites past this point or they will separate and become grainy.

3. Spread the meringue over the coconut filling, making sure it touches the edge of the crust all around the pie to prevent the meringue from shrinking away from the sides when baked. Form peaks by drawing a knife or spatula across the meringue in an upward motion.

4. Place in the oven to bake until the meringue peaks are golden brown, 10 to 12 minutes. Remove the pie from the oven and place on a rack to cool for at least 1 hour before serving. Sprinkle with toasted coconut and serve chilled or at room temperature.

Chocolate Chess Pie

CHESS PIE IS A PANTRY PIE, making use of nothing more than a few staples—milk, sugar, eggs and butter. For my preferred version, I make sure my pantry is always stocked with unsweetened chocolate, vanilla extract and nutmeg. Even better is when I also have whipped cream or fresh raspberries for serving. **Makes one (9-inch) pie / Serves 8 to 10**

2 cups sugar

¾ cup unsweetened cocoa, sifted

2 tablespoons all-purpose flour

½ teaspoon freshly grated nutmeg

½ teaspoon kosher salt

1 cup half-and-half

4 tablespoons (½ stick) unsalted butter

3 large eggs

2 teaspoons pure vanilla extract

1 unbaked (9-inch) Everyday Pie Dough (page 290)

1. Preheat the oven to 325°F.

2. Combine the sugar, cocoa, flour, nutmeg and salt in a large bowl and stir to mix.

3. Heat the half-and-half with the butter in a saucepan over low heat just until the butter melts. Let cool before whisking in the eggs and vanilla until thoroughly combined. Whisk the half-and-half mixture into the sugar mixture to combine.

4. Place the prepared pie shell on a rimmed baking sheet. Pour the filling into the shell and place on the center rack in the oven to bake until the custard is set around the edges but still slightly loose in the center, 55 to 60 minutes. It will set or firm up completely when it is out of the oven. Remove the pie from the oven and let cool several hours before slicing.

In the Kitchen

NUTMEG Like freshly ground black pepper, freshly ground nutmeg is much more fragrant and flavorful than the pre-ground stuff you buy in supermarkets. Grate with a Microplane or other fine grater, or if you have it, a nutmeg grinder. I provide measurements for nutmeg throughout this book, but it's best to use your eye and your instincts to tell you when to stop grating, rather than trying to grate into a tiny spoon. Just remember: nutmeg is strong, especially freshly grated nutmeg. Grate, then taste. You can always add more.

Mixed Berry Pie with Crumb Topping

THINGS FALL APART IN THIS BREEZY SUMMER PIE that's part crisp. Berries give into a pool of sweet juices, and a mix of butter, oats, flour and nuts is crumbled on top. Keep it all together with Flavored Whipped Cream (page 297) swirled with raspberry jam—or a scoop of vanilla ice cream.

Makes one (9-inch) pie / Serves 8 to 10

1 pint (2 cups) fresh blueberries

1 pint (2 cups) fresh blackberries

1 pint (2 cups) fresh raspberries

1 cup sugar

3 tablespoons cornstarch

1 teaspoon freshly grated nutmeg

½ teaspoon kosher salt

Zest and juice of 1 lemon

1 unbaked (9-inch) Everyday Pie Dough (page 290)

3 tablespoons unsalted butter, cut into small pieces

Crumb Topping (page 301)

1. Preheat the oven to 400°F.

2. Combine the blueberries, blackberries, raspberries, sugar, cornstarch, nutmeg and salt in a bowl and toss to mix. Add the lemon zest and juice and mix. Spread the berry mixture into the prepared pie shell and place on a rimmed baking sheet. Dot the top of the berries with the butter.

3. Add the crumb topping to cover the berries completely, pressing gently to adhere to the top of the pie. Place on a rimmed baking sheet.

4. Bake until the juices are bubbling around the edges and the crust is golden brown, 1 hour to 1 hour and 10 minutes. If the top of the pie is browning too quickly, cover loosely with foil until bubbling around the edges. Remove from the oven and let cool to set the berries before serving, at least 1 hour. Serve warm or at room temperature.

Individual Chocolate *Pots de Crème*

POTS DE CRÈME, LITERALLY "POTS OF CREAM," are similar to all-American pudding. But the French dish is thickened with egg yolks instead of cornstarch, so it's denser and richer. I serve them in small jelly jars (when outside, you can present them with their lids on). And for large gatherings, I place them on a buffet with a selection of flavored whipped creams. You will need eight to ten small jelly jars (they don't have to match) or 3- or 4-ounce ramekins to make this dish. **Serves 8 to 10**

2½ **cups half-and-half**

1 **vanilla bean**

8 **ounces bittersweet chocolate, finely chopped**

2 **ounces semisweet chocolate, finely chopped**

½ **cup sugar**

6 **large egg yolks**

Pinch of kosher salt

2 **tablespoons coffee-flavored liqueur**

Chocolate Swirled Whipped Cream (See Flavored Whipped Cream, page 297)

1. Preheat the oven to 325°F.

2. Place the half-and-half in a medium saucepan. Split the vanilla bean in half lengthwise with a small knife. Use the back of the knife to scrape loose the seeds and place in the pot with the pod. Heat the half-and-half over medium heat until it just begins to simmer. Remove from the heat and discard the vanilla bean. Add the bittersweet chocolate, semisweet chocolate and sugar and stir until the chocolate melts and the sugar dissolves.

3. In a large bowl, whisk together the egg yolks, salt and liqueur. Gradually add the chocolate mixture to the bowl with the egg mixture, whisking constantly, until the mixture is smooth.

4. Put 8 to 10 jelly jars or 4-ounce ramekins in a shallow baking dish and fill the dish with warm water about halfway up. Pour the chocolate mixture into the jars or ramekins, dividing it evenly among them.

5. Bake until firm around the edges but still slightly loose in the center, 30 to 35 minutes. Remove from the oven and carefully take the *pots de crème* out of the water and set aside to cool to room temperature. Cover and refrigerate to chill for at least 2 hours or up to 2 days. Remove from the refrigerator 1 hour before serving.

In the Kitchen

FLAVORED WHIPPED CREAM Whip **1 cup heavy cream** using a wire whisk or electric beaters until loose peaks form. Add ¼ **cup sugar** and **1 tablespoon pure vanilla extract** and whip until stiff peaks form. Swirl in any of the following ingredients with a rubber spatula to streak throughout:

- 2 tablespoons fruit jam (for berries or other fruity desserts)
- Pumpkin butter (for pumpkin pie)
- Chocolate sauce (for anything with chocolate or coffee)
- Applesauce or apple butter (for apple pie)
- Lemon curd (for berries or other fruity desserts)
- Coffee or hazelnut liqueur (for anything chocolate or coffee)

Say's Bread Pudding

THIS DISH CALLS FOR TWO ROUNDS: bourbon for the pudding and bourbon for the sauce. Perhaps that's why my mom didn't start making it until after my sister and I went off to college. As Peter recounts in the Introduction (page 10), we had to ban our underage employees from dipping into the pudding; my mother likes to make it with a heavy hand.

Makes one (9 x 13 x 2-inch) pan / Serves 10 to 12

12 tablespoons (1½ sticks) unsalted butter, melted

¾ cup light brown sugar

½ day-old baguette

4 cups milk

5 large eggs

¾ cups granulated sugar

2 tablespoons pure vanilla extract

1 cup raisins

¼ cup bourbon

Bourbon Icing (recipe follows)

1. Preheat the oven to 350°F. Brush a 9 x 13 x 2-inch baking pan with 4 tablespoons of the melted butter.

2. Sprinkle the brown sugar evenly over the bottom of the pan and set aside.

3. Slice or tear the bread into 1-inch pieces and place in a large bowl. Pour the milk over the bread and let stand until the bread is soft, 4 to 5 minutes.

4. Combine the eggs, granulated sugar, remaining butter and vanilla in a separate bowl and whisk together until well blended.

5. Pour the egg mixture over the bread mixture. Add the raisins and stir to mix.

6. Pour the pudding into the prepared baking pan, cover and bake, 50 to 60 minutes. Uncover, return to the oven and continue to bake until the pudding is puffy and golden brown on top, 15 to 20 minutes more. Remove from the oven, pour the bourbon over the pudding and set aside to cool slightly before serving, 10 to 15 minutes. Top with the icing while the pudding is still warm.

BOURBON ICING

MAKES ABOUT 1½ CUPS

Place **8 tablespoons (1 stick) unsalted butter** in a saucepan and melt over medium heat. Remove from the heat. Whisk in **2 cups confectioners' sugar,** about ½ cup at a time, and stir to mix until all the sugar is blended. Stir in **1 cup heavy cream** and **¼ cup bourbon** and whisk to blend thoroughly, until the icing is thick and creamy. Pour over the bread pudding.

Dark Chocolate Buttermilk Bread Pudding with Bourbon Hard Sauce

MY MOTHER INSPIRED MY LOVE OF THIS DISH (see Say's Bread Pudding, page 298). But Tennessee gets credit for the sauce: a shot of bourbon (or Jack Daniel's at my house), mellowed by butter, sugar and heavy cream. **Makes one (9 x 13 x 2-inch) pan / Serves 10 to 12**

1 (1-pound) loaf brioche, challah or other rich egg bread

8 tablespoons (1 stick) unsalted butter

1½ cups sugar

⅔ cup unsweetened cocoa

2 teaspoons pure vanilla extract

½ teaspoon kosher salt

4 ounces bittersweet chocolate, chopped

2 cups well-shaken buttermilk

5 large eggs

1 cup semisweet chocolate chips

Bourbon Hard Sauce (recipe follows)

1. Preheat the oven to 350°F. Lightly grease a 9 x 13 x 2-inch baking pan and set aside.

2. Slice or tear the bread into 1-inch pieces and place in a large bowl.

3. Melt the butter in a heavy-bottomed skillet over low heat. Add the sugar, cocoa, vanilla and salt, stirring constantly, until the sugar dissolves. Remove from the heat and stir in the bittersweet chocolate until melted.

4. In a separate bowl, whisk together the buttermilk and eggs. Pour the egg mixture and the chocolate mixture over the bread and stir to combine and soak the bread evenly. Add the chocolate chips and stir to mix. Pour the mixture into the prepared baking pan.

5. Cover with foil and place in the oven to bake, 45 minutes. Remove the cover and continue to bake until the pudding is puffy and bubbling around the edges but still soft in the center, 10 to 15 minutes longer. Remove from the oven and cool slightly. Pour the Bourbon Hard Sauce over the pudding and serve while warm.

BOURBON HARD SAUCE

MAKES ABOUT 2 CUPS

Combine **1 cup heavy cream** and **1 cup confectioners' sugar** in a saucepan and bring to a low boil, stirring constantly, until the sugar dissolves and the mixture thickens slightly, about 2 minutes. Remove from the heat and stir in ¼ **cup bourbon**.

Brown Sugar Apple Crisp with Crumb Topping

A PINCH HERE, A HANDFUL THERE. This crumb topping can be made last minute with the loose style of measuring my grandmother mastered. Serve warm with vanilla ice cream or cinnamon-flavored whipped cream. **Makes one (9 x 13 x 2-inch) pan / Serves 10 to 12**

8 tart apples (about 3½ pounds), peeled, cored and thinly sliced

1 cup light brown sugar

3 tablespoons all-purpose flour

2 teaspoons ground cinnamon

½ teaspoon kosher salt

Zest and juice of 1 lemon

Crumb Topping (recipe follows)

1. Preheat the oven to 375°F. Lightly grease a 9 x 13 x 2-inch baking dish with butter and set aside.

2. Combine the apples, brown sugar, flour, cinnamon, salt, and lemon zest and juice in a large bowl and toss to mix. Place in the prepared baking dish and spread evenly.

3. Sprinkle the topping over the apples and bake until the apples are tender and bubbling around the edges and the top is golden brown and crisp, 30 to 35 minutes. Remove from the oven and serve warm with a big scoop of vanilla ice cream.

CRUMB TOPPING

Combine **1 cup all-purpose flour, 1 cup old-fashioned rolled oats, ½ cup light brown sugar, ½ cup sliced almonds, 1 teaspoon ground cinnamon, ½ teaspoon ground cloves** and **½ teaspoon kosher salt** in a bowl and stir to mix. Add **12 tablespoons (1½ sticks) soft unsalted butter** and crumble into the flour mixture with your fingertips until the mixture forms moist clumps. Store refrigerated until ready to use or for up to 5 days.

In the Kitchen

VARIATIONS Change the spices in the topping to nutmeg and ginger. Try different varieties of apples or throw in a few pears. Or switch the fruit entirely. Some of my favorites include:

- Fresh peaches with a splash of bourbon
- Caramelized plums
- Chunky pears and pumpkin with a spoonful of maple syrup
- Straight-up rhubarb

Judy's Berry Trifle

THANKS TO MY SISTER, JUDY, THIS TRIFLE HAS BEEN A PART of my summer holidays as long as I can remember. She makes one large trifle using only raspberries, but I like to make individual servings in small glasses using mixed berries so you can see the different layers. It is important to make this ahead of time so the cake will absorb the flavor of the cream and berries.

Makes one (8- or 9-inch) trifle or 8 to 10 individual trifles / Serves 8 to 10

12 large egg yolks

1 cup sugar

¼ cup bourbon

2 cups heavy cream

Meyer Lemon-Coconut Pound Cake (page 312) or 1 (9 x 5-inch) loaf your favorite or store-bought pound cake

1 cup raspberry jam

3 pints (6 cups) fresh raspberries, strawberries, blueberries and/or blackberries

1. Beat the egg yolks and sugar in a heatproof bowl with an electric mixer on high speed until light and fluffy, about 2 minutes. Beat in the bourbon until well blended. Place the bowl over a double boiler and beat with a hand-held mixer until the mixture triples in volume, about 6 minutes. The temperature will reach about 150°F when tested with an internal thermometer. Remove from the heat and cool completely, stirring occasionally.

2. In a separate bowl, beat the heavy cream to stiff peaks and fold half of the whipped cream into the cooled egg mixture, being careful not to overmix. Just barely fold it in so the mixture is mousselike; it will still have some streaks where it is not thoroughly mixed. Refrigerate the remaining whipped cream until ready to use.

3. Slice the cake into ½-inch slices and spread each slice with about 1 tablespoon of the jam. Place the berries in a large bowl and toss gently to mix.

4. Layer the trifle by pouring about one-third of the custard in the bottom of the individual glasses, dividing evenly, or in a large bowl. Arrange the cake slices around the bottom edges of the glasses or bowl. Sprinkle about half the berries over the cake slices, dividing evenly among the glasses if making individual portions. Pour one-third more of the custard over the top of the berries, dividing evenly. Top with the remaining cake. Add the remaining berries, leaving a few for garnishing, and top with the remaining custard. Cover and refrigerate for at least 4 hours or overnight.

5. Remove from the refrigerator and let sit about 1 hour before serving. Just before serving, top the trifle with the remaining whipped cream and garnish with the remaining berries.

Double Chocolate Cake

THIS IS A SIMPLE, STRAIGHTFORWARD CAKE with chocolate and more chocolate. What else do you need? On second thought, a scoop of vanilla ice cream is a welcome addition for this, one of our best sellers. **Makes one (8- or 9-inch) 2-layer cake / Serves 8 to 10**

CAKE

1 cup milk

5 ounces bittersweet chocolate, chopped

2 cups all-purpose flour

1 teaspoon baking powder

½ teaspoon kosher salt

1 teaspoon baking soda

⅓ cup hot water

2 cups sugar

1 cup canola or safflower oil

4 large eggs

2 teaspoons pure vanilla extract

FROSTING

1 cup heavy cream

½ cup sugar

½ teaspoon kosher salt

10 ounces bittersweet chocolate

12 tablespoons (1½ sticks) unsalted butter, softened

CAKE

1. Preheat the oven to 350°F. Lightly grease and flour two (8- or 9-inch) cake pans.

2. Place the milk in a small saucepan and scald. Remove from the heat and stir in the chocolate until melted and combined.

3. Combine the flour, baking powder and salt in a large bowl and stir to mix. Dissolve the baking soda in the hot water.

4. In a separate large bowl, whisk the sugar and oil until combined. Add the eggs, one at a time, mixing well after each addition.

5. Add the flour mixture to the egg mixture in thirds, alternating with the chocolate mixture and beginning and ending with the flour mixture. Mix to combine. Add the vanilla and water mixture and stir to mix.

6. Divide the batter evenly between the prepared pans and bake until a wooden skewer inserted in the center comes out clean, 35 to 40 minutes. Remove the cakes from the oven and let cool in the pans, about 15 minutes. Run a small knife around the edges of the pans before turning the cakes out onto baking racks to cool completely before frosting.

FROSTING

1. Place the cream, sugar and salt in a saucepan over medium heat and stir until the sugar dissolves and the cream bubbles around the edges, 2 to 3 minutes. Remove from the heat and stir in the chocolate until it melts and is combined and smooth. Let cool to room temperature but still soft.

2. Place the chocolate mixture in a large bowl with an electric mixer or stand mixer fitted with the whisk attachment to combine the butter. With the mixer on medium-high speed, add one small piece of butter at a time, mixing well after each addition, stopping to scrape down the bowl several times, until all is incorporated. Let the frosting sit at room temperature until it becomes slightly thick and spreadable, about 1 hour.

continues »

ASSEMBLY

1. Once the cakes have cooled completely, use a long serrated knife to slice off the rounded top portion of each cake to make a flat, even surface. Discard the trimmings.

2. Place one of the layers bottom side up on a large plate or cake stand. Ice this layer with about 1 cup of the frosting, spreading a thick layer over the top and spilling over the sides of the cake. Add the other layer, bottom side up, and spread the remaining frosting over the top, spilling over the sides of the cake and spreading evenly on the sides and top. Slice and serve or refrigerate until ready to serve. If refrigerated, let sit at room temperature before serving, about 1 hour.

In the Kitchen

VARIATIONS At the Market, we use this cake as the base for our German Chocolate Cake recipe, adding caramel, coconut and pecans to the frosting. For extra flavor, you can also spread raspberry jam, orange marmalade or caramel between the layers. Or for a different cake entirely, the icing works great as a substitute on the Vanilla Cake with Milk Chocolate Frosting (page 308).

Vanilla Cake
with Milk Chocolate Frosting

IN SOME POCKETS OF THE SOUTH, a baker is judged by how many layers of this cake he or she can stack (the *New York Times* once reported 17 thin sheets in a similar cake in Slocomb, Alabama). At Foster's, we think four will work just fine. And for this simple cake, quintessential for any baking repertoire, two will more than do. **Makes one (8- or 9-inch) 2-layer cake / Serves 8 to 10**

CAKE

12 tablespoons (1½ sticks) unsalted butter

1½ cups sugar

2 large eggs

2 teaspoons pure vanilla extract

2½ cups all-purpose flour

2 teaspoons baking powder

½ teaspoon kosher salt

1¼ cups milk

continues »

CAKE

1. Preheat the oven to 350°F. Lightly grease and flour two (8- or 9-inch) cake pans. Have all the ingredients at room temperature before you begin.

2. Cream the butter and sugar in a large bowl with an electric mixer, stopping to scrape down the sides of the bowl several times until light and fluffy. Add the eggs, one at a time, beating well and scraping down the sides of the bowl after each addition. Beat in the vanilla.

3. Combine the flour, baking powder and salt in a separate bowl and stir to mix.

4. Change the mixer speed to low or by hand. Add the flour mixture to the butter mixture in thirds, alternating with the milk and beginning and ending with the flour mixture, stopping to scrape down the bowl several times and stirring just until all is incorporated. Do not overmix.

5. Divide the batter evenly between the prepared pans and bake until the cakes are springy to the touch and a wooden skewer inserted in the center comes out clean, 30 to 35 minutes. Remove the cakes from the oven and let cool in the pans about 15 minutes. Run a small knife around the edges of the pans before turning the cakes out onto baking racks to cool completely before frosting.

continues »

FROSTING

1 cup heavy cream

½ cup sugar

½ teaspoon kosher salt

2½ cups semisweet chocolate chips

½ pound (2 sticks) unsalted butter, softened

FROSTING

1. Place the cream, sugar and salt in a saucepan over medium heat and stir until the sugar dissolves and the cream bubbles around the edges, 2 to 3 minutes. Remove from the heat and stir in the chocolate until melted and is combined and smooth. Let cool to room temperature but still soft.

2. Place the chocolate mixture in the bowl with an electric or stand mixer fitted with the whisk attachment to combine the butter. With the mixer on medium-high speed, add one small piece of butter at a time, mixing well after each addition, stopping to scrape down the bowl several times, until all is incorporated. Let the frosting sit at room temperature until it becomes slightly thick and spreadable, about 1 hour.

ASSEMBLY

1. Once the cakes have cooled completely, use a long serrated knife to slice off the rounded top portion of each cake to make a flat, even surface. Discard the trimmings.

2. Place one of the layers bottom side up on a large plate or cake stand. Ice this layer with about 1 cup of the frosting, spreading a thick layer over the top and spilling over the sides of the cake. Add the other layer, bottom side up, and spread the remaining frosting over the top, spilling over the sides of the cake and spreading evenly on the sides and top. Slice and serve or refrigerate until ready to serve. If refrigerated, let sit at room temperature before serving, about 1 hour.

In the Kitchen

CRUMB-FREE FROSTING After icing between the stacked layers, frost the cake all over the outside with a thin coat of frosting and refrigerate until the frosting is firm. This will seal in all the crumbs of the cake and prevent them from mixing into the decorative layer of frosting.

Coconut Cake with Cream Cheese Frosting

IN *THE FOSTER'S MARKET COOKBOOK*, we layered coconut cake with lemon curd. In *Sara Foster's Southern Kitchen*, we topped it with a seven-minute frosting. Here, we go back to the basics to build a classic layer cake held together by tart cream cheese frosting.

Makes one (8- or 9-inch) 2-layer cake / Serves 8 to 10

1 cup canola or safflower oil

2 cups sugar

4 large eggs

1 teaspoon pure vanilla extract

2½ cups all-purpose flour

2 teaspoons baking powder

½ teaspoon kosher salt

1 cup milk

Cream Cheese Frosting (page 322)

3 cups sweetened flaked coconut

In the Kitchen

ADD-INS For extra flavor and color, we often make this cake at the Market with lemon curd or raspberry jam between the layers. My mother makes it with canned crushed pineapple and juice between the layers. Before frosting the cake, she pours the juice from the pineapple over the layers to make them extra moist.

1. Preheat the oven to 350°F. Lightly grease and flour two (8- or 9-inch) cake pans. Have all the ingredients at room temperature before you begin.

2. Combine the sugar and oil in a large bowl with an electric mixer or with a wooden spoon by hand and whisk until creamy and thoroughly combined. Add the eggs, one at a time, beating well after each addition. Add the vanilla and stir to mix.

3. Combine the flour, baking powder and salt in a separate bowl and stir to mix.

4. Add the flour mixture to the oil mixture in thirds, alternating with the milk and beginning and ending with the flour mixture, stopping to scrape down the bowl several times and stirring just until all is incorporated. Do not overmix.

5. Divide the batter evenly between the prepared pans and bake until the cakes are springy to the touch and a wooden skewer inserted in the center comes out clean, 35 to 40 minutes. Remove the cakes from the oven and let cool in the pans about 15 minutes. Run a small knife around the edges of the pans before turning the cakes out onto baking racks to cool completely before frosting.

6. Once the cakes have cooled completely, use a long serrated knife to slice off the rounded top portion of each cake to make a flat, even surface. Discard the trimmings.

7. Place one layer, cut side down, on a large plate or cake stand. Spread the top evenly with one-third of the frosting and sprinkle with about 1 cup of the coconut. Place the second layer on top of the iced layer. Spread the top and sides of the cake with the remaining frosting and sprinkle with the remaining coconut, pressing the coconut gently into the sides of the cake to adhere. Slice and serve or refrigerate until ready to serve. If you are serving this cake cold, remove from the refrigerator about 1 hour before serving to come to room temperature.

Meyer Lemon-Coconut Pound Cake with Lemon Glaze

MEYER LEMONS HAVE A DISTINCTIVELY SWEET flavor with a hint of orange. In this cake, they provide a refreshing counterpoint to rich coconut. Top off with a dollop of lightly sweetened whipped cream or soft ice cream. **Makes one (10-inch) Bundt or tube cake or two (9 x 5-inch) loaf pans / Serves 10 to 12**

CAKE

2 cups granulated sugar

¾ pound (3 sticks) unsalted butter, softened

6 large eggs

4 cups all-purpose flour

2 teaspoons baking powder

½ teaspoon kosher salt

½ teaspoon freshly grated nutmeg

½ teaspoons ground cardamom

¾ cup well-shaken buttermilk

Zest and juice of 3 Meyer lemons (substitute: lemons)

2 teaspoons pure vanilla extract

2 cups sweetened flaked coconut

GLAZE

1 cup confectioners' sugar

Zest and juice of 3 Meyer lemons (substitute: lemons)

Pinch of sea salt

CAKE

1. Preheat the oven to 350°F. Lightly grease and flour a 10-inch Bundt or tube pan or two (9 x 5-inch) loaf pans. Have all the ingredients at room temperature before you begin.

2. Cream the granulated sugar and butter in a large bowl with an electric mixer on high speed until light and fluffy, about 3 minutes, stopping to scrape down the sides of the bowl several times. Add the eggs, one at a time, beating well and scraping down the sides of the bowl after each addition.

3. Combine the flour, baking powder, salt, nutmeg and cardamom in a separate large bowl and stir to mix.

4. Mix together the buttermilk, lemon zest and juice and vanilla in another separate bowl and stir to combine.

5. Add the flour mixture to the butter mixture in thirds, alternating with the buttermilk mixture and beginning and ending with the flour mixture, stopping to scrape down the bowl several times and stirring just until all is incorporated. Do not overmix. Gently fold in the coconut.

6. Spread about two-thirds of the batter evenly into the prepared pan or pans and top with the remaining batter in the center of the pan to make a nice mound. Place on a rimmed baking sheet and bake 1 hour, undisturbed. Rotate the pan and continue to bake until the cake is golden brown and a wooden skewer inserted in the center comes out clean, 10 to 15 minutes more. Remove the cake from the oven and let cool in the pan for 15 to 20 minutes. Run a small knife around the edges of the pan before turning the cake out onto a baking rack to continue to cool.

GLAZE

1. While the cake is cooling, combine the confectioner's sugar, lemon zest and juice and salt in a small saucepan over medium heat, stir to mix and boil until the sugar dissolves and the mixture thickens slightly, about 2 minutes.

2. Brush the glaze over the top and sides of the cake. Serve the cake warm or room temperature.

Burnt Sugar Pound Cake with Bourbon Peach Glaze

BURNT SUGAR GIVES THIS otherwise traditional pound cake a marbled swirl, and a hefty shot of bourbon makes it woozy. **Makes one (10-inch) Bundt or tube cake or two (9 x 5-inch) loaf pans / Serves 10 to 12**

BURNT SUGAR

1 cup sugar

1 cup heavy cream

CAKE

2 cups sugar

¾ pound (3 sticks) unsalted butter, softened

6 large eggs

4 cups all-purpose flour

1 teaspoon ground allspice

2 teaspoons baking powder

½ teaspoon kosher salt

1 cup sour cream

2 teaspoons pure vanilla extract

continues »

BURNT SUGAR

1. Heat the sugar in a heavy saucepan over medium-high heat, without stirring, until it begins to caramelize around the edges, shaking the skillet often, about 1 minute. When it begins to caramelize, stir until golden and the sugar dissolves.

2. Carefully pour the cream down the side of the pan, being careful not to let it bubble up on you. Continue to cook, stirring often, until the cream is combined and the sauce turns a dark amber color and all the chunks dissolve, about 5 minutes. Remove and set aside to cool until ready to use (this can be made in advance and stored refrigerated until ready to use, for up to several days.)

CAKE

1. Preheat the oven to 350°F. Generously grease and flour a 10-inch Bundt or tube pan or two (9 x 5-inch) loaf pans. Have all of the ingredients at room temperature before you begin.

2. Cream the sugar and butter in a large bowl with an electric mixer on medium-high speed until light and fluffy, about 3 minutes, stopping to scrape the down the sides of the bowl several times. Add the eggs, one at a time, beating well and scraping down the sides of the bowl after each addition.

3. In a separate bowl, combine the flour, allspice, baking powder and salt and stir to mix.

4. Combine the sour cream and vanilla in a separate small bowl and stir to mix.

5. Change the mixer speed to low or stir by hand. Add the flour mixture to the butter mixture in thirds, alternating with the sour cream mixture and beginning and ending with the flour mixture, stopping to scrape down the bowl several times and stirring just until all is incorporated. Do not overmix. Add the burnt sugar into the batter and swirl, not mixing completely so that it looks marbleized.

continues »

1 cup peach preserves

2 teaspoons grated fresh ginger

¼ cup bourbon

Pinch of kosher salt

6. Spread the batter into the prepared pan or pans and bake until a wooden skewer inserted in the center comes out clean, 1 hour and 10 to 15 minutes. Cover with foil after 1 hour if the cake is browning too quickly. Remove the cake from the oven and let cool in the pan 15 to 20 minutes. Run a small knife around the edges of the pan before turning the cake out onto a baking rack to continue to cool.

GLAZE

1. While the cake is cooling, heat the peach preserves in a small saucepan over low heat until it liquefies. Add fresh ginger, bourbon and salt and stir to combine.

2. Let the mixture cool so it thickens slightly but remains a liquid. While still warm, pour over the cake and serve.

In the Kitchen

VARIATIONS Keep jamming. You can make this glaze with almost any jarred fruit. Just thin it out with bourbon, brandy or rum. You can also use simple syrup to make a glaze with white wine, oranges and warm spices or candied ginger. For the burnt sugar, you can use different flavored caramels—from coffee to sea salt. One of my favorites is Fat Toad Farm's Farmstead Goat's Milk Caramel.

Chano's *Tres Leches* Cake

FOR 22 OF OUR 25 YEARS, we've been blessed to work with Chano Valencia, an incredible baker. Of all his cakes, I think this one is my very favorite. Topped with strawberries, sandwiched with jam and soaked in cream, it makes for a super moist take on traditional strawberry shortcake. Just plan to make it ahead so the milk that pools at the bottom of the pan has time to soak in. **Makes one (9 x 13 x 2-inch) cake / Serves 12 to 15**

CAKE

3½ cups sugar

1½ cups canola or safflower oil

6 large eggs

1½ cups milk

2 tablespoons pure vanilla extract

4½ cups all-purpose flour

1 tablespoon baking powder

¼ teaspoon kosher salt

continues »

CAKE

1. Preheat the oven to 350°F. Grease the sides of a 9 x 13 x 2-inch baking pan and line the bottom with parchment paper (do not flour; it prevents the milk from soaking into the cake).

2. Combine the sugar and oil in a large bowl with an electric mixer or with a wooden spoon by hand and whisk until creamy and thoroughly combined. Add the eggs, one at a time, beating well after each addition.

3. In a small bowl, combine the milk and vanilla.

4. In a separate bowl, combine the flour, baking powder and salt and stir to mix.

5. Add the flour mixture to the oil mixture in thirds, alternating with the milk mixture and beginning and ending with the flour mixture. Mix just until the dry ingredients are incorporated.

6. Pour into the prepared pan and bake until a skewer inserted in the center comes out clean, 35 to 40 minutes. Remove the cake from the oven and let cool in the pan about 20 minutes. Run a small knife around the edges of the pan before turning the cake out onto a baking rack to cool completely.

continues »

SOAK AND TOPPING

2 cups whole milk

2 cups sweetened condensed milk

1½ cups coconut milk

1 tablespoon pure vanilla extract

2 cups strawberry jam

2½ cups heavy cream

½ cup sugar

2 pints (4 cups) strawberries, hulled and cut in half

SOAK AND TOPPING

1. While the cake is cooling, stir together the whole milk, condensed milk, coconut milk and vanilla in a large bowl to combine.

2. Once the cake has cooled, slice it in half crosswise with a large serrated knife to make two layers. Place the top layer of the cake on a rimmed baking sheet, cut side up. Using a wooden skewer or a fork, poke holes all over (you cannot create too many; it helps the liquid absorb) and slowly pour half the milk mixture over the cake on the baking sheet, about ½ cup at a time, spooning it back over the cake as it pools in the bottom of the pan until most of the liquid is absorbed. (There will still be a little liquid in the bottom of the pan but it will continue to absorb as it sits.) After most of the liquid is absorbed, spread half the jam over the top of that layer. Place the other layer, cut side up, on top of the soaked layer. Repeat the soaking process with this layer.

3. Whip the heavy cream to form soft peaks, add the sugar and continue to whip to form stiff peaks. Frost the cake all over with the whipped cream. Thin the remaining strawberry jam with 1 tablespoon water and pour over the top of the cake. Decorate the edges with the strawberries. Refrigerate for at least 2 hours or overnight before serving. Slice into portions and serve chilled.

In the Kitchen

VANILLA SALT FOR BAKING Fill an 8-ounce glass jar with sea salt or kosher salt. Split a vanilla bean in half and scrap the inside. Add the bean and seeds to the jar, submerging the bean into the salt. Place a tight-fitting lid on the jar and shake to distribute the bean and seeds. Let sit in a cool, dark place for at least a week and up to 6 months.

Carrot Sheet Cake with Cream Cheese Frosting

SPREAD IT OUT. For big groups, I prefer to serve carrot cake in a single layer, rather than stacked high. The sweet carrots make it rich enough that it doesn't need several bands of frosting.

Makes one (9 x 13 x 2-inch) cake / Serves 12 to 15

4 cups grated carrots

1½ cups roughly chopped walnuts

1 cup raisins

2 cups all-purpose flour

1 tablespoon unsweetened cocoa

1 tablespoon ground cinnamon

1 teaspoon ground cloves

2 teaspoons baking powder

1 teaspoon baking soda

1 teaspoon kosher salt

4 large eggs

1 cup canola or safflower oil

1 cup granulated sugar

1 cup light brown sugar

1 tablespoon pure vanilla extract

Cream Cheese Frosting (recipe follows)

1 cup finely chopped walnuts

1. Preheat the oven to 350°F. Lightly grease and flour a 9 x 13 x 2-inch baking dish.

2. Combine the carrots, walnuts and raisins in a large bowl and stir to mix.

3. In a separate bowl, sift together the flour, cocoa, cinnamon, cloves, baking powder, baking soda and salt and stir to mix.

4. In another bowl, combine the eggs, oil, granulated sugar, brown sugar and vanilla and whisk until well blended.

5. Slowly fold the flour mixture into the egg mixture and stir to blend just until the dry ingredients are moist and blended, being careful not to overmix. Fold in the carrot mixture and stir just until combined.

6. Scrape the batter into the prepared pan and bake until the cake is firm to the touch and a wooden skewer inserted in the center comes out clean, 35 to 40 minutes. Remove the cake from the oven and let cool in the pan, about 15 minutes. Run a small knife around the edges of the pan before turning the cake out onto a baking rack to cool completely.

7. Once the cake has cooled completely, use a long serrated knife to slice off the rounded top portion of the cake to make a flat, even surface. Discard the trimmings.

8. Place the cake, cut side down, on a large platter or rimmed baking sheet. Spread a thin layer of the frosting to cover the top and sides of the cake to form a crumb layer. Place in the refrigerator to chill for about 30 minutes until the frosting is firm before continuing to coat.

9. Fill a pastry bag, fitted with a decorative tip, with about 2 cups of the remaining frosting and set aside. Remove the cake from the refrigerator and spread the top and sides of the cake with the remaining frosting. Gently press the finely chopped walnuts into the sides of the cake. Pipe around the top and bottom edges of the cake with the frosting in the pastry bag to make a decorative finish.

10. Slice into portions and serve, or refrigerate until ready to serve. This cake keeps well refrigerated for several days.

continues »

CREAM CHEESE FROSTING

Cream together **8 tablespoons (1 stick) soft unsalted butter** and **12 ounces soft cream cheese** in a large bowl with an electric mixer on high speed until light and fluffy. Slowly add **4 cups confectioners' sugar, sifted**, about 1 cup at a time, beating well and scraping down the sides of the bowl after each addition until smooth. Add the **zest and juice of 1 lemon** and **2 teaspoons pure vanilla extract** and continue to mix on high speed to make the frosting light and fluffy, about 1 minute.

PICK-ME-UP DESSERTS

DESSERT DOESN'T HAVE TO MEAN a hot oven or a mess of flour. There is an abundance of good bakeries that make excellent cookies and cakes you can incorporate into your own menu. See what's available in your area, or go simple, providing toppings for ice cream or relying on fresh fruit such as figs or berries. A little something sweet goes a long way.

- Espresso–Ice Cream Floats with Shortbread
- Ice Cream Mix-Ins Buffet (page 289)
- Mixed Cookie Platter
- Brownie Ice Cream Sundaes with Chocolate Sauce and Sea Salt
- Artisanal Chocolate Bars and Tangerines
- Figs with Honeycomb and Goat Cheese and Blue Cheese
- Mixed Berries (or Sliced Stone Fruit) with Pound Cake and Whipped Cream

ACKNOWLEDGMENTS

WE OPENED FOSTER'S MARKET in May 1990 at the beginning of gardening season. Because the Foster's building had previously been a lawn mower repair shop, folks pulled into our gravel parking lot hoping to fix their rusty equipment. Instead, they saw that we'd taken out the gas pump and replaced shelves of nuts and bolts with fresh flowers and vegetables. With our staff of three, I stood on the porch and watched people drive away as quickly as they came, never even slowing down to take note of the nature of our new business.

Thankfully, we had a few curious customers who lived in the neighborhood and watched the renovation. Judith Olney was among them, and I cannot describe how excited I was to meet her—a fellow food enthusiast in Durham. Then there was Peg Palmer. She practically kept us in business in our early days, dining daily for breakfast, lunch and dinner while her kitchen was remodeled at her home nearby. Shelly Lieberman has come into the Market almost every day of our 25 years. Frank Skidmore comes daily for a grinder or Cubano sandwich. Other customers slowly trickled in, too, from Duke and the surrounding neighborhoods.

But our real break was thanks to Bridgette Lacy, whose article for Durham's *Herald-Sun* in late April 1995 changed everything. She gave people an idea of what was inside—pastries, fresh salads and sandwiches—and then the word was out. Cars slowed down on the Boulevard and more pulled into the lot, delivering us customers and friends whom we still greet regularly.

I'd list all of our customers by name here if I could: the Duke students who we've loved meeting and hated to see move on over the years; the moms, dads and countless kids that have grown up along with us; the doctors who drop by after a night shift to have a beer at 8 a.m.; the businessmen and women who gather for meetings at our large table in the back. To all of you, I offer a special thanks for your patronage and enthusiasm. You make this all worth it, day after day.

Our purveyors and farmers who supply us with incredible resources—you've made the past 25 years possible in so many ways, not to mention delicious: Betsy and Alex Hitt of Peregrine Farm in Graham, Ken Dawson of Maple Spring Gardens in Cedar Grove, Stuart and Alice White of Bluebird Meadows in Hurdle Mills, and my cousin Rose at Lyon Farms in Creedmoor. At the beginning there was also Mrs. Barker, who sold what she deemed ugly tomatoes at the Market's back door. They were so ripe and juicy they often did not make the salad case, but they enriched our soups and sauces, as well as tomato sandwiches that we greedily kept to ourselves in the kitchen.

The early crew who literally helped lay the foundation for Foster's: my sister Judy bricked the entrance, made endless runs to the hardware store and did most anything else on the list to launch the Market, including opening the red wine at the end of the day. Boukie, my lifelong friend from Tennessee, designed our logo and sign, painted walls, installed the bathroom mirrors, fed the cat and made me keep my sense of humor.

Our staff, which is to say, our family—from Elizabeth Laine, our first kitchen manager, who whipped the kitchen into shape and was

responsible for some of the early recipes that we still sell, including her beloved pimiento cheese with smoked Gouda, to Chris Law, our current kitchen manager, who has added his own inventive touch and more than kept us afloat. Laura Cyr and Wendell Wilson taught me a great deal from their simple and creative approaches to food. Gretchen Sedaris brought way more to the kitchen than just her talents with baking. Tim Youngblood suggested we serve omelets and paved the way to our brunch menu. Shay Charles was my right hand for more than a decade and helped me open the Chapel Hill Market. Jennings Brody took our candy sales and displays to new levels. Jan Vandervort kept my mom in line when we first opened and helped grow our staff and improve our customer service. Eric Muhl, aka Chico, who has weathered 16 years with us (including one incredible ice storm). Chano Valencia, our baker of 20-something years, who is the backbone and visionary behind our baked goods. The entire staff at Foster's has made our business special. Thank you for supporting and contributing to this book and Foster's Market in your own unique ways.

My husband, Peter Sellers: thank you for your enthusiasm for eating and for your endless support from day one—even the time we had to put the payroll on the credit card and I didn't know we had to pay sales tax! You are also our most committed breakfast patron. I love looking out to see you seated in the back over a cup of coffee each morning. Patrick Edwards, my business partner and nephew: thank you for working so hard every day for more than 20 years—your dedication has helped make Foster's what it is today. You've done everything possible to help run the business, even pulling dish shifts in the early days and watering the flowers. You mean so much to me and to our business.

The behind-the-scenes team—new and old friendships that I will cherish forever—that helped put this book together: Emily Wallace, my coauthor, for her creative input, knowledge, humor and dedication that made this project better each day; Frank Edwards, our photographer, for his original eye and for truly capturing my recipes with beautiful and stylish photographs; Sandy Lane, photo assistant, stylist and all-around girl Friday, for her sharp wit, her "little touches" to the food and photos and her willingness to hop in whenever help was needed; Marian Cairns, our food stylist, for the creativity she brought to each dish and detail.

The entire Story Farm family that put this together and that helped see me through my first foray into self-publishing with grace: Bob Morris, our publisher and the man with the vision. Ashley Fraxedas, our editor, for her guidance in organizing and refining this work, while encouraging us along the way; Jason Farmand, our designer, for his keen aesthetic.

Wendy Goldstein and other friends and family who tested recipes: this book is better for your relentless pursuit of perfection and deliciousness. Linwood Bradley at Southern Season and Nomadic Trading Company—thank you for setting the table by providing us with an endless supply of beautiful plates and props.

All of my family and friends who contributed recipes, props and, most importantly, who have given encouragement and inspiration not just to this book, but to my continued journey as a cook and business owner—I am truly blessed. My parents' and grandparents' guidance and love were immeasurable, and the family gatherings they hosted were, in a sense, what brought me to the creation of Foster's Market and the desire to share good food with community.

Twenty-five years. I am humbled.

INDEX

Italicized page numbers indicate photos.

Snacks
Mayo
Dip
Grits
Salsa
Breakfast
Syrup
Flour
Butter
Sugar
Soups & Stews
Wine
BBQ
Honey
Family Dinners
Flour
Oil
Beer
Salsa
Butter
Ketchup
One Pot Cooking
Soy
Butter
Sugar